ON FRIENDSHIP AND FREEDOM

THE CORRESPONDENCE OF IGNAZIO SILONE AND MARCEL FLEISCHMANN

ON FRIENDSHIP AND FREEDOM

THE CORRESPONDENCE OF IGNAZIO SILONE AND MARCEL FLEISCHMANN

Maria Nicolai Paynter

UNIVERSITY OF TORONTO PRESS
Toronto Buffalo London

Toronto Buffalo London
www.utppublishing.com

ISBN 978-1-4426-4996-5

(Toronto Italian Studies)

Library and Archives Canada Cataloguing in Publication

Paynter, Maria Nicolai, author, translator, editor
On friendship and freedom : the correspondence of Ignazio Silone and Marcel Fleischmann / Maria Nicolai Paynter.

Letters translated from the French by Maria Nicolai Paynter; letters translated from the German by Aine Zimmerman.
Includes bibliographical references and index.
ISBN 978-1-4426-4996-5 (cloth)

1. Silone, Ignazio, 1900–1978 – Friends and associates. 2. Silone, Ignazio, 1900–1978 – Correspondence. 3. Fleischmann, Marcel, 1891–1984 – Friends and associates. 4. Fleischmann, Marcel, 1891–1984 – Correspondence. 5. Authors, Italian – 20th century – Correspondence. 6. Communists – Italy – Correspondence. 7. Businessmen – Switzerland – Correspondence. 8. Friendship. 9. Liberty. I. Title.

PQ4841.I4Z635 2016 853'.912 C2016-901196-8

University of Toronto Press acknowledges the financial assistance to its publishing program of the Canada Council for the Arts and the Ontario Arts Council, an agency of the Government of Ontario.

Canada Council for the Arts
Conseil des Arts du Canada

Funded by the Government of Canada
Financé par le gouvernement du Canada
Canada

Life is an ethical adventure.
Love is beautiful.

DARINA SILONE

To Sofia Maureen

and to my sisters

Nicoletta and Franca

Contents

Preface

The genesis of this work is rather fortuitous. Four years ago, when I was no longer focusing my research on Ignazio Silone,[1] I received an unexpected phone call from Gloria Fleischmann, the widow of Werner Jürg, Marcel Fleischmann's only son. In her husband's studio, she had found a folder with the correspondence between Silone and Marcel Fleischmann – Silone's Swiss "Maecenas" – and wanted to safeguard it for the future. We met, and I suggested that she consider contacting Yale University, since it had awarded Silone the degree of Doctor of Letters Honoris Causa in 1966; the University of Pavia, where some of his original manuscripts were already held; or the Centro Studi Ignazio Silone, in Silone's native town of Pescina dei Marsi, where scholars could find a wealth of archival material and personal possessions donated by Darina Silone. Mrs Fleischmann opted for this destination. Even as I refrained from influencing her decision, I was happy when she made it because I knew that Silone intended to donate his archives to his native town, and also because, during the years of my research, I had come to appreciate the importance of the Centro Studi as custodian of Silone's legacy. Much progress has been made from the early days when Diocleziano Giardini, who enjoyed Darina Silone's trust, singlehandedly worked as a volunteer, organizing and gathering material, conducting research of his own, and making himself available to visiting scholars, myself included. A milestone was reached in 2000 when Silone's widow donated copies of his archives and other possessions to Pescina.[2] At present, the Centro Studi, under the regional and local administrations, sponsors high-level events, the most important of which is the yearly edition of the Premio Silone. Local scholars, such as Liliana Biondi and the late Vittoriano Esposito, have for years lent their assistance in keeping the dialogue with all who are interested in Silone both open and professional.[3]

When I began this project, the first decision I had to make concerned the translation. Should I publish in Italian or English? I opted for the latter in order to reach a broader audience. Ignazio and Darina Silone wrote almost always in French, Fleischmann and Elsa Schiess in German.[4] I could translate from French and other languages but not from German. For this I secured Aine Zimmerman's professional help.[5] Once the letters were translated and examined, I faced a dilemma: should I abide by Silone's wish that personal correspondence should not be published or – given the accessibility to the now organized archives – was my concern unwarranted? Opting to go ahead, I was also mindful that, after her husband's death, Darina Silone had sought to gather all the correspondence she could find, even launching an appeal with a letter of 19 July 1979 to the publisher of the *New York Times Review of Books*. And, two years later, she had reached out to Jürg Fleischmann with a similar plea for help.[6]

What is the importance of this correspondence? Scholars who write on the value of epistolary writings argue that they yield an authenticity and immediacy that is not normally found in historical documents. Prominent among them, Wilmarth Sheldon Lewis, speaking at the American Philosophical Society's dinner on 19 April 1963 as the editor of the *Horace Walpole Correspondence*, reminded the audience that as early as 1761 Walpole had noted: "Nothing gives so just an idea of an age as genuine letters; nay, history waits for its last seal from them […] Familiar letters written by eye witnesses … that let us more intimately into important events are genuine history; and as far as they go, more satisfactory than formal premeditated narratives."[7]

The validity of this observation is evident when one thinks, for instance, of the importance of Leopardi's letters[8] for the insight that they offer about the poet and his time, of Gramsci's letters[9] for encompassing the trajectory of the Italian Communist Party, and of the letters of the members of the Italian Resistance,[10] who wrote to their families before facing the firing squad. No premeditated narrative could provide more vivid testimonials.

The body of scholarly work that has been produced in the field and the numerous volumes of collected letters written by artists, scientists, statesmen, and other people of consequence legitimate Walpole's claim and attest to the need and the importance of preserving epistolary writing. This task is now greatly facilitated by the resources of technology. In fact, by simply contacting the Centro Studi Ignazio Silone via the Internet, readers can learn about the wealth of epistolary writings that still remain unexamined.

The correspondence published here for the first time spans the years 1934 to 1976 and is largely of a personal nature. Because of this, it does not yield as much historical information as one might have hoped (especially about the first decade), but, as I argue in the Introduction, even what is not said offers the occasion for pause and reflection, and by the end the reading proves to be most rewarding.

Editorial Note

While my aim is to facilitate future scholarship, I am also writing for the general public. Therefore, rather than abiding by the technical requirements of a strictly critical edition of the correspondence, I offer a more unencumbered presentation of the same.

All the correspondence in this volume, including several writings by Darina Silone and by Fleischmann's companion, Elsa Schiess, is presented in English translation. Unless otherwise indicated, Silone's letters and picture postcards were handwritten in French and signed by him. Most of Fleischmann's letters were typewritten, in German, and bear his handwritten signature. Handwritten initials ES (for Elsa Schiess) are found in many of the letters,[11] suggesting that she filed them away for him.

We do not have a cohesive body of the correspondence that the two friends exchanged; with some exceptions, the letters do not constitute an ongoing dialogue, and the postcards merely show the writers' desire to share their experience and stay in touch.[12] The writings are presented chronologically, with author's name and sequential numbers used to simplify the cross-reference process. The writers' initials are used in the footnotes as follows: S, DS, F, and ES, indicating Silone, Darina Silone, Fleischmann, and Elsa Schiess, respectively. A chronology listing people, activities, and events related to the correspondence facilitates a contextual reading.

To achieve greater textual unity, I adopt the same format for all the letters: single spacing, indented paragraphs, addressee and salutation flush left, with all the dates (including the few that appear at the end of the text) at the beginning, written according to British usage (day, month, year). Also, in keeping with current copy editing practice, words underlined in the originals appear in italics.

All translations seek to faithfully render the quality and tone of the originals; when appropriate, however, corrections that do not alter the meaning are silently made. The persons mentioned in the letters are identified in the footnotes, with asterisks indicating possibility rather than certainty. Italics are used for book titles and for the *Kleine Pension*, as Fleischmann affectionately called his villa at 53 Germaniastrasse. Undated letters are assigned tentative dates within square brackets, with footnotes explaining the basis for the assumption. All picture postcards are described and the messages are translated. When no date is given, the postmark is used to indicate possible dates.

Throughout the book, passages that are not quoted directly from English editions appear in the original, followed by a translation. All translations from German are by Aine Zimmerman. She began her task by revising some letters previously translated as working copies by Gregory Zwygart and Angineh Djavadghazaryans, and then went on to translate the rest. Unless otherwise noted, all other translations are mine.

Chronology[1]

1891 *13 January.* Marcel Fleischmann is born in Zurich, Switzerland, the first of four sons of Michael Fleischmann (13 June 1857–6 July 1926) and Helene Fuchs Fleischmann (6 November 1864–11 July 1919). His brothers were Carlo (28 April 1892–24 August 1965); Edgar (19 August 1897–20 February 1923), who died in an accident during an avalanche; and Kurt (26 December 1903–25 March 1974).

1896 Gabriella Seidenfeld Triedmann is born. Silone's companion in the antifascist struggle and in life for over a decade following their 1921 meeting, she assumes the battle name of Serena. In June 1933, to secure her right to Swiss residency, she marries Edy Meyer (aka Eduard Mayer, Meier, or Maier), a Swiss citizen nineteen years her senior, divorcing him one year later. In the correspondence, Gabriella's new surname is variously spelled.

1897 *24 January.* Elly Maeder, Marcel Fleischmann's future wife, is born.

1898 *17 April.* Elsa Schiess, who will become Fleischmann's companion, is born in Herisau, Appenzell, Switzerland.

1900 *1 May.* Secondino Tranquilli (Ignazio Silone) is born in Pescina dei Marsi, Abruzzo, Italy, the second of seven children of Paolo Tranquilli (1870–1911) and Marianna Delli Quadri (1872–1915). His siblings were Domenico (1897–1911), who died in an accidental fall; Romolo (1904–32), who died in prison; plus three sisters and one more brother,

1 A more complete chronology was published by Maria Moscardelli on the *Ignazio Silone Web.* I draw some information about Silone from this source.

who were victims of infant mortality: Elvira (1895); Maria (1903); Cairoli (1907–8), and another Maria (1909–10).

1915 *13 January.* An earthquake devastates the Marsican area. Only 1,500 of the 5,000 inhabitants of Pescina survive (ISRS, xliv). Silone's mother is among the victims. Romolo Tranquilli is found alive after five days. Secondino and Romolo are entrusted to the care of Maria Vincenza Del Grosso, their maternal grandmother.

December. Travelling from Pescina to San Remo, where he will continue his studies, Silone gets to know Don Luigi Orione (1872–1940), the priest (elevated to sainthood in 2004) who takes him and his brother Romolo under his care. Silone writes about him in *Emergency Exit.* Their correspondence, spanning the years 1916–18, was published by Giovanni Casoli in DOeS.

1917 *30 March.* Darina Elizabeth Laracy, Silone's future wife, is born in Dublin, the first of four daughters of Patrick Joseph Laracy (1882–1960) and Mary Cecilia King (1888–1948). Her sisters were Cecily (1923–2009), Moira (1929–2007), and Eithne (1931–).

September. Silone returns to Pescina from Reggio Calabria, where he completed his secondary education. He attends the meetings of the Fucino Farmers' League. His political activism begins.

1918 Silone, declared physically unfit to serve in the Italian army engaged in World War I (WWI), tries to cope with the loneliness that he experiences. In May he spearheads a riot to prevent the arrest of soldiers on leave from the war front. The police headquarters are set on fire, and some policemen are hurt. In July he is tried, convicted, and sentenced to pay damages.

11 November. The armistice is signed to end WWI.

1919 *August.* Silone is elected secretary of the Roman Socialist Youth. In October he becomes a member of the Central Committee of the Italian Socialist Youth.

In November he travels to Berlin where he admires the abilities of the leaders of the German Communist Youth. He meets Antonio Gramsci.

23 September. Werner Jürg Fleischmann, Marcel's only son, is born in Zurich. He will be known as Jürg.

1920 Silone is editor of the socialist weekly *L'Avanguardia.*

1921 Silone is editor of *Il Lavoratore* and *Avanti!*

21 January, XVIII Conference of the Psi [the Italian Socialist Party] is held in Leghorn. Silone sides with Amadeo Bordiga (1889–1970) and is among the founding members of the Pcd'I (Italian Communist Party).

April. Silone returns to Pescina. During the campaign for the political elections to be held in May he forcefully speaks against the Fascist Party candidates. Fearing unrest, the police ask him to leave the town.

June. He travels to Moscow as a member of the Italian delegation attending the Third Congress of the Comintern. He meets Lenin and is impressed by his charisma.

November. In Fiume (Riyeka), at a meeting of the Communist Youth, Silone meets Gabriella Seidenfeld Triedmann. They become companions in life and in political activism, adopting the battle names of Sereno and Serena.

1922 *29 October.* Following the March on Rome, King Victor Emmanuel III asks Mussolini to form the new government.

December. Silone moves from Trieste to Berlin with Gabriella Seidenfeld.

1923 *April.* Willy Münzenberg, the German leader of the International Communist Youth, sends Silone and Gabriella to Spain. Their mission is to help the Spanish communist movement. They are arrested in Madrid. Avoiding extradition to Italy, they move to Barcelona. There, writing for the weekly *La Batalla*, Secondino Tranquilli adopts for the first time the pseudonym "Silone."

Elsa Schiess joins Marcel Fleischmann's family as housekeeper. In time she becomes Marcel's companion.

1924 *1 January.* Silone is arrested in Madrid and is detained in the Carcel Modelo. In February he is extradited to Italy via Marseille. He escapes. Is in Paris (16 February –14 June) as editor of the weekly *La Riscossa.* On 11 November he is arrested and expelled from France but is again in Paris the following day.

1925 *16 July.* Silone is rearrested in Paris for non-compliance with the order of expulsion. He spends two months in the Santé prison and is expelled again on 21 September.

Silone returns to Italy and works in the Press and Propaganda unit of the Pcd'I, then directed by Gramsci.

1926 Rome, *7 July.* Silone and Gabriella, identified by an ex-communist turned fascist informer, are stopped and released with an injunction to return to Pescina.

27 July. The Prefect of L'Aquila informs higher authorities that Silone has not complied with the injunction and that an order has been issued for his arrest.

Silone continues his undercover political activism in Genoa and other northern locations. He writes articles for *L'Unità, Stato Operaio,* and *Battaglie Sindacali* under the pseudonym "Pasquini."

1927 Moscow, *May.* Silone is part of the Italian delegation attending the 8th Enlarged Plenum conference of the Comintern. A confrontation with Stalin ensues when he and PalmiroTogliatti ask to see the documents proving the allegations of betrayal against Leon Trotsky. This marks the beginning of the crisis that Silone will later recall in *The God That Failed.*

Following the arrest of Guglielmo Jonna, the head of the Soccorso Rosso (Red Aid), and his disclosure of its operations to the fascist police, Silone and Gabriella escape to Lugano and then to Basel, continuing their undercover work.

1928 *13 April.* Romolo Tranquilli is arrested. He is accused of the 12 April massacre at the Milan Fair and of attempted regicide. He declares his innocence, to no avail. In prison he suffers police brutality.

23 April. Silone writes to Romolo asking him to be strong. He tells him that he trusts him, suffers with him, and that all will be done to prove his innocence.

Silone plans to travel to Italy to help his brother. Chief of Police Bocchini informs Mussolini that Guido Bellone, the inspector general of the political division responsible for the control of Secondino Tranquilli, "the well-known Communist subversive," has received a telegram announcing his intention to come to Italy. But Silone cannot carry out his plan because a warrant has been issued for his arrest.

1 September. Silone writes to his grandmother that he will somehow find the money to pay the legal fees for Romolo's defence.

Silone continues to engage in antifascist activities in Paris and Berlin.

1929 Pescina, *2 February.* Silone's grandmother sends a plea for pardon to the King of Italy on behalf of her grandson Romolo Tranquilli.

Ascona, *July.* Silone's health has been deteriorating. On sick leave from the Communist Party, he is treated at the Curhouse Collinetta.

Silone begins to write *Fontamara.*

1930 Davos, *8 January.* Silone informs Romolo that he is experiencing hardship and must decrease the meagre monthly amounts of money he has been sending him.

Liege, *30 March.* Following ongoing disagreements, at the meeting of the Central Committee of the Communist Party, Silone is ousted.

13 April. In a letter found by Biocca and Canali, Silone writes to Guido Bellone to communicate his decision to end their relationship. The letter, as published by the historians, is handwritten, has no addressee, and is signed "Silvestri."

Zurich, *23 December.* Silone, found without a residence permit, is arrested. His Swiss friends intervene to spare him from expulsion. He obtains a residence permit on the condition that he will not engage in political activities.

1931 *13 January.* Silone and Fleischmann meet for the first time on the occasion of the latter's fortieth birthday.

Silone meets Aline Valangin (1889–1986), a remarkable intellectual, pianist, and psychoanalist married to Wladimir Rosembaum, a noted lawyer. An intense romantic relationship develops. Aline, the first reader of *Fontamara,* is instrumental in its publication.

4 July. The PCI sanctions Silone's expulsion.

1932 *February.* The Swiss authorities grant Silone the status of political refugee.

June. The first issue of *information* appears. For its importance see *ISiE.*

27 October. Romolo Tranquilli dies in the Procida prison.

1933 *February.* Silone takes up residence at Marcel Fleischmann's Kleine Pension, 53 Germaniastrasse, Zurich.

April. Fontamara's first edition, dedicated to Romolo Tranquilli and Gabriella Seidenfeld, is published in German translation by Nettie Sutro. The original Italian version is published by Nuove Edizioni Italiane.

June. To secure the permit to remain in Switzerland, Gabriella Seidenfeld marries Edy Meyer (aka Eduard Mayer, Meier, or Mayer [1877–1967]).

1934 Silone publishes *Die Reise nach Paris* (*Viaggio a Parigi,*) a collection of short stories translated into German by Nettie Sutro.

Silone publishes *Der Faschismus: Seine Entstehug und seine Entwicklung* (*Il fascismo. Origini e sviluppo),* translated into German by Gritta Baerlocher.

Silone meets Nicola Chiaromonte, the Italian intellectual and antifascist activist. In 1956, their common interests and mutual respect lead to the co-founding of the monthly *Tempo Presente.*

October. Gabriella Seidenfeld divorces Edy Meyer.

1935 *10 January.* In Italy, the fascist police record that Silone is still abroad and is among those who are to be arrested in given circumstances.

16 January. The chief of the fascist political police reports that Tranquilli does not hide his deep hatred of fascism, blaming it for the death of his brother, whom he sought to help when he tried to lend himself as an informer.

In Lugano, Ascona, and Zurich, Silone remains under police surveillance.

1 July. The Italian Consulate in Berlin notes that the state secret police have ordered the seizure of Silone's *Der Faschismus.* In December, the Italian government orders that the book must not circulate in Italy.

1936 *12 January.* The Swiss police record that Silone is still living in Zurich, at 53 Germaniastrasse, and that "his lover Gabriella Seidenfeld" also lives in Zurich.

Silone's *Pane e vino,* translated by Adolf Saager, is published as *Brot und Wein.*

30 August. In an open letter, Silone declines the invitation to write for *Das Wort,* saying that he refuses to become a fascist and a red fascist at that.

31 October. Silone's residence permit expires.

1937 *1 September.* In an open letter to left-wing newspapers, Silone defends André Gide against Moscow's false accusations that he is an agent of the Gestapo.

1938 Silone publishes *La scuola dei dittatori,* in a German translation by Jacob Huber (pseudonym of Jacob Humm) as *Die Schule der Dictatoren,* and in an English translation by Gwenda David and Erich Mosbacher as *The School for Dictators.*

1939 *20 April.* The Italian Interior Ministry asks the prefect of L'Aquila to find some episode in Silone's life to be used to redefine his image abroad where he publishes books that are damaging to the regime.

10 September. The Italian fascist police issue a warrant for Silone's arrest and a request for extradition from Switzerland. The Swiss government rejects the request.

1941 *9 December.* Silone and Darina meet at Fleischmann's villa.

Silone's third novel, *Il seme sotto la neve,* translated into German by W.J. Guggenheim, is published as *Der Samen unterm Schnee.* The book is dedicated "To Darina," and Silone personally gives her a copy thus inscribed: "Alla compagna Darina – *Unum in una fide et spe. libertas.*"

1942 *14 December.* Silone is arrested for having engaged in political activism.

In jail he writes his *Memoriale dal carcere svizzero* (*Memoir from a Swiss Prison,* translated by Stanislao G. Pugliese) and another important writing about freedom that is published for the first time in the Introduction to this volume.

30 December. Concern over Silone's health causes the authorities to release him, pending his trial. He is sent to a sanatorium in Davos.

1943 *January–June.* Silone is confined to Davos. The sentence of expulsion (for engaging in political activism) has been commuted to internment.

He then moves to Baden and finally returns to Zurich where he remains until the end of World War II.

8 September. Italy announces the armistice with the Allied Army. Marcel expresses his enthusiasm in a letter to Silone.

1944 *July.* As indicated in one of Silone's letters, Jürg Fleischmann marries Jane Cook. The exact date of the marriage is unknown.

Baden, *14 August.* Silone completes *Ed egli si nascose* [*And He Hid Himself*]. The play is published the same year in the Italian original, and in the German translation by Lotte Thiessing as *Und er verbag sich.*

12 October. Silone returns to Italy with Darina Elizabeth Laracy.

Rome, *20 December.* Silone and Darina marry in Campidoglio.

1945 The New York Museum of Modern Art (MoMa) acquires Braque's *Man with a Guitar* and Picasso's *Ma Jolie* from Marcel Fleischmann.

1946 *2 June.* Silone is elected to the Assemblea Costituente (Constituent Assembly).

4 July. Silone officially adopts "Ignazio" as his first name.

1947 *24 January.* Silone legally adopts this surname.

1948 Jürg experiences business troubles. His marriage ends.

1949 *November.* The Silones learn that Fleischmann is about to lose the Kleine Pension.

1950 Silone becomes the director of the Associazione Italiana per la Libertà della Cultura (Italian Association for Cultural Freedom).

2 February. Jürg Fleischmann marries Gloria Goldberg (1924–). They have two children: Jessica (1952–) and Anthony (1956–).

9 February. Having lost the Kleine Pension, Fleischmann and Elsa Schiess move to a modest apartment at 78 Plattenstrasse, Zurich.

Florence, *June.* At a UNESCO conference Darina Silone meets the young Indian poet Keshav Malik.

Brussels, *3 November*. Silone delivers his famous speech "Habeas animan!" at the second Congress for Cultural Freedom.

1952 Silone publishes his first post-exile novel, *Una manciata di more* (*A Handful of Blackberries*).

1956 Silone and Nicola Chiaromonte found the cultural journal *Tempo Presente.*

Silone publishes *Il segreto di Luca* (*The secret of Luca*).

1959 *17 April.* Fleischmann writes an important letter to Silone about his visit to the Nuremberg cemetery.

1960 Silone publishes *La volpe e le camelie* (*The Fox and the Camellias*), dedicated to Marcel Fleischmann.

1963 *13 April.* Silone and his wife arrive in New York. They visit Princeton, Yale, and Harvard universities, among others.

25 May. Silone writes to Fleischmann from the George Washington University Hospital, in Washington, D.C., where he is recovering from lung illness.

December. Silone and his wife travel to Israel.

1965 Silone receives the Marzotto Prize for *Uscita di sicurezza.*

1966 *June.* Silone receives the Doctor of Letters degree *Honoris causa* from Yale University.

21 November. Having read Silone's *Emergency Exit,* Fleischmann writes an important letter to his friend.

1967 Silone resigns from the Congress for Cultural Freedom.

Nettie Sutro dies. *4 October,* Fleischmann writes that more should be done to commemorate her.

1968 Silone publishes his second play, *L'avventura di un povero cristiano* (*The Story of a Humble Christian*), for which he receives the Super Campiello Prize.

Tempo Presente ceases publication.

1969 *19 March.* Silone receives the Jerusalem Prize. In his acceptance speech he urges the Jews – who have suffered more than other peoples – to consider the plight of the Palestinian refugees.

Silone receives the degree of Doctor *Honoris causa* from the University of Toulouse.

1970 Silone is widely celebrated in the media on his seventieth birthday. *28 June,* Swiss television broadcasts a documentary about his Zurich years, including his stay at the Kleine Pension.

1971 At the initiative of the publisher Stefano De Luca, a group of Silone's friends produce *Dal villaggio all'Europa (omaggio a Silone).*

Silone receives the Cino del Duca International Prize.

1972 Silone receives the degree of Doctor *Honoris causa* from the University of Warwick.

Silone receives the Order of Merit of the Italian Republic.

1 December. Silone writes to Fleischmann that he intends to bequeath his archive to Pescina.

1973 *13 January.* Elsa Schiess dies. It is Fleischmann's eighty-second birthday and the sixty-eighth anniversary of the earthquake that killed Silone's mother.

The Italian government awards Silone the Penna d'Oro for Literature.

The French government awards Silone the Légion d'Honneur.

In Switzerland, Silone receives the Gottfried Keller Literary Prize.

1977 Gabriella Seidenfeld dies in Rome. She is buried in the Jewish section of the Cimitero Monumentale del Verano.

1978 *22 August.* Silone dies in Geneva, with his wife at his side. His ashes are entombed in Pescina dei Marsi, as he requested in his last will.

1982 The Campiello d'oro prize is awarded posthumously to Silone.

1984 *6 August.* Fleischmann dies in Zurich. He is buried in the family tomb at the Friedhof Manegg.

2000 *1 May.* Darina Silone donates the Silone archives and other possessions to the town of Pescina dei Marsi, Centro Studi Ignazio Silone.

2003 *25 July.* Darina Silone dies in Rome. At her request, her ashes are brought back to Ireland to be scattered at sea.

Abbreviations

ALIS	Stanislao G. Pugliese, *Bitter Spring. A Life of Ignazio Silone*
CCF	Congress for Cultural Freedom
Colloqui	Michele Dorigatti and Maffino Maghenzani, *Darina Laracy Silone. Colloqui*
DOeS	Giovanni Casoli, *L'incontro di due uomini liberi: Don Orione e Silone*
ISiE	Deborah Holmes, *Ignazio Silone in Exile. Writing and Antifascism in Switzerland 1929–1944*
ISBTV	Maria Nicolai Paynter, *Ignazio Silone: Beyond the Tragic Vision*
ISRS	Bruno Falcetto, ed., *Ignazio Silone. Romanzi e Saggi*, vols I–II
LdE	Luce d'Eramo, *L'opera di Ignazio Silone. Saggio critico e guida bibliografica*
LdEIS	Yukari Saito, ed., *Luce d'Eramo* IGNAZIO SILONE
LDV	Dario Biocca, *La doppia vita di un italiano*
MSP	Stanislao G. Pugliese, trans., *Memoir from a Swiss Prison*
NZZ	*Neue Züricher Zeitung*
OSS	Office of Strategic Services
OVRA	Opera Vigilanza Repressione Antifascista
PcdI	Partito comunista d'Italia
PCI	Partito Comunista Italiano
Psi	Partito socialista italiano
PVSL	Maria Nicolai Paynter, *Perché verità sia libera. Memorie, confessioni, riflessioni e itinerario poetico di David Maria Turoldo*

SCP	Dario Biocca and Mauro Canali, *L'informatore: Silone i comunisti e la polizia*
SL	Aldo Forbice, ed., *Silone, la libertà. Un intellettuale scomodo contro tutti i totalitarismi*
SPCI	Giulia Paola Di Nicola and Attilio Danese, *Silone, percorsi di una coscienza inquieta*
StAM	Antonio Gasbarrini and Annibale Gentile, eds, *Silone tra l'Abruzzo e il mondo*

ON FRIENDSHIP AND FREEDOM

THE CORRESPONDENCE OF IGNAZIO SILONE AND MARCEL FLEISCHMANN

Introduction

This work aims to provide the reader with new, original material that, when coupled with what is already widely known about Ignazio Silone, can help broaden our understanding of the man as a human being. The correspondence that is published here for the first time is a significant source that needs to be explored, particularly after the revisionism that has resulted in a second "caso Silone."[1] Equally important is the introduction of Marcel Fleischmann – a remarkable man, thus far hardly known, and now revealed through the expression of his and Silone's conceptions of friendship and freedom. At their sides were two remarkable women: Darina Silone and Elsa Schiess. Darina is already well known for her intellectual stature and as Silone's wife, but will be even better known through her letters. Elsa is introduced here for the first time. As they get to know her, readers will discover a woman of generous spirit and a very poetic soul with an immense capacity for love and understanding.

I begin this introduction with a recollection of the first meeting of Secondino Tranquilli and Marcel Fleischmann in order to provide new readers with essential background information needed to help them understand the "four remarkable people" in the biographical section that follows. To facilitate an informed reading of the correspondence contained in the second part of the book, I provide a brief recollection of the historical milieu that prevailed in Switzerland, followed by a note on the importance of Silone as a literary figure and a thinker, and on his and Fleischmann's thoughts on friendship and freedom. Finally, pondering the Silone archives, I note the scant scholarship that has thus far been dedicated to the correspondence, and anticipate that the present study will open the door to others interested in exploring this very promising field.

A Friendship Is Born

Zurich, 13 January 1931. Marcel Fleischmann is celebrating his fortieth birthday. Among his guests is Secondino Tranquilli, an Italian political refugee who will soon be better known as Ignazio Silone, the author of *Fontamara.* Silone is almost thirty-one. A lifelong friendship between two men who apparently have little in common is about to start.

Silone's history prior to this meeting may be outlined as follows. His childhood years, spent in the Marsican town of Pescina dei Marsi, are unremarkable, save for his natural inclination to observe and analyse reality. Born into a working-class family with traditional Christian values, he suffers the premature loss of his father and several siblings. Then, in the earthquake of 13 January 1915 that devastates the region, he loses his mother. His younger brother, Romolo, and his grandmother are the only other survivors. As an orphan, he is uprooted and left at the mercy of various educational institutions. That experience and his realization of the hypocrisy and corruption that prevail in the circles of power compel him to engage in socio-political activism. In just a few years he becomes an effective leader of the Italian Socialist Youth. In 1921 he is in Leghorn where he participates in the founding of the Italian Communist Party. His remarkable dedication and talent earn him the admiration of such leaders as Antonio Gramsci and Camilla Ravera. In the following years he joins the antifascist struggle, and, together with his comrade and companion Gabriella Seidenfeld, he carries out the missions assigned to them by the party. They face the risks and endure jail and all the hardship without reservation, until, at the 1927 Comintern meeting held in Moscow, Silone realizes that communism is no different from red fascism. The resulting crisis – as documented in *The God That Failed* – as well as other considerations, compels him to abandon political activism and to become a writer. The relative peace he finds in Switzerland is muted by his anguish over the fate of his brother Romolo, who is in jail and needs his help, and by his own bad health and financial hardship.

Fleischmann, on the other hand, a native of Zurich, has always enjoyed a privileged life. He is a member of a wealthy family of Jewish grain merchants belonging to the upper bourgeoisie. In his villa, located in one of Zurich's most prestigious neighbourhoods, he has amassed a remarkable art collection. His friends are artists, musicians, writers, and other intellectuals; some of them are refugees to whom he offers hospitality with great generosity. That same generosity compels Fleischmann to help his new friend. In February 1933, four months after his brother Romolo's death in the Procida prison, Secondino Tranquilli accepts Fleischmann's invitation and takes up residence at the villa that Marcel calls the Kleine Pension.

It should be noted that Fleischmann is not motivated by self-serving considerations. He enjoys a good life. He has a beloved son and a devoted assistant in Elsa Schiess, who provides the security he lost when he became a widower. Secondino Tranquilli cannot support himself and his companion, Serena (as Gabriella Seidenfeld is called), and is not yet famous, as he will suddenly become after the publication of his first novel in April 1933. What compels this reserved and proud man to accept Fleischmann's invitation? Certainly need! He has not had a place of his own since he was uprooted from his family's home in Pescina. Now, as a writer, he can benefit from the stability that his new friend offers him. Neither man, at this point, can foresee that the stay will last more than a decade.

As Luce d'Eramo[2] and I demonstrated in our ample discussions of Silonian criticism, Silone's literary fortune dates back to the publication of *Fontamara,* and he has since become renowned worldwide. Scholars still interested in learning more about his life and his thought continue to produce significant works that merit readers' attention. Noteworthy among these are Pugliese's engaging biography and a well-researched book about Silone's Swiss years by Deborah Holmes.

Surprisingly, nothing has been written to date about Marcel Fleischmann, not even by those who benefited from his generosity and could easily have left their testimonials. My contribution, in this regard, provides a good starting point. The biographical profile that follows aims to provide information which, together with the chronology, will help to contextualize the correspondence.

The Historical Milieu

The years that Silone spends in Switzerland are, historically, the most dramatic of the century. In Italy Mussolini celebrates the "Decennale" – the first decade of his regime. Then, in January 1933 Hitler is named chancellor of Germany. Two years later, having conducted an aggressive propaganda campaign, Mussolini invades Abyssinia while waging war on all political enemies. For instance, even though Silone has pledged to the Swiss authorities that he will refrain from all political activities, the Italian fascist police keep him under constant surveillance, plan for his arrest, and order the seizure of his new book about fascism. When the

Rome-Berlin Axis is formed in October 1936, Silone's situation becomes even more dangerous. The assassination of the Rosselli brothers only a few months later sends a stern warning to all who oppose fascism. In May 1938, Hitler's official visit to Italy, prepared for and carried out with great fanfare, is meant to display the power of the two strongmen. Only six months later, during Kristallnacht, the Nazis vandalize, loot, and burn Jewish shops and synagogues with impunity. In that same month, Italy proclaims its own Racial Laws. The "Pact of Steel" is signed the following year, and on 10 June 1940 Italy declares war on France and England, thus entering World War II. In 1941 Germany and Italy declare war on the United States. Germany implements the "final solution" that will exterminate millions of Jews, as well as political enemies and other human beings deemed to be unfit to live in a world dominated by a "pure race." The enormity of this madness is such that the initial reaction is psychological denial. But soon reality sets in and countless innocent people, having to flee their homes, seek refuge wherever they can find it. Switzerland is a magnet for them, and Fleischmann's home provides a temporary safe haven for many.

Mussolini's deposition and arrest on 25 July 1943 provides some hope, but his rescue by the Germans throws Italy into even greater chaos. In September he establishes the Italian Social Republic in German-dominated northern Italy. This marks the onset of a de facto civil war, especially once Badoglio – the general who has succeeded Mussolini – switches sides, joining the Allies and then declaring war on Germany on 13 October 1943. Not until the war is finally over, in 1945, does Silone return to Italy.

During all these years Switzerland remains under threat of German occupation and needs to appease the Nazi regime. As a result, the situation for political refugees is increasingly precarious. Some rules pertaining to them become more stringent. For instance, in 1938 German non-Aryans need a special visa to cross the border; in 1939 border crossings are closed, and people who shelter Jews hiding from the Nazis are subject to prosecution. Writing on "The Conditions of Literary Exile in Switzerland, 1929–44," in her book *Ignazio Silone in Exile,* Deborah Holmes describes the situation faced by the majority of foreign writers and other intellectuals.

There appears to be no solution in sight. After the outbreak of the war, the Swiss general Henri Guisan, who wants to explore new possibilities, has to contend with the newly elected president, Marcel Pilet-Golaz, and most members of the Federal Council, the Swiss Foreign Office, high-ranking army officers, and influential Swiss citizens, who successfully argue for a politics of continued appeasement with Germany.

Under the circumstances, Silone can no longer honour his pledge to refrain from political activism and seeks to find ways, other than with his writing, to intervene in history. He befriends Allen Welsh Dulles, an American diplomat working for the Office of Strategic Services (OSS), and together they explore possible ways to rescue Italy from Mussolini's disastrous leadership. Silone writes and distributes a pacifist manifesto, "Il terzo fronte," a passionate appeal to Italians, reminding them of the promises made by the Duce and the suffering caused by his regime and urging them to engage in civil disobedience. "Silone reminded Italians that fascism had promised them an empire and instead had made Italy a colony of Germany; it had promised prosperity and had reduced Italians to beggars; it had promised social peace and fraternity between workers and owners through its sham ideology of the corporate state, but had instead turned a blind eye to rampant corruption, cronyism, and the sacking of the public sphere in favor of a few wealthy 'sharks.' The Fascist regime had promised the restoration of Italian society but had dragged the people into the 'barbarous cult of the swastika.'"[3]

Silone also cooperates with the *Partisan Review*, working tirelessly in support of Dwight Macdonald's initiative to help refugee intellectuals held in concentration camps leave Europe for America.[4] Then, when Clement Greenberg and others urge him to leave Switzerland for his own safety, he declines the invitation, choosing to abide by the dictates of his conscience.

Some Perceptions of Silone

Whatever one might think about Silone the man – and opinions may vary depending on the individual's point of view – it is generally recognized that he was one of the most highly regarded writers and thinkers of the twentieth century. He published short stories, novels, plays, essays, a satire, and autobiographical writings. His major works were translated into many languages, and from the early 1930s significant scholarship was dedicated to his opus. Luce d'Eramo's study remains of fundamental value for understanding, on the one hand the popularity that Silone enjoyed abroad, and on the other the cold and even hostile reception he found in Italy for the two decades following World War II. D'Eramo's work, published in 1971, and still only available in Italian, needed updating; more needed to be done to reach a wider public. To this end, I wrote about "Silone's Literary Fortune" from 1933 to 2000 and also published a new article noting the tendency of scholars, in the following decade, to read (or reread) Silone's work in order to find clues to his character.[5]

Even though interpretations of an author's words may vary, the essence of his thought – his main concern – invariably emerges. For Silone it was the need to understand human history. To explore this topic, many noted scholars convened at an international symposium titled *Silone: Reader of the Signs of History.*[6] They spoke of the writer's concept of history and his awareness of the seduction of power, with the tragic consequences that it entails. Also, in an interview occasioned by his receiving the Ignazio Silone International Prize, Giuseppe Mazzotta pointedly noted,

> Credo che Silone sia tra i pochi che abbiano colto il segreto che ha segnato di tragedia la storia del ventesimo secolo. Ha capito, cioè, l'intreccio di teologia e politica, ne ha smascherato le insidie e ne ha sottolineato l'inevitabilità. [...] Silone ha stabilito una distanza critica da queste che al suo spirito profondamene francescano non potevano che apparire cupe idolatrie. E ha stabilito una distanza critica anche perché ne ha riconosciuto il fascino e per qualche tempo si è sottomesso ad esso. Il potere, quindi, come, allo stesso tempo, gioco diabolico e tentazione. Dalla lucida diagnosi dell'ambiguità del potere è sorta, io credo, la vocazione letteraria di Silone.[7]
>
> [I believe that Silone is among the few who have grasped the secret that has left an imprint of tragedy on the history of the twentieth-century. He understood the interweaving of theology and politics, unmasked its deceptions and underlined its inevitability. [...] Silone established a critical distance from what could only appear as dark idolatries to his deeply Franciscan spirit. And he established a critical distance also because he recognized the allure of power and for some time was subjected to it. Power, then, as diabolic game and temptation at the same time. Silone's literary vocation stems, I believe, from this lucid diagnosis of the ambiguity of power.]

In Silone, the nexus of truth, history, and utopia is found in the figure of Christ. Pondering the past, he notes how the two millennia of the Christian era have not sufficed to bring justice to the oppressed and that the history of the world remains on the page of the agonizing Christ. In his play, significantly titled *And He Hid Himself*, he states: "In the sacred history of man on earth, it is still, alas, Good Friday. Men who 'hunger and thirst after righteousness' are still derided, persecuted, put to death."[8]

Silone, like Carlo Levi and Ennio Flaiano,[9] feels that what is deemed to be "civilization" is a dubious concept when revisited and compared to the supposedly "uncivilized" realm inhabited by the historically oppressed. But whereas Levi leaves Lucania looking back "with affectionate sorrow" at the "dark civilization and motionless time that he leaves behind" and goes on to resume his previous journey, and Flaiano suggests that human nature is best represented by the Africans whose humanity has not been corrupted by 2000 years of "civilization," Silone's heroes see it as their duty to intervene in history. They come to realize that they are in fact their brothers' keepers, and that only the individual's acceptance of self-sacrifice for the sake of others can save humanity. This is why Berardo, the hero of *Fontamara*, endures torture and, before confessing to a crime he has not committed, expresses his newly found awareness as follows: "If I turn traitor, everything is lost. [...] If I turn traitor, Fontamara will be damned forever. If I turn traitor, centuries will pass before such another opportunity occurs again. And if I die? ... I shall be the first peasant to die not for himself but for the others. For the other peasants. For the unity of the peasants."[10]

When Silone wrote *Fontamara*, he implicitly began a creative process similar to the one he attributed to medieval painters, who, he noted, always drew and redrew Christ's Holy Face. In his works, Berardo's self-sacrifice as *figura Christi*[11] is followed by Cristina's in *Bread and Wine*; by Luigi Murica's in *And He Hid Himself*; by Pietro Spina's in *The Seed beneath the Snow*; by Luca's in *The Secret of Luca*; and by Cefalù's in *The Fox and the Camellias*. In *A Handful of Blackberries*, Silone broadened the scope of his "drawing and redrawing" by showing how individuals can lose their freedom when they are mired in political ideology and how they can instead live in harmony by simply respecting one another. His concern over freedom also compelled him to write *The School for Dictators*. And it is noteworthy that in *The Story of a Humble Christian*, Pope Celestine V resigns when he realizes that he cannot be a true Christian and a good pontiff at the same time.[12]

For six decades Silone engages in the most important intellectual and political debates of the times with his writings, his journalistic initiatives, his passionate speeches, and significant interviews. Bruno Falcetto lists them in "Opere e scritti di Ignazio Silone."[13] A mere glance at the titles and the dates suggests that Silone seeks to intervene in history as a freedom sniper throughout his life.

On Friendship and Freedom

Precisely as a freedom sniper Silone resumes political activism and, in December 1942, having disseminated "Il terzo fronte," he is arrested. While in jail he writes his *Memoriale dal carcere svizzero* (*Memoir from a Swiss Prison*). He also writes a beautiful piece about freedom that is published here for the first time. Its importance justifies the long digression:

> Yesterday towards evening you went along the lake. The mist blended the water and the sky into a vast grey without horizon; it softened the vulgar noise of the electric ads and draped the frail winter nudity of the poplars. You went along the lake and the lake, seen through the mist, was without horizon. Today you are in prison. Yesterday's vast sky is distant beyond the prison bars and the dusty windows. Only the keys of the jailer who stops to glance through the peephole interrupt the silence. Four stone walls exclude the world. You are in jail. The reason is very simple. You personify something more formidable than a thousand Panzer divisions: the freedom of the mind. You have refused to burn incense on the altar of the official idols, have refused to stifle your brain by singing the litanies of journalistic liturgy, have refused to obey the commandment: you will hate your neighbour. You have refused to accept that political freedom be held captive by a handful of platitudes; that personal freedom be imprisoned by virtue of a licence for individual egotism. And the mere conquest of your own freedom has not satisfied your thirst: you wanted the same for others as well. You have become evidence that human dignity can survive even its present suicidal mania, that the value of human personality is above all theories, all fanaticisms, all politics. In a society where liberty has degenerated to a propaganda slogan, where truth is seen as eccentricity, where dignity and charity risk being denounced as treason, within a society that depends upon the brutalization of its slaves, you are an apparition – for some nostalgic – for others scandalous – arrived from another world, a dangerously beautiful world, a dangerously possible world. The things that you have said are not all that new, most of them are at least two thousand years old, but truth is always sensational; even after two thousand years it continues to amaze and frighten, it continues to scandalize. It is not after all very surprising that you are in jail. But four stone walls are not sufficient to stifle the truth; even your silence speaks to us.
>
> Your silence proclaims to us that freedom demands as many duties as the rights that it confers. It proclaims that the choice of spiritual freedom implies the acceptance of persecution as its extreme and logical consequence.

It proclaims that spiritual freedom not only does not diminish but also reinforces itself when material freedom is sacrificed for its defence. It proclaims that freedom is nothing else than mankind's supreme good. Imprisonment has not isolated you. The door has been locked to the unwelcome acquaintances; it has united you to all who in the past have been persecuted for the sake of truth and to all who now, listening to the echo of your silence, realize that it is in order to show them the path of freedom and dignity that you renounce the vast sky and accept the humiliations that the jailers inflict upon you. These humiliations are testimony of their impotence to touch you. They do not have the key to the door that separates your spirit from theirs. They ignore that the pride of one's own spiritual dignity can reach a degree of intensity where it demands the sacrifice of exterior, superficial dignities. Those who speak as if imprisonment had deprived you of a treasure, as if your spirit were at the mercy of material surroundings, pay too much honour to those who have locked the door of your cell. They can prevent you from walking down the street, but the freedom of your spirit is beyond their reach. You cannot see the sky and the lake blend in the mist, but the universe of your spirit is without horizon. Prison does not exist for a free being, it is not you, it is we who need to know it.

Heroism has an existence independent of quality – astonishing and distant only when it is the supreme gesture of a faint-hearted man. For those who are accustomed to act according to their beliefs, this is not a gesture, nor a series of [gestures],[14] it is not effort, nor sacrifice; it is simply the natural climax of their soul. To free oneself of all constraints except for the love of truth is to exorcize fear. There are those who need to know it. You are in prison. It is the final verdict on the pitiful and petty bestiality of those who persecute you. By imprisoning you, they create a heroic legend out of something that for you is quite natural. They are mistaken if they think that they can dominate, humiliate, possess you. It is they who are dominated, humiliated, possessed by a historical, ineluctable process of which they are the unconscious tools: that is to say that truth in all ages needed to be persecuted in order to triumph. The path of persecution is the path of achievement. "Vicisti Galilaeus [sic]" [You have won, Galilean][15] – the last word of the persecutors before disappearing into darkness.

The internal monologue expresses a vision that both Silone and Fleischmann share. The end of the first paragraph brings to mind a scene in *The Seed beneath the Snow* where Pietro Spina's attention is totally absorbed by a picture of the Crucifixion bearing St Paul's words: "Judaeis quidem scandalum, gentibus autem stultitiam" ["Unto the Jews a stumbling block, unto the Gentiles foolishness"]. This "scandalum," represented in the individual's willingness to sacrifice for the sake of others, is also for Silone, Fleischmann, and the poet David Maria Turoldo the essential, redeeming force that legitimates the "the scandal of hope."[16] Silone further clarifies the concept in a letter to Luce d'Eramo. He writes:

> La frase di San Paolo su Cristo che è "uno scandalo," che Lei cita, è di quelle che amo di più. Essa ricorre varie volte nei miei libri, specialmente in alcuni capitoli di "Il seme sotto la neve," in un senso però diverso dal Suo. Non credo che si possano far risalire allo "scandalo"di Cristo le non poche turpitudini di cui è ricca la storia della Chiesa. Soprattutto non credo che Cristo sia proprietà della Chiesa e che abbia bisogno del permesso della Curia per agire tra gli uomini. Penso, sono convinto che egli non è solo in Chiesa, ma ovunque si lotta e si soffre per la giustizia in purezza di cuore.[17]

> [St Paul's sentence, that you quote, on Christ being "a scandal" is among the ones I love the most. It recurs several times in my books, especially in some chapters of *The Seed beneath the Snow*, in a sense, however, that is different from yours. I don't believe that we can trace back to the "scandal" of Christ the considerable number of turpitudes in which the history of the Church abounds. Above all I don't believe that Christ is the property of the Church and needs permission from the curia to act among men. I think, I am convinced that He is not only in Church, but is wherever people fight and suffer for justice with a pure heart.]

This spirit of Pauline friendship also informs the letter that Silone writes to Fleischmann on the occasion of the latter's fiftieth birthday, to which he adds a typewritten copy of the "First Letter of St Paul to the Corinthians," chapter 13, with the following footnote: "Au lieu d'amitié, certain auteurs traduisent le mot charité, d'autres le mot amour; mais, puisque charité a un peu changé de signification dans les temps modernes et puisque Paul ne pensait pas seulement aux rapports entre hommes et femmes, peut-être le mot amitié convient le mieux"[18] [Instead of friendship, some authors translate the word as charity, others as love; but since in modern times charity has somewhat changed in meaning, and since Paul was not thinking only about the relationship between men and women, it is possible that the word friendship is the most appropriate]. Friendship, as understood herein, is a recurring topic in the correspondence. The others are freedom, goodness, and free will: freedom as the supreme goal, and goodness and free will as means to achieve it by moral choice and exemplary conduct. Whereas Silone and Fleischmann come from different social and economic backgrounds, and Silone's apolitical friend does not share the writer's political passion, the two men have similar moral values and a genuine need to help anyone in need.

Even as fighting for justice with a pure heart is the aspiration of both Silone and Fleischmann, it would be wrong to yield to the temptation of perceiving either of them as a "hero" and risk transforming human experience into legend. At the same time, the tendency of examining a fictional work to draw conclusions about its author's life should also be resisted.

The Silone Archives

Little has thus far been published of the wealth of correspondence pertaining to Ignazio Silone. The Fondazione di Studi Storici "Filippo Turati" (where much of the original material has been held since 1985) makes it available to the public, but thus far no extensive collection of correspondence has been produced in print, nor is a digitized version of the archives available online. Electronic access is presently being facilitated by the work of state archivists Sebastiana Ferrari and Martorano Di Cesare, who have been entrusted with the organization of the material held at the Centro Studi Ignazio Silone.

In a few isolated instances, a certain number of letters have been collected and published: the letters that Silone wrote to Luce d'Eramo; his letters to Don Orione;[19] his correspondence with Angelo Tasca; his exchanges with Ivan Anissimov; and the letters published by Margherita Pieracci Harwell in *Un cristiano senza chiesa e altri saggi.*

Sixty-four items are published in the appendix of a recent volume edited by Yukari Saito[20] (mostly letters addressed by Silone to Luce d'Eramo during the composition of *L'opera di Ignazio Silone,* a flap copy for the book, five notes from her to him, and some letters they exchanged with Mondadori, publishers of the volume). The letters are of clear importance for all who are interested in knowing more about the friendship that the two intellectuals shared, their thoughts about literature and the creative process, d'Eramo's commitment to her monumental task, and Silone's generous support and guidance during many years.

Silone's correspondence with Don Orione, edited by Giovanni Casoli, encompasses his formative years and is quite revealing. His exchanges with Anissimov[21] are useful for an understanding of both writers' views on the topic of freedom, and his correspondence with Angelo Tasca[22] sheds light on the precarious situation he faced before his expulsion from the Communist Party. Finally, in his exchanges with Margherita Pieracci Harwell[23] Silone discusses his views on Christianity in terms similar to those found in his letter to Luce d'Eramo quoted above.

Over the years, some of Silone's personal letters to his grandmother, his brother Romolo, Gabriella Seidenfeld, Aline Valangin, publishers, translators, intellectuals, and other interlocutors have been found and published. They provide valuable insight, but much more can be done to facilitate a deeper understanding of Silone, as a human being, a socio-political activist, and a writer.

Contextualizing the Silone-Fleischmann Correspondence

Caution about the possibility that their letters could be read by others must have prevented both friends from putting their thoughts about current events in writing. Apparently, "censorship of civilian mail was the exception rather than the rule but did occur."[24] And even though Silone and Fleischmann do not write about the possibility that their letters may be intercepted, there is some evidence of the legitimate concern they experienced on account of other evidence of restricted freedom. In one of his letters Silone worries that his friend might get in trouble for hosting a revolutionary writer. In another, he reassures Fleischmann, who fears that the books he is storing for Max Raphael[25] could get him into trouble. There is also evidence that the Swiss authorities censored Silone's work, asking him, for instance, to change some passages of *The Seed beneath the Snow.*

While not dismissing the legitimate controversy regarding Silone's alleged role as a fascist informer, it is regrettable that the tendency to paint a negative picture of the man has not been limited to his public life. There have been arbitrary claims of unstable temperament and split personality, of suspected impotence, and of homosexuality. The voyeuristic and homophobic instincts of such readers may find additional fodder in some of the letters they now read. For instance, in one of them, Fleischmann writes that, missing his friend, he went to put flowers in his room. In others, the two discuss tentative plans to spend some days together, alone, in silence. But, to understand, the letters must be read objectively and in the appropriate context, beginning with an appreciation of Silone's previously noted conception of friendship and silence. In this regard, a poem by the poet David Maria Turoldo, who received the Silone Prize in 1989 for his affinity with the writer, comes to mind.

It is an internal monologue that the notoriously silent Silone could have also composed:

Non perdere tempo a scrivere tradirai di meno, vai torna a vedere, vai ad esempio sulla sera, d'autunno da solo a Varenna, sul molo, in silenzio nell'ora della luce obliqua e velata: alle spalle	Don't waste time writing You'll betray less, go go back to see, go for instance, at dusk, in autumn alone to Varenna on the pier, in silence when light is oblique and veiled: behind
le case anch'esse in punta di piedi dai ripidi vichi ferme a guardare. Meglio se persona amica t'accompagna ma in silenzio – qualcuno che ti sia indiviso: gioia	the houses too on tiptoe from the steep alleys are staring in stillness. Better if a kindred friend is with you but in silence – someone that is one with you: joy
lo esige onde farsi ancora più godibile: è l'ora della pace. Vai	demands it to make itself even more enjoyable: it's the hour of peace. Go
e vedi e guarda e lascia che ti prenda la grazia e tu ami perfino di essere quello che sei. E meglio è	and see and look and let grace take a hold of you and you'll even love to be what you are. And it's better
se qualcuno potesse appena affidare ai colori (ma quali? e come?) il prodigio: con la passione di Van Gogh,	if someone could just entrust to colours (but which ones? and how?) the prodigy: with the passion of Van Gogh
perché duri, e grazia ancora continui a sperare: ma tu non dire nulla![26]	so that it may last, and grace may still continue to hope: but you, don't say a word!

This is the state of mind that one notices in some of the letters. For instance, at the prospect of a possible meeting, Fleischmann says that he is as happy as a child, and Silone replies, "I truly believe that after a few hours we will begin to be silent and only exchange a few brief words; this is, for me, the highest point that a friendship can reach."[27] Both friends display uncommon sensitivity; especially uncommon for men living in an age dominated by fascism and its prevailing idea of manhood so well represented by its impact on the life of the protagonist in Moravia's novel *The Conformist* and Bertolucci's film of the same name.

A letter that Fleischmann wrote to his grandson almost four decades later is also quite revealing. Like Turoldo, he wishes he could express his feelings as an artist. He writes about the affinities of character he shares with his grandson: "Most precious to us in our ethic [sic] approach to life is genuine truth, modesty, love for mankind with all its shortcomings, a sense of fairness and a deep-rooted feeling for beauty – beauty in the light of inner cleanness and serenity, uprightness of character and responsibility." And then he adds: "If I were gifted to express my feelings as an artist, be it in writing or painting, I would enjoy expressing the features of your soul in the subtle way I sense them."[28] Turoldo also reminds the reader of his and Silone's struggles in the pursuit of freedom in these verses that he composed honouring the writer:

Grazia ad usura, Amico ora ripaga alte solitudini e sogni e battaglie; tu a cercare verità che libera io che verità sia libera: oltre ogni Fontamara[29]	Abundant grace – my Friend now repays deep solitudes and dreams and struggles: you in search of truth that renders free I that truth be free: beyond every Fontamara

If, as I have been arguing, a reading of the Silone-Fleischmann correspondence offers an occasion for pause and reflection, it is also important to notice how the nature of the two men emerges from apparently ordinary letters. For instance, when Silone writes to his friend for his fortieth birthday, he notes that 13 January is also the anniversary of the 1915 Abruzzo earthquake and then draws poignant analogies as follows: "thus are connected, in life, bereavement and birth, sorrow and joy. [...] It will soon be a year that I have been living in your home: the material aid that this represents for me (and indirectly for Serena) is great, but it is very small when compared with the spiritual aid; even if this manifests itself through the invisible paths that lead to the soul, and they don't consist of moralizing speeches and sermons, but of the example of a life that humanizes and harmonizes itself ever more each day. For many things, you are, in my eyes, the man that I would like to be and perhaps will be at the end of my life."[30] Again, silence rather than words speaks for them. The spiritual dimension of life is what truly matters, as well as possessing an exemplary character, as Fleischmann already does and he admittedly does not. His lifelong aspirations, in this regard, are already expressed during his youth in several letters to Don Orione.[31]

The correspondence of the Swiss years is primarily revealing of the men's characters and aspirations, even though Silone, for obvious reasons, does not write about his return to political activism. The letters that the two friends exchange between 1945 and 1976 are rather different, in both tone and content. While previously Silone was immersed in the intellectual climate that pervaded Zurich and that was associated with such intellectuals as Aline Valangin, Jean Paul Samson, Fritz Brupbacher, Jacob Wasserman, Martin Buber, Ernst Toller, Klaus Mann, Kurt Tuscholsky, and countless others, upon his return to Italy he initially felt like a Zurichian in exile. Whereas in Zurich he benefited from Fleischmann's hospitality at the Kleine Pension and was only away from it when health and other circumstances made it necessary, now, in better health and in his own country, he can resume a "normal" life. But, despite a loan he received from Fleischmann before his departure,[32] he and his wife cannot find decent rental accommodation and must live in a hotel for almost two years. In her letters to Fleischmann and Elsa Schiess, Darina Silone speaks about their precarious economic situation and the efforts that are needed to return to normalcy, both for her and Silone and for the Italian people as they usher in the birth of the new Republic.[33]

Fleischmann also resumes a more "normal" existence. In some of his letters he appears to be under pressure to help his son and his brother Carlo, who evidently feel that Silone, who is now a member of the Assemblea Costituente, might be of assistance in their business endeavours. But he also tries to help others – for instance, asking Silone, who knows Arturo Toscanini,[34] to recommend Willi Reich[35] to him. Silone, however, cannot provide that assistance.

In the later years one notices their constant desire to meet again, to spend some time together, and also their inability to do so due to intervening circumstances. Mutual affection and concern are evident. Silone's warmest letters are those he writes when his friend celebrates a new milestone. Fleischmann treasures them and on several occasions mentions that, as a birthday gift to himself, he shares with others the letter Silone wrote to him in 1941. In fact, he thinks that there isn't another letter of such beauty, and Silone should consider publishing it.[36]

Fleischmann is older than Silone, and more sentimental. He loves, and needs to feel that others love him. And Silone reassures him, reminding him that he was never prone to show his feelings but still misses the days when they were together. In one letter he writes, "During the last years, I went through some difficult moments; many times I had to choose between pride and honesty, and I felt very strong nostalgia for our life in common, not in the sense of being able to speak with you, but simply being together. At the time when I had the impression that the hardships had been overcome, and I was again in harmony with myself, I told Darina: what if we went to Switzerland to spend a little time with Marcel Fleischmann and Elsa?"[37] Silone again reiterates that silence can express one's feelings better than words. And also, when he informs his friend that he will dedicate *The Fox and the Camellias* to him, he tells him that this is very appropriate since the novel's main theme is friendship and solidarity among men "in a totally natural manner."

For over three decades, the two friends endeavour to bridge the distance, reminiscing about the past and sharing both joys and sorrows. For instance, Fleischmann writes about the physical decline of their mutual friends and the sorrow he experiences when they die. At Nettie Sutro's funeral,[38] Marcel and many others felt that not enough had been said about that remarkable woman, so they thought of publishing a more worthy testimonial. To this end, Silone wrote a piece in remembrance of his generous friend.

Even when they write about practical matters, their letters show that they are frank with one another. Quite revealing, in this regard, is their concern about Darina and Elsa. Both suffered from depression: Elsa more severely. Marcel sought to help her in every way he could and, when the treatments failed, he agonized over her, wondering about his own shortcomings. Silone, on the other hand, does not seem to engage in soul-searching when Darina is having a drinking problem. In one of his letters he says that she is almost sober, but he does so matter-of-factly, and one senses his frustration as he watches her neglect herself and her health.[39] As he repeatedly admitted in his letters, Silone did not possess the same degree of inner goodness that his friend did, but he did care for his wife and showed her his love until the very end.[40]

Silone also writes to his friend about his work, and praises him for his artistic sensitivity as shown by his ability to capture in his letters the beauty of some of the places he visits.[41] The aging process is often mentioned. Silone's stoicism helps him cope. Fleischmann experiences depression. At the end of his life, having lost Elsa and now living in a rest home, he becomes a recluse, and yet he welcomes Darina's visit, soon after his eighty-fifth birthday, and is moved to tears by her affection. The testimonial letter she wrote to Marcel's son after her visit is quoted in Fleischmann's biographical profile.

Finally, simply reading Fleischmann's letters allows readers to get to know a remarkable human being who was previously merely known as a "grain merchant" and Silone's "Maecenas." Readers will also become immersed in the atmosphere that prevailed in Switzerland in the years from 1934 to the end of the war. When reading the letters of the later years, they will get to know Fleischmann's companion, Elsa Schiess, and the views that she Marcel shared about human life, religion, friendship, goodness, and individual responsibility.

From Silone's letters, readers learn about his Swiss years and the hardships he endured on many fronts. They will also notice the privileges he enjoyed as a result of Fleischmann's generosity and that of other Swiss friends, including Fritz Brupbacher; Nettie Sutro and her husband, Erich Katzenstein; the Oprechts; Aline Valangin and her husband, Wladimir Rosenbaum; and many others. It will not surprise them to notice that even though he was agonizing about the war[42] and had returned to political activism as his own individual way to make a difference, Silone would try to amuse Marcel by drafting a humorous piece, ostensibly intended for Fleischmann's brother Carlo, to "celebrate" him on his fiftieth birthday.[43] When Silone was arrested and his friends were concerned, he reassured them by writing that "imprisonment becomes almost a holiday when it does not bring detachment, indifference and hostility on the part of one's friends but offers their solidarity and affection new possibilities of manifesting themselves. I do not believe that there is, in life, a more precious reality."[44] Silone also writes about his and Darina's travels. Some of the postcards they sent from their favourite spots are included in this volume, and Marcel and Elsa seem to appreciate the chance of keeping up to date. They all keep in touch until life makes it no longer possible.

Four Remarkable People

Ignazio and Darina Silone

Ignazio Silone was born Secondino Tranquilli on 1 May 1900 in Pescina dei Marsi, a small town in Abruzzo that was also the birthplace of Cardinal Mazarin;[1] he died in Geneva on 22 August 1978. His pseudonym was inspired by the Marsican leader Quintus Poppedius Silo and St Ignatius of Loyola.[2]

Silone's father, Paolo Tranquilli, was a modest landowner; his mother, Marianna Delli Quadri, worked as a weaver. Through their words and example, they sought to teach their son the moral values that he would always seek to uphold as a most precious legacy.[3] Naturally bent on internalizing experience, the young Secondino was an attentive listener and a critical observer. The stories and legends his grandmother told by the fireside during the long winter months and those he heard from his mother, sitting at her side when she worked at the loom, would later be credited with the power to inform his narrative style.

In the preface to *Fontamara*, he writes about the art of storytelling as follows: "We learned it when we were children, sitting on the doorstep, or around the fireplace in the long nights of winter, or by the hand loom, listening to the old stories to the rhythm of the pedal. […] The art of putting one word after another, one line after another, one sentence after another, explaining one thing at a time […] is just like the art of weaving …"[4] But, even though the method is apparently simple, the narrative deeply transcends the limits of linearity, as the author's natural tendency to mythopoesis helps him create stories that are both realistic and symbolic.

Silone's life was tragically affected by the earthquake of 13 January 1915, when his mother was found among the victims. Having already lost his father in 1911, he began an orphan's precarious existence, moving for years from place to place with the caring support of Don Luigi Orione, to whom he confided his youthful anxieties as well as the "irresistible fire" he felt within. In a letter dated 29 October 1916 he asks the saintly priest to pray for him so that, atoning for his sins, he can begin his second life. The tone is melodramatic, but the self-awareness is striking. He writes: "Io ho molta paura di me stesso e vorrei vivere in un ambiente isolato, ma ho in me un fuoco irresistibile che mi spinge a fare del bene e vorrei essere in mezzo al mondo" ["I am very afraid of myself and would like to live in an isolated environment, but I have within an irresistible fire that compels me to do good and would like to be in the world"]. Then, in a letter of 11 February 1917, he continues his self-analysis and reiterates his will to overcome temptation: "Prima ero o molto cattivo o molto buono. Quando facevo il buono e cadevo in fallo, subito mi scoraggiavo e diventavo molto cattivo. Adesso mi sono convinto che a me è impossibile, nei primi passi, non ricadere nell'errore e perciò ora, se anche inciamperò, se cadrò, mi rialzerò subito e proseguirò il cammino ..." ["Before I was either too bad or too good. When I was being good and took a fall, I got discouraged and became very bad. Now I am convinced that it is impossible for me, at first, not to fall again, therefore, now, even if I stumble, if I fall, I will quickly get up and continue on the [right] path ..."].[5]

Silone returned to Pescina and began his political activism in the summer of 1917. In the beginning of the following year, writing to Don Ferretti – the head of his former high school – he abandons the pious posture he had maintained with Don Orione and talks instead of the small house he has been given – as a victim of the earthquake – and of its fame as "la casa dei diavoli" [the house of the devils] because of the din that he and his friends make (singing, laughing, eating, drinking, dancing). It is now 1918. World War I continues, and most of his friends are being drafted while he is deemed unfit to serve for health reasons. He worries that he will soon remain alone and, since youth is but a fleeting moment, the future is too dark to think about, and death is too bitter a thought, he tells Don Ferretti that he will take a wife, but not in the traditional sense.[6]

The letter's humorous tone does not diminish its impact. Faced with events too tragic to bear, the young man could only escape into a rowdy *carpe diem*; but that was not to last. His "inner fire" demanded more from him and, "to do good," he engaged in political activism, denouncing the widespread corruption related to the reconstruction process. Again writing to Don Orione (28 July 1918) he tells him, "io credo (lo credono tutti che mi conoscono) di essere socialista" ["I believe (all who know me believe) that I am a socialist"]. But then – he wonders – how can he speak about the soul and forgiveness? He must be an incoherent materialist! As Casoli notes, in this apparent conflict one finds, *in nuce*, Silone's later definition of himself as "a Christian without a church and a socialist without a party."[7]

Silone was only eighteen when he became a socialist. A year later he was elected secretary of the Italian Socialist Youth; in 21 January 1921 he participated in the congress held in Leghorn, and was among the founders of the PCd'I (the Italian Communist Party). That same year he was part of the Italian delegation to the third meeting of the Comintern held in Moscow. Then, at the November meeting of the Communist Youth held in Fiume (Rijeka), he met Gabriella Triedmann Seidenfeld, the young Jewish woman who would become his companion for the following decade. Using several battle names, including Serena, often mentioned in Silone's and Fleischmann's letters, they worked together in the antifascist underground movement, operating in Italy, France, Spain, and Germany. They endured arrest, extradition, and constant surveillance. In 1927 at a Comintern meeting in Moscow, Silone realized that the ideals he had embraced in his youth had been betrayed and that Russian communism was nothing more than "red fascism." By the end of that year, following Guglielmo Jonna's arrest and his betrayal of his comrades to the fascists, Silone and other communist leaders had to leave Italy. They moved to Lugano first and then to Basel.[8] Expelled from Switzerland, Silone escaped to France, spent some time in Germany, and then returned to Switzerland where he was in 1928 at the time of his brother Romolo's arrest.

Romolo Tranquilli was falsely accused of a bombing in Milan that killed eighteen people and wounded many others during an apparent attempt on the life of King Victor Emmanuel III. Upon learning about his brother's detention, Silone wrote to reassure him that justice would prevail:

> [M]ai come ora sento così fortemente i vincoli della fraternità che ci legano! Io vivo, ora per ora, tutta la grande bugia nella quale il caso ti ha gettato; io spero con te, ora per ora, soffro con te, resisto con te. Ciò che vorrei dirti in questo momento te lo immagini e colle condizioni attuali esso è indicibile. Ma io ti assicuro che tutto sarà fatto perché la verità sulla tua innocenza finisca col trionfare. Nell'attesa sii forte e paziente.
> Ti abbraccio e ti bacio con grande affetto
> tuo fratello
> Secondino Tranquilli.

[I never like now felt so strongly the brotherly bonds that unite us! I am living, hour by hour, all of the great lie that chance visited upon you; I hope with you, hour by hour, I suffer with you, I resist with you. What I would like to tell you in this moment you can imagine, and with the present conditions it cannot be said. But I assure you that all will be done so that your innocence will end up triumphing. As you wait, be strong and patient.
I hug you and kiss you with great affection
your brother
Secondino Tranquilli][9]

Ten days later, Silone tried to return to Italy, where he hoped to enlist the help of Chief Inspector Guido Bellone in Romolo's defence. But the fascist police had intercepted his telegram to Bellone and had issued a warrant for his arrest, so he could not carry out his plan.[10] Through Gabriella and with all other possible means he tried to help his brother from afar, but his own precarious situation did not allow him even to satisfy some of Romolo's requests for his material needs. In a letter of 23 December 1930 he tells his brother that he has been able to collect 100 liras "with great effort" and is sending them in addition to the 300 he has already sent.[11] He then appeals to the Comité de Défense des Victimes du Fascisme for their intervention. A petition, signed by such influential persons as the Nobel laureate Romain Rolland and Henri Barbusse,[12] spares Romolo's life, but he remains in jail where he must serve twelve years for belonging to the Communist Party. He suffers from tuberculosis, aggravated by the consequences of the police brutality he experienced at the time of his arrest. Silone does not appear to fully realize the gravity of his condition and is unable to prevent his premature death, in October 1932.[13]

During the years of Romolo's incarceration, Silone experienced severe hardship: his bad health, his ideological crisis and the reaction of the party leaders, his lack of means to satisfy even basic material needs – all these caused enormous concern. In the spring of 1929 he took a leave from the party for health reasons, and in July he was treated for respiratory ailments in Ascona at the Curhaus Collinetta. In the fall he resumed some of his propaganda activities within the party, and in January 1930 he left Ascona for Davos. There he continued to be treated for bronchiectasis, and also benefited from what he described to Gabriella as "psychoanalysis or rather, to be more precise, analysis."[14]

His health was improving, but he still lacked the financial wherewithal to meet his material needs, especially since the party had relieved him of all leadership roles. To try to improve his circumstances, he asked his friend Fritz Brupbacher to see if any of his acquaintances might need a tutor or a translator, and began to write his essay on fascism in the hope that its publication would bring him some income.[15]

It is noteworthy that he did not seek the help of Guido Bellone, a powerful man twenty-nine years his senior whom he had presumably met in the wake of the 1915 earthquake and with whom he had remained in contact.[16] On the contrary, notwithstanding his needs, he decided to put an end to their relationship, and in his letter to Bellone of 13 April 1930 he specifically asserted that no material considerations influenced his decision.[17]

The letter, first published by historians Dario Biocca and Mauro Canali, revealed an unsuspected aspect of Silone's life. Apparently, this man who was generally considered to be a moral figure, had been a fascist informer between 1923 and 1930. This revelation caused a long controversy and resulted in considerable new scholarship. Those who believed that Silone was duplicitous and those who did not engaged in a spirited debate, which remains unresolved. Since the dispute has been widely covered by the media, and the scholarship that has been published is readily available, the reader can be spared another summary. Having pondered the opposing viewpoints, I will simply say that in my view, the most logical appraisal of the facts is the one presented by Mimmo Franzinelli.[18]

In an article published in 2011, the author of *I tentacoli dell'OVRA* (and a noted authority on the practices of the Organization for Vigilance and Repression of Anti-Fascism) rightfully argues that historians must be careful and suspicious when dealing with police sources, since they can be easily used to prove opposite viewpoints, adding that police papers often pose problems that they cannot resolve:

> Talvolta capita che su di esse si accendano I riflettori dei mass media ed è una cosa negativa perché sfalsa tutto. Il caso Silone è celeberrimo, se ne è scritto abbondantemente e in modo non rispettoso della sua personalità, della sua identità, della sua arte, poiché usando solo le carte di polizia si è travisato un personaggio che è molto più sfaccettato, multiforme, problematico rispetto a come è stato reso. Di fatto Ignazio Silone è stato tramutato nella spia peggiore che il fascismo abbia mai avuto dentro il Partito comunista, ma la realtà è ben diversa.[19]

> [It sometimes happens that they attract the spotlight of the mass media, and this is a bad thing because it offsets everything. Silone's case is very

famous, a lot has been written about it, and in a way that was not respectful of his personality, his identity, his art, because, using only police papers, they have misrepresented a personage that is much more multifaceted, multiform, and problematic than he was made to be. As a matter of fact Silone was turned into the worst spy that fascism ever had inside the Communist Party, but the reality is quite different.]

Given all that is known about Silone, how can one reconcile the struggles he faced and the moral lessons he imparted through all of his writings with his letter to Bellone? A possible explanation is that Silone was a triple agent acting on behalf of the Communist Party. A document found in Luce d'Eramo's archives states that Umberto Terracini, one of the founders of the Italian Communist Party, told her that "Silone era stato incaricato dal PCI clandestino di utilizzare le conoscenze che aveva nella polizia politica, fingendosi di essere informatore per sapere notizie riservate sui metodi e sui tranelli usati contro gli antifascisti"[20] [Silone had been asked by the underground PCI to use the acquaintances he had in the political police, pretending to be an informant in order to learn about the methods and traps that were used against the antifascists]. This may have been the case, but it cannot be proven because those who could say more, beginning with Silone, are no longer alive.

This is why, years after the publication of my last book, I am still unable to answer the questions I raised at that time: Why did Silone do it? What did he gain from it? Why did he endure so much hardship? If he was a fascist spy why were the fascists after him? Why upon his expulsion from the PCI was he not unmasked by Togliatti? If he was a valuable informer why could he not secure his brother's release from jail? Historians are still at work and will possibly find the answers to the questions that still remain. Meanwhile, as long as the different views are presented, it would be useful if corrections and retractions were forthcoming when warranted. One cannot forget that the late Christopher Hitchens, having published an accusatory article in *The Nation* about Silone and realizing that he had been party to "a widely and prematurely disseminated falsehood," wrote this retraction: "In the circumstances, I feel that I should alert *Nation* readers to a possible grave injustice ..."[21] This example of remarkable integrity should be followed whenever a person's reputation is concerned.

As a reader, I must also express my dismay at the questionable tendency, that some have shown, to partially read (or reread) Silone's works and use them to reinvent his life – whether their aim was hagiographical or simply sensation-seeking, as, for instance, when some insinuated that Silone might have had a homosexual relationship with Bellone because he wrote that it was "physically" impossible for him to go on. The fact that Silone was then physically ill was ignored, and his addressing Bellone in the formal "Lei" was left unnoticed. Is that how one would have written to a lover in common Italian practice?

On a number of occasions Silone stated that he had a secret, and that it was to be found within the pages of his novels. This caused some to argue that the secret is in his "confession" of duplicity through the character of Luigi Murica in the play *And He Hid Himself.* But if Silone was busy reinventing himself to cast his new image in a positive light, why would he want to point the reader in the opposite direction? Also, he said that the secret was to be found in his novels! And if in the play, then why not begin with the scriptural meaning of the title, and its source as indicated by the epigraph, "et abiit et abscondit se ab eis. Johannes, XII 3"? If Silone's suggestion should be heeded in one case, why then ignore his note to the reader in this specific case? Also useful in this regard are Carlo Ossola's comments in the preface to the new Italian edition of the play.[22]

If we take Silone literally when he speaks about his secret, we fail to remember that some writers intentionally make intriguing claims. Boccaccio, for instance, caused speculation about his birthplace: was it Certaldo or Florence? And when Flaubert declared "Madame Bovary c'est moi," what did he really mean? Was he "confessing" some hidden truth? The perils of reading fiction as fact are obvious. As Darina Silone noted when speaking at the centenary celebration of Silone's birth, Dostoevsky did not have to be an assassin to write *Crime and Punishment,* and Tolstoy did not have to give birth to describe Kitty's labour pains in *Anna Karenina*;[23] and, one might add, Moravia did not have to live Cesira's life to have her narrate it, in the first person and with all of its nuances, in *Two Women.*[24]

Silone did derive his inspiration from the reality of his life, his native region, and the land of his exile, but the autobiographical elements are only incidental. For instance, even though both his brother Romolo and Berardo, the hero of *Fontamara,* are innocently arrested and suffer police brutality, Romolo's death, unlike Berardo's, does not result from a decision to give his life for the sake of others and Silone does not, even implicitly, aim to make a martyr of his brother.

Unfortunately, even a noted scholar like Alexander Stille unwittingly encouraged the tendency to reinvent the author's life based on a rereading of his books when he wrote that now that Silone's heroic image no longer influences the reader, "the undercurrent of deceit and betrayal" becomes evident, and those who previously read the novels "as straightforward denunciation of social injustice" can marvel at Silone's ability to reinvent himself "by killing Secondino Tranquilli and becoming Ignazio Silone."[25]

As the correspondence reveals, Secondino Tranquilli was never killed, and no self-reinvention took place. Silone did not like his first name (which in Italian means jail warden), and in his letters he often uses only his surname or truncated versions of it. As a writer he was Ignazio Silone, but in his daily life and even in his correspondence he did not use his new name until 1947, when he officially adopted it.[26] His decision to become a writer was not part of a self-reinvention; it was the natural progression of his life. From his early years in the Communist Party, both Antonio Gramsci and Camilla Ravera had noticed his writing talent and sought to have him use it.[27] In 1930, as he prepared to leave the party, he needed to find a way to earn a living and a new venue in which to continue his struggle for freedom and justice. He used the talent he had, and writing became his means. It is important to remember that, in a letter he sent to Gabriella while writing *Fontamara*, he says that they had talked about his becoming a writer in the past, but he was not ready; now he finally is. In July 1930 he writes:

> *Fontamara* è ancora nella fase di elaborazione: vi sono alcuni capitoli così vivi che io parlo con essi. Credo che siano i primi contadini di carne ed ossa che appaiono nella letteratura italiana. Non ho mai provato nello scrivere ciò che provo ora. Delle notti mi sveglio all'improvviso e devo alzarmi per prendere appunti. Altre volte sono in giardino e corro in camera per modificare un passaggio di un capitolo. Ti avevo detto altre volte che il tempo di produrre non era ancora arrivato e io mi consideravo sempre nel periodo della preparazione. Ora credo che il tempo di produrre è giunto. Qualcosa di nuovo è in me.[28]

> [*Fontamara* is still in its elaboration phase: some chapters are so alive that I speak with them. I believe that they are the first peasants in flesh and blood that appear in Italian literature. I never felt what I feel now while I write. Some nights I suddenly wake up and have to get up to take notes. Some other times I am in the garden and run to my room to change a passage in a chapter. I had told you, on other occasions, that the time to produce had not yet arrived and I considered myself in a period of preparation. Now I think that the time to produce has arrived. There is something new within me.]

And in August:

> Buba cara, nella tua lettera c'è qualcosa che mi ha un po' offeso ed è che tu pensi che forse io non ho piacere di venire con te! Come ti è potuta venire una simile idea? Certamente è colpa mia che non so bene spiegare le cose e immagino che tu, per intuizione, devi sapere tutto. Così è per la mia salute. Come puoi credere che io non ti dico la verità? Dunque, gnocco, le cose stanno così. Io sono guarito, cioè la psicanalisi è finita (anzi per essere preciso: l'analisi). Non c'è più nulla da analizzare, tutto è chiaro. Io mi sento bene. Ora è il periodo che si chiama ricostruzione: riabituarmi alla vita normale, collettiva, dimenticare il passato ecc ... [...] Cucchila, se tu fossi con me in mezz'ora ti spiegherei con più chiarezza cose che a scriverle ci vorrebbe un pacco di carta. Dunque, sta' sicura che io desidero tornare nella bobite, come la più bella cosa della mia vita. Appena il medico mi dirà volerò.[29]
>
> [Buba, dear, in your letter there is something that has a little offended me, and it is that you think that maybe I don't like going with you! How could you get such an idea? Certainly it is my fault if I can't explain things well enough and imagine that you should know everything by intuition, about my health as well. How can you think that I don't tell you the truth? So, dumpling, this is how things stand. I am cured, that is, the psychoanalysis ended (or rather, to be exact, the analysis). There is nothing else to analyse, all is clear. I feel well. This is the period called reconstruction: to get re-accustomed to normal, collective life, forget the past etc. ... [...] Cucchila, if you were with me, in a half hour I would explain more clearly everything that in writing would require a package of paper. So, rest assured that I wish to return to Bubaland as the most beautiful thing in my life. As soon as the doctor tells me, I will fly ...]

Evidently, having decided to move on, and having written to Bellone, he experiences the peace of mind that he needs to become a writer. The tone of the second letter is playful and affectionate. As he writes in his *Memoir from a Swiss Prison,* he suffered "an atrocious crisis" but one that granted him salvation when God did not let go of him and his "spiritual homeland" nurtured his intellect and his spirit:

> In Switzerland I became a writer; but, more importantly, I became a man. Not only did I gain a clearer conception of society, not only did my political thinking break free of the Bolshevist nightmare, discovering in my daily encounters with a free, democratic and peaceful people the possibility

> of a form of human existence that I had previously thought impossible; more significantly, I rediscovered a Christian and divine aspect to the very meaning of man's existence on earth, the very meaning of reality in a holy, Christian sense that had been present for me in my early adolescence but which I lost as I grew older. [...] It appeared evident to me that the highest aspiration of man on earth must be above all to become good, honest and sincere. My work as a writer has been the testimony of this struggle of mine and its internal maturation.[30]

These words were not dictated by the opportunism of a man who wants to create a new, moral self-image. On the contrary, the correspondence shows that both Silone and Fleischmann sincerely endeavoured to fulfil this "highest aspiration" throughout their lives.

But even as his writing and his health were giving him reason to be more optimistic about the future, Silone was tormented by the thought of his brother Romolo, whose freedom he could not secure. The tension he must have felt is unimaginable and must have been in part responsible for his decision to meet with Togliatti and sign a declaration of solidarity with the party.[31] That same month, December 1930, he was arrested by the Swiss authorities and only avoided extradition thanks to the intervention of Fritz Brupbacher and other influential Swiss socialists. He obtained the residence permit that was then granted to refugees who pledged not to engage in political activism and began his legal exile that would continue until his return to Italy in 1944.[32]

Arrested once more in 1942 for having broken the pledge by disseminating propaganda fliers (urging the Italians to organize a "Terzo Fronte" [Third Front][33] of civil disobedience against fascism), he wrote about that period as follows:

> Exactly twelve years ago, in December 1930 (as today, a few days before Christmas), I was a guest in this very prison [...] the authorities wished to examine my case as I had arrived in Switzerland lacking a passport. [...] I was thirty years old, I had just recently left the Communist Party, to which I had sacrificed my youth, my studies, and every personal interest; I was gravely ill and without any means of support; without family [...] I had been expelled from France and from Spain; I could not return to Italy, in a word, I was on the threshold of suicide.[34]

Even though his final exit from the party was only sanctioned by his expulsion in 1931, Silone's life drastically changed when he abandoned political activism and began to write *Fontamara*. In a long letter to Rainier Biemel he speaks of the crisis he endured, the meaning of art, and the role art played in his life.[35]

Silone records the completion of *Fontamara* in a letter dated "Winter Solstice 1931." That same year, other determinant events helped to strengthen his resolve to move on. As he notes in one of his letters,[36] he met Marcel Fleischmann in January 1931, when the latter was celebrating his fortieth birthday, and benefited from his hospitality at the Kleine Pension, 53 Germaniastrasse, Zurich, from February 1933 to October 1944. To appreciate the importance of Fleischmann's generosity, one must not forget that Silone was in poor health and even poorer financial circumstances. To survive, he wrote occasional pieces, did translations, and gave lectures and private lessons. In the latter capacity, he was invited by Wladimir Rosenbaum and his wife, Aline Valangin, to give Italian lessons to their nephew. Thus he arrived at "La Barca," the eighteenth-century palace the prominent couple had bought in 1929 in Comologno, transforming it into a sort of Gertrude Stein salon where avant-garde refugee artists were often hosted and regularly gathered. In her memoirs,[37] Valangin writes about her first meeting with Silone as follows:

> Grandi occhi, un po' affaticati, mi scrutavano. Diventai immediatamente seria. Questo non era un uomo qualsiasi. La sua voce era opaca, tossiva leggermente, era formale, a distanza, ma le mie vibrazioni, che allora non capivo, mi avvertivano che qualcosa stava per accadere.[38]
>
> [Big eyes, a bit tired, scrutinized me. I became immediately serious. This was not any man. His voice was opaque, he coughed slightly, was formal, kept a distance, but my vibrations, which I did not then understand, were warning me that something was about to happen.]

And something did happen. The woman, eleven years his senior, was attractive and intelligent; she was a pianist, a writer, and a Jungian psychoanalyst. Unlike him, she did not harbour traditional moral values, had an open marriage, and, feeling neglected by her husband, didn't disdain other men's attention. Their passionate affair lasted less than two years, ending when Silone, unlike Rosenbaum, would not accept Aline's "lies" and "betrayal."

Whereas before he had written her romantic letters that either elevated her to mystical status or expressed erotic desires, and had written about "La Barca" as a place of primordial innocence and bliss, now he writes about her as a nymphomaniac whose presence is reminiscent of a "whited sepulchre." Unmoved by her tears and promises, he tells her that his decision is not dictated by jealousy; it is simply his rejection of falsehood. His disgust is not personal; it is the reaction of a sensitive person at the sight of garbage – at the sight of her lies that offend her and man[kind] in general.[39]

But Silone was not capable of harbouring enduring resentment and was always grateful to those who helped him. How could he forget that Aline, as the first enthusiastic reader of *Fontamara*, had done everything within her power to help him publish it?[40] He didn't forget. And, as a result, the two went on to share a lifelong friendship.[41]

While he was involved with Valangin, Silone no longer lived with Gabriella, but their relationship remained strong and meaningful. She loved him unconditionally and hoped to have him back. To this end she often wrote to Romolo and offered him support as the "cognata" (sister-in-law) that he deemed her to be. Then, when Silone got his conditional residence permit to remain in Switzerland, she acquiesced in a marriage of convenience with Edy Meyer, an elderly Swiss citizen.[42] With Silone's help, she opened the Libreria Internazionale (a failed initiative to promote Italian culture) and was at his side whenever he made it possible.[43] Her presence is documented in the writer's correspondence with Angelo Tasca during the 1930s, and by the fact that when writing to Silone in those years, Fleischmann often mentions her and sends her his regards. Even when she moved to Rome after the war, she benefited from Silone's enduring affection and gratitude. Darina Silone, who donated Gabriella's autobiographical manuscript to the Centro Studi, entered the following handwritten comment at the bottom of the last page: "N.B. Gabriella Maier morì a Roma nell'estate del 1977 e fu sepolta nel reparto ebraico del cimitero del Verano. Silone l'appoggiò materialmente e moralmente fino all'ultimo"[44] [N.B. Gabriella Maier died in Rome in the summer of 1977 and was buried in the Jewish section of the Verano cemetery. Silone assisted her materially and morally until the end].

In Marcel's Kleine Pension,[45] where Silone officially resided from February 1933 to October 1944, he found both material and spiritual support. Its location, at the top of a hill, its decor, as a veritable art gallery, the sensitivity and magnanimity of its owner, the constant coming and going of both illustrious and less well-known refugees who – like Silone – received more than material help – all these were antidotes for the despair caused by the turmoil of the times.

Even though he was often away, mainly for health reasons, Silone could always count on the safety and warmth of his new home. Replying to an inquiry by the German journalist Andreas Mytze, Fleischmann noted: "Silone was seriously ill most of the time he stayed with us. He suffered from bronchiectasis due to lung infections. He spent a great deal of time recovering from this at various places."[46] This explains the correspondence the two exchanged even as they both resided at 53 Germaniastrasse.

The Kleine Pension was also the site of Silone's first meeting (9 December 1941) with Elizabeth Darina Laracy,[47] the woman who was to become his wife. As she would tell her sisters, she was "hypnotized" by Silone's mind and, despite the seventeen years that separated them, she went on to become his lifelong partner, supporting him with remarkable wisdom and self-abnegation. Her letters to Marcel and his companion, Elsa Schiess, attest to this and are precious expressions of shared concerns and friendship.

Like Fleischmann, Darina Silone – as she liked to be known – has not received the attention she deserves as the remarkable intellectual and indefatigable promoter of culture and humanistic ideals that she was. She was born in Dublin on 30 March 1917, the first of four daughters of Cecile King and Patrick Joseph Laracy. Her first name, Elizabeth, was her maternal grandmother's; the name "Darina" was inspired by a George Russell poem. In the *Colloqui* with Michele Dorigatti and Maffino Maghenzani she speaks of her family: her open-minded parents; her maternal grandfather, Martin, who taught her to read by the age of three and instilled in her a lifelong love of learning; her formal studies; her youthful years; the adventurous and perilous life she lived both before and during the war; her marriage to Silone; the years they spent together; and her meetings with such personalities as Jacques Maritain, Indira Gandhi, and Martin Buber.

While the information contained in the volume is of obvious historical value, the modesty and reticence that Darina Silone evidently displayed do not allow her more complex human identity to fully reveal itself. The privilege I had in knowing her compels me to say more. To begin with, one often wondered what she could have become if her role had not been a supporting one: that of the woman *behind* the great man. She had so much potential! Had Silone given her the same support that he received, could she have become a writer, as Moravia's wives did? Or, given her credentials, could she not have become an effective diplomat? She was intelligent, learned, creative, and always eager to know more and share her knowledge. She was a polyglot and possessed both beauty and poise. William Weaver describes her as "beautiful and captivating [...] a tall, blonde Viking of a woman" who spoke with "a soft melodious accent."[48] She loved travelling and did not disdain the limelight. As her sister Eithne noted, she was fifty years ahead of her time. Much of the hardship she endured in her marriage and in life in general stemmed from this. Darina was also a romantic soul. A handwritten note she sent to Silone in December 1942, while he was in a Swiss prison, reveals both her love and admiration for him and her gentle spirit. Citing the gospel of Matthew, 5:10 ("Blessed are those who are persecuted for righteousness' sake, for theirs is the kingdom of heaven"), she writes: "Mio carissimo, non L'ho mai sentito tanto vicino, né tanto libero, come ora"[49] [My dearest, I never felt you so close nor so free as I do now]. This comment about freedom suggests that her thoughts were similar to the ones that Silone expressed in the piece he wrote about freedom that is published here (pp 10–11) for the first time. Their romantic relationship had already begun when Silone wrote from the Swiss prison to Marcel and asked that some Christmas gifts be sent to both Gabriella and Darina.[50] For some time he was ambivalent: he still loved Gabriella and, knowing what he meant to her, he did not want to hurt her. But now there was Darina! In May 1943, writing to Gabriella, he first speaks of "friendship" and seeks to clarify the state of their relationship: "A me sembra che noi siamo arrivati a una grande data della nostra amicizia e che strada facendo essa si è molto approfondita liberata purificata" [It seems to me that we have arrived at a great point of our friendship and that along the way it has become much deeper liberated, purified]. But then he adds: "Cara, io non saprei immaginarmi la mia vita senza di te. Tuo, Infante"[51] [Dear, I could not imagine my life without you. Your Infante]. And this postscript: "L'accordo con la Sig.na L. è nel modo da te desiderato: appena potrà, andrà via; finché resterà qui eviteremo di vederci; espressioni personali, anche in forma di lettere, regali, fiori e simili, saranno eliminate" [The agreement with Miss L[aracy] is as you desire: as soon as she can, she will leave; while she is here we'll avoid seeing each other; personal expressions also in the form of letters, gifts, flowers and the like will be eliminated]. Evidently he maintained this promise by suggesting that Darina go to Arosa for a period of rest.[52]

The following month he continues to reassure Gabriella, stating that she is more than a friend, a companion, a wife, and even a mother to him; that nobody can destroy what she is to him; and that in life what matters is what one gives rather than what one receives. Therefore, she should feel strong and satisfied, should be good and generous as she is by nature, and should nourish her spirit with good readings.[53] It is an artful and tactful let-down – but still a let-down. And yet, according to a letter to Fleischmann, in July Silone and Gabriella are in Baden together.[54] Nevertheless, he finally has to tell her that he has made a decision and can no longer equivocate. In a much colder tone, he writes that she should understand that things had already changed between them (before he met Darina) and should accept his decision so that they can remain friends and he can continue to help her, as far as it is within his means to do so.

The liberation of Rome came shortly thereafter, and Silone returned to Italy with Darina. As the correspondence reveals, after their marriage, on 20 December 1944, she industriously tried to build a home for them, despite their scant means, and immersed herself in their new life with the optimism of a new bride. Silone evidently appreciated her efforts, but his reticence about spending the little money they had gave her pause. Darina was a brilliant, progressive young woman, Silone a famous writer and politically minded personality. Their agendas, if they did not conflict, did not always converge. Initially, as director of *Avanti!* Silone worked very long hours, leaving his wife feeling alone in a foreign land. She remained attached to her parents and sisters and kept in contact with them, occasionally returning to Ireland to share both happy and sad events. She travelled and worked a lot, mainly interpreting and translating, but that was not sufficient to fill the void. Fascinated by his intellect, she did not regard the great age difference as an obstacle. After all, the distance can be bridged when two people are on the same wavelength in so many ways. But Silone was not only seventeen years her elder; he was a man of his region and his times. His intellect and talent and the uncommon life he had lived had made him a man of the world, but his perception of the woman in a supporting role may have remained anchored to his old-fashioned upbringing; and his sensitivity to Darina's feelings may not have been sufficient to fill some of the void that, as a young woman, she came to feel.

Even as her husband remained close to Gabriella Seidenfeld, corresponded with Aline Valangin and Elinor Lipper,[55] and was flattered by the accolades he received from intellectuals such as Luce d'Eramo,[56] Darina found a soulmate in the Indian poet Keshav Malik, whom she met in Florence in 1950 while attending a UNESCO convention. He was seven years her junior and quite different from the Italian men whose idea of manhood had been forged during the fascist era. He possessed the qualities she most admired in a human being, and she perceived him to be living evidence of the goodness of man. In the *Colloqui*, she states: "Keshav Malik, un ragazzo che mi colpì per la trasparenza e che comunicava una dimensione di purezza indefinibile negli atteggiamenti e nei pensieri; in quei giorni a Firenze dialogammo a lungo su tanti argomenti e mi sembrò di toccare con mano i valori assoluti della bontà: l'India ha giocato un grande ruolo nella mia vita. Le amicizie sono delle oasi dove ci si ritempra"[57] [Keshav Malik, a young man who impressed me with his transparency and as one who transmitted a dimension of purity in his attitude and his thoughts; during those days, in Florence, we spoke at length on many topics and it seemed to me that I was touching with my hand the absolute values of goodness: India has played a great role in my life. Friendships are oases where one restores oneself].

This friendship went on to become something more, albeit at a distance, and Darina benefited from it for the rest of her life.[58] Malik, who is recognized as one of India's foremost poets,[59] remembers Darina as "a person with a big heart" who left "a deep inerasable mark" on his nature. The following two poems, inspired by her, speak of the intensity of his feelings for her.[60]

In the first, the subject, having to confront and accept the irrationality of reality, feels overwhelmed. The whole earth trembles; darkness ensues. And yet, the yearning still remains "to touch a lost loved face." The sorrow for the departure is mitigated by the power of remembrance that makes it possible for the fading star to shine anew and reason to flow again in the passionate veins.

The second poem is an invitation to spiritual resistance; to place individual suffering in the universal context; to focus on the signs of life, even in the midst of dreadful days; to have courage; for, even as "these things have been, shall be," it is "the truly living" – those who live the life of the spirit – who will, at the end, "cry victory."

A Departure

Now no sooner, some sorcerer
fixes a phantasmal beam
upon a backtracking venous stream,
my pulse count begins to mount
and I'm obliged to rise from my seat,
midget caught in the vortex
of a clueless reality,
those wheels within intricate wheels.

Yes, with the rising of your craft
shadows are hovering about me
and beneath my feet
as if a quaking earth.
A great dish seems to have now been slapped
on the golden cornea of the sun,
and there then is as though the absolute night.

Yes, I'm kneeling down in prayer,
invoking the strength to remain calm
confronted by the kingdom of unfathomable causes.

See how, within minutes,
traps are wont to be flung open upon us
ushering us mankind into dark abysses! –
and yet my hands seek
to touch a lost loved face
but how may hands affect
what fate wills.

And so, perforce, my eyes close
but ears to hear the more
the furor of the world's heaving ocean
but wherein of us is no sign seen.

So how may I tell myself:
no matter life or death
never to forget the glorious corolla of that cool fire
that unfailingly inheres in us all,
and takes away the taste of bitter
from the reigning dark.

O fading star anew beam the brighter,
so the stream of reason
once more overflows to the brims of my veins.

Beyond All Doubt

Beyond all doubt
doubt surrenders ghost
and the slain resume their cycle of births;

with life, the suppressed seed bursts –
promise fulfilled.

So follow in the wake of those longest rays
which reshape dormant clay into pulsing flesh
flesh into flower –
from age to age the breath of courage praised.

Beyond the shell-shock of day
the one undeviated way:
certain it, that death gives in,
clods thrust out the gold of waving corn –
and that the rigor of the glacial age thaws:

the flinching eyes drawn
to the flame of love that is the sun
as tides drawn to their full height
by the moon –
life quickened in the dereliction of wastes.

Not say these things are not,
that the soul loathes to haul
the burden of its duties
beyond the prescribed routine
and the reach of claws
towards the wealth of spirit,
that the sleep of death is not vanquished.

These things have been, shall be,
and the marshalled legions of the truly living
cry victory.

Beyond all doubt
there is the greater faith,
so afresh the dream's hewn in the hardest stone,
the animated face soaring above the field of dead,
brightness of light gratis from the heart,
hand picking untold shining truths
from the overhanging night –
this is only right.

One can only imagine what these verses must have meant for Darina. And yet she evidently loved her husband and tried to cope with the conflicting feelings she harboured. She continued to work a lot, even when she found the tasks intellectually unsatisfying; but she eventually began to suffer from depression and, as one of Silone's letters to Marcel reveals, she let herself go and resorted to alcohol.[61] Nevertheless, as the strong, principled woman she was, she overcame the crisis and, resuming her active role as Silone's wife, went on to spend the following years assisting him, advising him, and morally sustaining him until his last day. Silone's love for her also lasted until the end. The affectionate tone of his letters of this same period, signed "with love" and his pet name, and his concern about Darina's well-being attest to this.[62] Also, and most important, by naming her his principal heir, he entrusted her with his most precious possession: his literary legacy. After Silone's death she dedicated herself to securing it and protecting it in all possible ways. She completed and edited *Severina*, his last, unfinished work; she recorded his final hours in her beautiful piece "Le ultime ore di Ignazio Silone"; she pressed Mondadori to realize her ambition to publish his *Opera Omnia* in the Meridiani series and was only satisfied when Bruno Falcetto produced the two wonderful volumes titled *Ignazio Silone. Romanzi e Saggi.* She also facilitated new translations and editions, endeavoured to collect all of his correspondence, secured the cooperation of generous volunteers like Diocleziano Giardini to assist the researchers who visited Pescina,[63] met or corresponded with scholars, and intervened in the debate over the new "caso Silone." In this regard, and much to her distress, the media did not faithfully report her statements, and she had to rectify them. Her position was that since she had not known Silone at the time of his alleged involvement with Bellone she could not help to clarify the matter, but she could certainly say that Silone was and remained a socialist and would not have objected to the historians' efforts to inquire about his past. She also felt compelled to write about Silone's interaction with Allen Dulles and the CIA. In a letter to the editor of the *Times Literary Supplement*, she recalled how the two had met, and noted that Silone had tried to act as "an Italian patriot serving the interests of his country" and that he believed that the Congress for Cultural Freedom was initially financed by the "innocuous Fleischmann Foundation" and later by the Ford Foundation.

There were times when Darina sent me articles she thought I should read, with her short comments. On this one she wrote: "Faccio quello che posso. Darina" [I do what I can. Darina].[64] To help me better understand, she also shared these comments that Silone wrote to Allen Dulles on 31 August, 1943: "Mais je ne suis pas aussi naïf de croire que mes billets et messages puissent même dans une mesure minime, influencer la détermination d'une politique obéissante a des forces bien plus lourdes. Mon but, en réalité, est plus modeste: contribuer a établir des rapports de compréhension réciproque entre vous et les forces de la démocratie sociale italienne. Il faudrait imprimer sur le édifices de l'AMGOT la devise de Clemenceau: "La guerre est une chose trop sérieuse pour la lasser aux militaires" [But I am not so naive as to believe that my notes and messages can, even minimally, influence the determination of much heavier politics. My goal, in reality, is much more modest: to contribute to establish rapports of reciprocal understanding between you and the forces of Italian social democracy. We should print Clemenceau's motto on the AMGOT buildings: "War is something too serious to be left to the military"].

Darina also lamented that those who tried to make another "caso Silone" out of her husband's interaction with the OSS and Allen Dulles[65] did not acknowledge that, from the documents found in the Washington National Archives, "Silone emerge tutt'altro che una spia, invece un patriota italiano che cercava di fare il suo dovere in tempo di guerra (guerra che putroppo 'loro' troppo facilmente dimenticano) un uomo politico, socialista, che cercava di dialogare con gli alleati per cercare di influire sulla loro politica verso l'Italia"[66] [Silone emerges not as a spy, but rather as an Italian patriot who tried to do his duty during wartime (a war that "they" all too easily forget), a political man, a socialist, who tried to engage in a dialogue with the Allies in order to try to influence their policy towards Italy].

As I stated in the *Introduction*, in recent decades Silone's scholars and biographers have produced meaningful works encompassing the important moments and events in the writer's life, but the archives contain a wealth of material that merits further attention. A case in point is some correspondence of the Swiss period that is still largely unknown. Of particular interest are many letters of 1940 to 1943, which document American assistance to people living in internment camps under German domination, Silone's work on the victims' behalf, and the conditions they had to endure.

In a letter of 19 August 1940, Clement Greenberg writes: "The *Partisan Review*, at the initiative of Dwight Macdonald, has organized a fund for refugee intellectuals, writers and artists in France and elsewhere." And he urges Silone to come to America where he can be instrumental in the fundraising effort. When Silone replies that he wishes to remain in

Switzerland, he is given the task of reaching out to those who are in need of help. In another letter of 23 October of the same year, Nancy Macdonald thanks Silone for his good work on behalf of the International Relief Association and informs him that they are trying to get visas for those who wish to relocate, including Ante Ciliga.[67]

Also of great importance are the letters that Silone receives from many people interned in the various camps. Among these is Juan Andrade, who was arrested by the Vichy regime and the Gestapo, and who addresses Silone as "Dino," the battle name of their days in the Spanish underground movement. (It was in an article published in *La Batalla*, a journal where Andrade had a great deal of influence, that Silone first used this pseudonym.) Their friendship is evident from the affectionate tone that both Andrade and his wife use in their letters.[68] Silone is entirely responsive to them and to all who write to request his help.

The Andrades' letters are exemplary records of the times, testifying to the human price paid by those who, like Silone, had chosen to fight totalitarianism in all its forms. Some of the other prisoners bear witness to the camps' horrible conditions, whether the infamous camp at Le Vernet or any other. They lack food, clothing, medicine, and basic necessities and hopelessly yearn for news of their loved ones and their own destiny. Even those who, like Umberto Terracini,[69] are moved from the camp to "better" quarters suffer the same limitations and write to Silone about them.

It is noteworthy that Silone never mentioned all the work he did on behalf of so many. This suggests that, like Marcel Fleischmann, he only sought to alleviate human suffering however he could. Even his new romance with Darina and his concern for Gabriella's feelings did not distract him from his humanitarian work. His state of mind during this period is revealed by his famous letter of 13 January 1941 to Marcel and by his writings of the following years, when he serenely endured prison and confinement.[70]

Regardless of the position one takes on Silone's political past and his sincerity, his struggle for freedom cannot be questioned. With his actions and his writings he sought to share what he learned by direct experience and as a penetrating reader of the signs of history. His initiatives – whether he was promoting the idea of a Third Front to combat fascism, collaborating with Allen Dulles at the end of the war, participating in the work of the Congress for Cultural Freedom, delivering his momentous speech *Habeas animam!*, engaging Anissimov on the freedom of Russian writers, or delivering courageous appeals such as the one in his 1969 speech in Jerusalem upon receiving the International Prize for Literature, when he asked the Israelis, as a people who had suffered exile like no other, to consider the lot of the Palestinian refugees. These and many other thoughts and deeds reveal a man who had lofty ideals and sought to be coherent, *etiam peccata*.

The Centro Studi archives also contain many letters that Silone received after his return to Italy from personalities such as Henry Kissinger and Adlai Stevenson, the writers Thomas Mann, Richard Wright, and Czeslaw Milosz, among others, and artists who were inspired by him, such as Emilio Vedova.[71] But even as these should stimulate further research, it is the human value of the correspondence contained in this volume that will give readers a better understanding of Ignazio Silone, while also enabling them to get to know Marcel Fleischmann.

With two remarkable women at their side, each left an indelible mark for future generations to behold: Silone with his socio-political activism and his writings and Marcel with his words and his philanthropic deeds. Fleischmann's letters – his ability to capture the essence of Silone's thought through the pages of his books, his humility, and his simple yet profound reflections on human imperfection and noble aspirations – suggest that he had found in Silone a spiritual alter ego. In both cases, the men were committed to doing good as the only way to exorcize the all-pervasive evil of the times.

As their letters reveal, both men found their vision and their hopes best represented in Silone's favourite novel, *The Seed beneath the Snow*. In a letter of 8 September 1943 Fleischmann tells Silone that he is rereading the novel and finds it twice as moving, going "so far as to judge people by how this confession affects them" and also judging them "by whether the book shakes them up, and whether they agree with the ending – the most beautiful of all sacrifices. Human beings could be good ..." As if to underscore the legitimacy of this hope, while he is writing the radio announces the signing of the armistice. "Now," he says, "every word is too much!"[72]

But the war was yet to end. Upon his return to Italy after the liberation of Rome, Silone was politically engaged as a member of the new Psiup (Italian Socialist Party of Proletarian Unity) and was later elected to the Assemblea Costituente. As an "autonomist" he was concerned that Italy might fall victim to the power struggle between the Russians and the Americans, and sought to promote his vision of a united Europe. In 1947, at a meeting in Rome on European unity and world peace, he spoke about the European mission of socialism, concluding with this warning: "se non faremo l'Europa, la nostra generazione potrà considerarsi fallita" [If we do not make Europe, ours will be a failed generation].[73]

Silone's disappointment with the political realities of the post-war years found their expression in his journalistic and literary work. The first novel he wrote in Italy, *Una manciata di more* (*A Handful of Blackberries*) was particularly effective in rendering the idea of the dehumanizing power of the Communist Party. As if to confirm the validity of his stance, when the novel came out in 1952, the communist critic Carlo Salinari wrote a virulent review, ridiculing Silone and defining him as a "poor man" who had failed both as a politician and as a writer. Having tried unsuccessfully to re-enlist Silone within the PCI, the Italian left created a hostile climate on both the political and the literary fronts. But Silone continued to fight for the ideas he believed in – the same ones he had expressed as early as 1941 in "Le idee che sostengo" ("The Ideas I Stand For").[74] His initiatives and his travels to promote his vision of freedom and social justice are documented by his biographers and outlined by Maria Moscardelli on the Silone website. Of particular importance was his founding, with Nicola Chiaromonte, of the cultural journal *Tempo presente*.[75]

On the personal level, Silone remained anchored to the moral values of his childhood; the same ones he had reclaimed in a 1924 letter to Gabriella when he stated that, with her help, he had overcome a deep spiritual crisis and felt reborn as he returned to be a guy from Pescina: "Deep down each person has a given temperament, and I realize that all my present thoughts are those I already thought when I was fifteen years old. Thus you – a red Jew – have brought me back to the spiritual condition that I was in when I entered the seminary, or when I campaigned for Scellingo, the Deputy of the poor."[76] This spiritual rebirth did not include, even later, a return to the Christian faith as represented by institutionalized religion. In this regard he wrote:

> Mi pare di avere espresso a varie riprese, con sincerità, tutto quello che sento di dovere a Cristo e al suo insegnamento. Riconosco che, inizialmente, m'allontanò da lui l'egoismo in tutte le sue forme, dalla vanità alla sensualità. Forse la privazione precoce della famiglia, le infermità fisiche, la fame, alcune predisposizioni naturali all'angoscia e alla disperazione, facilitarono i miei errori. Devo però a Cristo, e al suo insegnamento, di essermi ripreso, anche standone esteriormente lontano. Mi è capitato alcune volte, in circostanze penose, di mettermi in ginocchio, nella mia stanza, semplicemente, senza dire nulla, solo con un (forte) sentimento di abbandono; un paio di volte ho recitato il Pater noster; un paio di volte ricordo di essermi fatto il segno della Croce. Ma il "ritorno" non è stato possibile. [...] Mi sembra

che sulle verità cristiane essenziali si è sovrapposto [sic] nel corso dei secoli un'elaborazione teologica e liturgica d'origine storica che le ha rese irriconoscibili. Il critianesimo ufficiale è diventato un'ideologia. Solo facendo violenza su me stesso, potrei dichiarare di accettarlo; ma sarei in malafede.[77]

[I think that I have sincerely expressed at various times all I feel that I owe to Christ and His teachings. I recognize that initially selfishness, in all of its forms, from vanity to sensuality, cast me away from Him. Perhaps the early loss of my family, the physical illnesses, hunger, and some natural propensity to anguish and desperation facilitated my errors. But I owe it to Christ and His teachings if I recovered, even while remaining externally away. At times, in painful circumstances, it happened that I got down on my knees, in my room, simply, in silence, only with a (strong) sense of abandonment; a couple of times I recited the Lord's Prayer; a couple of times I remember to have made the sign of the Cross. But the "return" was not possible. [...] It seems to me that over the centuries, a theological and liturgical elaboration of historical origins has superimposed itself on the essential Christian truths, rendering them unrecognizable. Official Christianity has become an ideology. Only by doing violence to myself could I say that I accept it, but I would be in bad faith.]

In his last will Silone remained committed to this stance. He asked that he be cremated and, if possible, that his ashes be placed at the foot of the bell tower of the abandoned church of St Berardo in Pescina. He also requested that the funeral should not have a political or confessional character, and that, "Sul carro, o sulla bara, vi sia una croce. [...] Non desidero un'epigrafe, basterà una pietra di montagna con nome e cognome; sul muro accanto, una piccola croce" [On the hearse or the coffin there should be a cross [...] I don't wish to have an epigraph, only a mountain stone with name and surname; on the adjoining wall, a small cross].[78]

The image of the crucified, agonized Christ, ever present in Silone's thought and work, was to contain his final vision. A simple cross stands on his tombstone. At his funeral, his widow recited the Lord's Prayer, as he had requested.

Even as she continued her battles to preserve her husband's legacy at great personal cost and with very limited means, Darina Silone remained open and accessible to all who sought her assistance. As Keshav Malik urged in his poem, she remained willing to "follow in the wake of the longest rays" and willing to handpick "untold shining truths / from the overhanging night." In her eighties, she was still an avid reader, sought to uplift her spirit with music and poetry, and always kept herself informed by reading newspapers, biographies, and historical works. She thought that life was "un'avventura etica" [an ethical adventure][79] and, having fully lived hers, she wanted to be fully aware at her death. According to Don Flavio Peloso, who administered the last rites to her, she was. She died on 25 July 2003, and as she requested, her sisters brought her ashes back to Ireland, placed a small portion in the family grave, and scattered the rest at sea.[80]

Marcel Fleischmann and Elsa Schiess

Marcel Fleischmann, a member of a noted family of grain merchants of Hungarian descent and an art dealer, was born in Zurich on 13 January 1891 and died on 6 August 1984. He is buried in the family tomb at the Friedhof Manegg, in Zurich's Wollishofen Quartier. The tomb, where three generations of Fleischmanns have found their resting place, reminds the visitor of the one that Moisè Finzi-Contini had set up *sibi et suis* in Bassani's celebrated novel,[81] but with some remarkable differences: as Swiss citizens, the Fleischmanns were not persecuted and could reunite after death as their patriarch envisaged. Also, unlike the ostentatious tomb of the Ferrarese, the neoclassical beauty of the Fleischmann tomb reveals both artistic sensitivity and a philosophical understanding of human life.[82]

The eldest of Michael Fleischmann's four sons,[83] Marcel did not entirely share his father's interest in the import-export business. His natural bent was humanistic and artistic. As his correspondence with Silone clearly attests, he dedicated his life to the pursuit of goodness and the enjoyment of beauty – through art as well as nature. Even though he lent his collaboration to the "Fleischmann & Comp. Getreidenhandel,"[84] it was his brother Carlo who followed in their father's footsteps as a successful merchant, also sharing with him the diplomatic limelight. In fact, in 1924, when the king and queen of Romania paid their first official visit to Switzerland, Michael was present as honorary consul-general, and Carlo, rather than Marcel, accompanied him as honorary consul.[85]

Like Marcel, Dr Carlo (as he was known) was a learned man and a philanthropist. In a recent interview, his nephew Kaspar Fleischmann recalled how Carlo, after the death of his father, "took over the management of the former Fleischmann and Company, a company principally trading in grain, and quite successful in the import and export of raw materials." And also how, "In the late 1950s, Dr Fleischmann decided to invest a considerable amount of money into a foundation which he had established to provide financial support for art, culture and education in Switzerland."[86]

Whereas his brother Carlo never married, Marcel married Elly Maeder and, after his wife's early death, raised their only son, Werner Jürg, with great love. He cherished him, and in his letters to Silone, noted how pleased he was that the young man, who had moved to the United States, was hard working, ambitious, and successful, yet had also not lost his natural ability to pause and let the beauty of nature uplift his spirit.

Marcel Fleischmann was a very sensitive and generous man. For many years in his Kleine Pension he was a welcoming host to countless refugees and occasional visitors. In his letters to Silone he mentions them quite naturally, but one notices that they number some of the most prominent intellectuals and artists of the time. In a letter written on 13 January 1941, the occasion of Marcel's fiftieth birthday,[87] Silone expresses his gratitude and leaves an essential portrait of the Pauline quality of Marcel's generosity in providing many, including the writer Manés Sperber and the art historian Max Raphael,[88] with a material and spiritual "safe haven."

It is surprising that other testimonials by the many who were so generously helped have not been recorded,[89] not even after the end of the war, when there would have been no fear of repercussions. This omission makes it all the more necessary to preserve and share this correspondence.

Marcel, unlike his brother Carlo, did not covet the great economic benefits that he could have derived from being more involved in the family business, and yet he was exceedingly generous. Not only did he give Silone free hospitality from February 1933 until his return to Italy in October 1944, he also lent him enough to live on for the following two years.[90] How could he afford to be so magnanimous with so many? As one of the heirs of Michael Fleischmann, he must have enjoyed financial well-being, and he also worked with his brother in the accounting and finance department of the family business until the beginning of 1950, when their already difficult relationship further deteriorated, and he left the firm.[91] His activity as an art dealer is never mentioned in the letters, and public records indicate that he sold most of his valued possessions after the end of the war[92] when he no longer needed the proceeds for his philanthropic deeds.

Regarding his art collection, it is interesting to note the impression it made on Darina Laracy when she had her first meeting with Silone on

5 December 1941: "Silone era ospite di Marcel Fleischmann, mecenate di origine ungherese che con passione e generosità aiutava intellettuali in esilio da tutte le dittature. Senza questa ospitalità dopo duri anni di fame e di lavori pagati malissimo, Silone non avrebbe mai potuto avere la tranquillità di scrivere. La casa di Fleischmann era situata in un quartiere molto elegante di Zurigo, con vista sul lago e vi si arrivava con la funicolare. [...] Ricordo l'impressione nel vedere alle pareti degli originali di Picasso, Modigliani, Matisse, Cézanne, Braque, forse anche Van Gogh ... da non credere ai propri occhi" [Silone was a guest of Marcel Fleischmann, a Maecenas of Hungarian origins who, with passion and generosity, helped intellectuals in exile from all dictatorships. Without this hospitality, after hard years of deprivation and badly paid work, Silone could never have had the tranquillity to write. Fleischmann's house was in a very elegant area of Zurich, with a view of the lake. One arrived there by a funicular. [...] I remember my impression at the sight, on the walls, of original works by Picasso, Modigliani, Matisse, Cézanne, Braque, and maybe even Van Gogh ... something unbelievable].[93]

As of that date, Fleischmann was apparently collecting rather than dealing. But his name appears on the provenance records for Braque's *The Guitar Player,* the ownership of which was disputed and then settled between the French Centre Pompidou and the heirs of Alphonse Kann, who sought restitution under the protection afforded to Jewish families whose art was stolen during the war.[94]

Alex Danchew wrote about the open issues related to the provenance of this work, noting that even after André Lefèvre's records were made public the matter remained to be resolved: "Against *The Guitar Player* is the cryptic notation, 'Fleischmann, Zürich,' indicating Lefèvre bought the painting from the Zürich dealer Marcel Fleischmann, another figure deeply compromised by his trade in Jewish goods."[95]

Surprised by the claim, I endeavoured to find evidence supporting it, but to no avail. I then wrote to Professor Danchew to ask how he had learned that Marcel Fleischmann was "deeply compromised" as an art dealer. In his kind reply he stated that he did not recall and did not at present have access to the material used for his book. He also suggested venues for further research, but there too I found no information to justify the claim. On the contrary, I found that Marcel Fleischmann's name does not appear in the critical Art Looting Intelligence Unit (ALIU) Reports.[96] Also, the 1945 *Report on Visits of Investigation into Looted Works of Art and Their Whereabouts in Switzerland* concludes that, save for a few exceptions (Fleischmann not among them), "neither the

Swiss museums nor the more important Swiss collectors have acquired looted works of art."[97]

Another source of essential information that neither Dagen nor Danchew mentions, since it doesn't deal with *The Guitar Player*, is now available online and merits careful consideration. In *The Jacques Seligmann & Co. Records 1904–1978*, under "General Correspondence: Fleischmann, Marcel, 1939–1946," there are twenty-four items, consisting of letters, memoranda, and notes. Item 1 is a letter dated 19 June 1939, addressed to Marcel by the noted art collector, historian, and critic C.M. Hauke. Recalling a pleasant meeting they had had in Zurich, the latter asks Marcel if he is still thinking of sending his collection to the American institution he had in mind "for exhibition purposes and safe-guard." Item 5 is a memo, dated 19 December 1945, listing twenty-four works in the Marcel Fleischmann Collection, as seen at the Lincoln Warehouse in New York City by Germain Seligmann with Dr Drey.[98] The list includes three works by Picasso, one by Delacroix, three by Braque, one by Courbet, one by Modigliani, eight by Rouault, one by Chagall, one by Klee, one by Utrillo, one by Dufy, two by Soutine, and one by Goseg. Two columns indicate the prices in Swiss francs respectively quoted by Max Hirschberg[99] and Paul Drey. Several letters addressed to Hirschberg during the period December 1945 to March 1946 record Seligmann's interest in acquiring some of the works in the Fleischmann Collection, including *Man with a Guitar*. In a letter dated 26 December 1945, Hirschberg answers that, "Picasso's 'La Jolie' and Braque's 'Man with Guitar' are reserved for the time being, but not for an indefinite period of time." He also reminds Seligmann that "Mr. Fleischmann is a native Swiss citizen and therefore a blocked national under the freezing order."[100] As of March 1946 there was no evidence that any deal had been concluded, and Seligmann – who had evidently coveted the two works – wrote to withdraw his previous offers.

How and when did Fleischmann acquire his collection? The task of retracing the history and provenance of his remarkable possessions is not within the scope of my work. However, it is fair to note that Marcel appears to have been more interested in enjoying and protecting the art works than in their sale. Even the tentative prices that are quoted – subject to a 40 per cent commission, as shown in one of the notes – are not indicative of an intent to profit. In his correspondence with Silone, Fleischmann often mentions his love for the visual arts, music, and literature, but he only speaks of his art collection once, when he writes that his friend Tony Degen, who is going to New York on 8 April 1947, will be looking after his collection.[101]

Fleischmann's role as an art dealer is best understood when placed in an appropriate context, beginning with the awareness of the societal impact of the creation and movement of art throughout history – an awareness that he obviously possessed and that quite likely informed his decisions. But even focusing only on the Nazi era, given the wealth of scholarship of the last six decades, one can appreciate the complexity of his situation. Feliciano's comprehensive work *The Lost Museum*[102] provides essential insight in this regard. With depth and passion, the author writes a painstaking account of the Nazi regime's massive and systematic confiscation of art works, noting the contempt that was visited on the so-called "degenerate art" and its creators, including Braque, and the tragic years during which precious exemplars were lost and even *perished.*

Another indispensable work is Jonathan Petropoulos's *The Faustian Bargain.*[103] Focusing on the more practical aspects of the problem, the author immerses the reader in the situation as it then was, discussing how dealers competed for the art works, and what compelled them to engage in what he calls "Faustian bargains." Quoting from Feliciano, he notes that while Paris was the place where dealers were stocking up on art, Switzerland was their outlet. This was the case because "Switzerland did not have as many import or export restrictions. [...] Switzerland also had a legal framework that made it a preferred center for trade: after possessing a work for five years, an 'owner in good faith' had a legal right to the work (regardless of whether it was stolen)."[104] This is important to bear in mind because it clarifies the legal conditions under which Fleischmann would have operated if he had engaged in art dealing during the Nazi era, and it would help place any such activity in the appropriate legal and moral context.

The image of Marcel Fleischmann that emerges from the correspondence is not that of a person of dubious moral character; in fact he seems to have been quite the opposite, at the cost of disappointments and deceptions.[105] As an art lover he appears to have been most attracted to the aesthetic value of the art works, even asking Silone in one of his letters if his empty walls are not "crying for paintings."[106] As a dealer he dealt with people of impeccable reputation and credentials; as a man, he was imbued with human compassion to the point that, rather than feeling gratified by all the help he gave others, in one of his letters he expresses regret that he was not coherent till the end; that he had not given all of himself because he was unable to "give up" his family.[107] His son, Jürg, his brothers Carlo and Kurt, and their respective families were at his life's core. In time, his union with Elsa Schiess further enriched his emotional life. She was a remarkable woman who, though he did not make her his second wife, was his devoted companion and soulmate.

Elsa Schiess was born in the small pastoral town of Herisau, Kanton Appenzell, in 1898 and died in Zurich on 13 January 1973, the day of Marcel's eighty-second birthday.[108] She joined the Fleischmann family in 1923, and when Marcel became a widower, she helped raise the four-year-old Jürg with great dedication. As the correspondence reveals, she was also very generous and helpful to others. Silone noted as much when he wrote, "She belongs to the number of people who forget their own worries when friends need help."[109] Anthony Fleischmann confirmed this, and told me about his father's love and gratitude for his *de facto* second mother, her remarkable goodness, and the regret that his grandfather expressed after her death for not having married her.

Much like a real mother, Elsa was at Jürg's side whenever she could be of assistance, visiting trade shows with him, and even travelling to New York in 1947 to help him and his first wife, Jane Cook, get settled in their new home. Writing to Silone, Marcel shows his sensitivity through his concern that she will be travelling in winter and then, upon her return, by noting that she needs to rest, since travelling has never been easy for her.[110] During the following years he also writes about Elsa's struggle with depression, and his letters reveal that he shared her anguish even as he provided her with the best medical help available at the time, in the best clinics. His love for Elsa is evident, as is his appreciation of the positive impact she had on his life. They shared the same values, including a selfless need to be of assistance to others and a genuine desire to help build a better world. Their disregard for material considerations and their inability to harbour resentment are manifested by their reaction to adversity. Even though they cherished their Kleine Pension, when they were forced to sell it in order to satisfy a debt that Jürg could not repay to his uncle Carlo, they moved to an apartment at 78 Plattenstrasse without regrets. In a letter to the Silones they express their satisfaction with their new home in a way that would have been unnatural in other people under similar circumstances.[111] It is noteworthy that, whereas Darina Silone writes about the distress she felt upon hearing the "atrocious news" and her hope that Carlo would be assailed by remorse, Marcel simply states that he was not hurt by *what* happened but by *how* it happened.[112]

It is in fact at this time that he leaves the firm and writes to Silone that he should no longer have his business mail sent there and also that Germaniastrasse (i.e., the Kleine Pension) will soon be changing its name.

This he does for his son whose business and marriage are evidently failing, and he does it without claiming credit and without casting blame.

Lamentably, after the break-up, Carlo even compelled his friends to distance themselves from Marcel, and the two brothers no longer spoke to each other. Nevertheless, when Carlo died, Marcel regretted that for health reasons he was unable to bid him a last farewell.[113]

As Marcel often acknowledges, Elsa's presence in his life was essential, nurturing, and reassuring. For this he was eternally grateful and sought to make his feelings known, whether by expressing regret for the suffering he caused her – "El suffered a great deal during her life, and I know I caused her much sorrow, and I have been castigating myself for not being more loving to her, for not trying harder. And now it is too late! Our lives are now that much poorer for Elsa's absence" – or by expressing his love through poetic gestures and words. For instance, for Elsa's seventy-fourth birthday he had a bracelet engraved with these words: "El, je voudrais mourir pour voir si les anges te ressemblent" [El, I would like to die to see if the angels resemble you]. Also, when he had to inform the Silones of her death, he wrote that Elsa fell gently into sleep: "Elsa s'est endormie ce matin doucement." Elsa was an equally sensitive soul. Her last words, spoken in French like Marcel's loving ones for her, were, "Mais la vie repare ceux qui s'aiment, tout doucement, sans faire de bruit" [But life makes amends for those who love each other, very softly, without making noise].[114] Even then, she sought to reassure her companion. When she is no longer at his side, Marcel recalls his listening to Bach's *Et Resurrexit* with her, and looks forward to the end of his days, when they can be reunited.

The correspondence is dated from 1934, but it encompasses a period of forty-five years – from Silone's recollection of his first meeting with Marcel in 1931 to the latter's last letter to his friend, dated April 1976. As the two friends age, they cope with the process in different ways: Marcel, yielding to depression, becomes increasingly isolated and seeks refuge in the memories of the past; Silone, more stoically, continues to work and endeavours to bring solace to Marcel, dedicating one of his books to him, honouring him in a documentary about his Swiss years, and constantly reminding him of his and Darina's undying friendship and gratitude.

Marcel's sadness in his later years is deep yet not pathetic. On his birthdays he rereads the letter Silone wrote to him in 1941 and revisits the past, which he so intensely lived. Despite his failing vision, he continues to write and to share his feelings with his friend. In the closing years of his life, some of his letters – now addressed to his grandson – denote convivial and pedagogical intents. It is evident that he is also writing for posterity. His poetic nature and the essence of his character clearly emerge from the letters. Because of their importance, I sought and received permission to quote from them extensively:

Zurich, 17 December 1974 [115]

My dear Tony,

Your fine letter which came right from your heart found its way to mine and caressed it lovingly. It arrived in due time: you are probably not aware of the fact that the curve of my life has had a downward trend for quite some time already and that as of late it has been decaying more and more rapidly. I am practically constantly bedridden and just to get up for the meals means already quite an effort, the ailments of age becoming a growing bother.

I am writing you all this merely to explain why I have to dictate my letters instead of writing them myself, but I know you will bear with me and can read through the lines. From this introduction you will see also that I can follow your so well meant and encouraging recommendation to enjoy life in its last phase, only in theory.

Your letter made me happy as it reflects your trust and showed me that you are willing to open me your heart. As you so rightly stated, we have a lot in common, especially that rather outstanding sensibility which, though making us feel the depths much stronger than others, allows us to reach moments of sublimeness [sic] and height that are beyond reach for the majority of men. Most precious to us in our ethic [sic] approach to life is genuine truth, modesty, love for mankind with all its shortcomings, a sense of fairness and a deep-rooted feeling for beauty – beauty in the light of inner cleanness and serenity, uprightness of character and responsibility. If I were gifted to express my feelings as an artist, be it in writing or painting, I would enjoy expressing the features of your soul in the subtle way I sense them.

[...] you are probably too demanding and exacting toward yourself, physically and morally. Remember the saying "All the secret of prolonging one's life consists in not shortening it" and "culture is what remains after one has forgotten everything one had learned." We are living in terrible times and they are likely to become still a lot worse. In order to cope with life, you will need all your strength. Actually, the more conscious and responsible a person is, the tougher the task. Obviously you – and there we are very similar – do not appear to be satisfied with mere superficial floating on the surface but want to dig into the true values of man's being and then want to abide by them. In thoughts I stretch out my hand to you to give you strength.

[...] Through your father I heard that for your test at Princeton you chose the theme "Arabs and Israelis." I appreciate your choice; the Jewish people must survive. They have given mankind more spiritual and cultural values than any others. The world may not fall back into medieval thinking. I would be anxious to read your paper – would you see your way to send me a copy of it?

[...] For many years I have kept a small copy-book into which I noted some thoughts I have come across in my readings or which passed my own mind and which I consider to be essential truths. I often wondered what would become of this booklet which is particularly dear to me, once I am dead. Now I know. I shall hand it to your father or ask Friedel to pass it on to you lateron, [sic] so you may keep it as a personal souvenir from me and may perhaps carry on with the entries yourself. It contains many beautiful but also some quite daring and dangerous thoughts some of which may be 'consumed' perhaps only at advanced age, and cautiously so. For instance: 'To reach the source/spring, one must swim against the current" or "who [sic] swims with the current certainly makes leaway [sic] but in downward direction."

From the content of your letter I sense that you take things rather serious [sic] and make yourself reproaches for errors of omissions committed in the past. Don't forget, God created man to live and to make mistakes. Man would suffocate in the mistakes currently made had the Lord not provided him with a fabulous gift – the ability to forget. Do you know the saying: "God appreciates me when I work and loves me when I sing"?

I am writing you these words in a rather melancholic frame of mind because I am afraid that the time I am still alive will not be long enough that we could meet again. Our souls and our mind will, however, remain united nevertheless, even after I shall have left my physical shell, the same as is the case with my beloved Elsa whom I always feel within and around me.

After having reread your letter for the third time, it struck me again in what a sensitive and serious way you respond to the problems of life. This is certainly very fine. Once upon a time, some fifty years ago, when I was faced with a particularly critical and crucial phase of life, my best friend wrote me that it is actually immaterial what one does in life and how one does it, all that matters is the spirit – and the spirit only – in which it is being done. Your approach to things and the spirit which guides it, is irreproachable and noble. This is the most valuable present you can make to your parents and myself, and last but not least also to yourself. You are basically peaceful in a very unpeaceful world and therefore I really am, as a last resort enjoying you.

[...] Let me add that, whatever a person with a fine character as yours is doing, is well done and correct, because you care and try. Your letter has been the nicest Christmas present I could possibly have received.

I love you dearly,

Grandpa Marcel[116]

In another letter, dated 30 June 1978, also to his grandson, he records additional important thoughts.[117] He writes:

Meines Freundes Ugnatius [sic] Silone's Motto heisst: Ich bein ein Christ[sic] ohne Kirche und ein Sozialist ohne Partei. So möchte ich sagen, dass auch El[sa], Friedel und ich keiner besonderen Religion bedurften, indem unser Motto, das erstmals von El[sa] ausgensprochen wurde, heist: "Est gibt nichts Gutes, es sei den man tut es.

[My friend Ignazio Silone's motto is: "I am a Christian without a church and a Socialist without a party." I would like to state that Elsa and I do not need to adhere to any specific religion. As Elsa would say, "There is no good in this world unless one does good."]

Marcel's affinity with Silone is hereby underscored. But his desire to express his and Elsa's concept of religion in such humanistic terms should not be understood as a rejection of his Jewish roots. As noted in the previous letter, he is proud of his heritage and feels that the Jewish people have given the world more spiritual and cultural values than any other people. He is concerned about the future of Israel and its safety and yearns to visit it again. In one of his letters, he tells Silone that during his visit he hopes to regain the sense of wonder that he has lost due to so many tragic events.[118]

Writing again to Anthony, only a few weeks before Silone's death, on 22 August 1978, Marcel notes in his postscript that a well-known writer [Silone] has sent him a book thus inscribed: "To Marcel Fleischmann, l'ami de tous ceux qui souffrent" [To Marcel Fleischmann, the friend of all who suffer]. Marcel was then eighty-seven years old. He was evidently gratified by his friend's recognition of his compassion. He was also deeply moved when Darina Silone visited him in 1981 at the Belvoir rest home to show him her affection and remind him of Silone's eternal gratitude. Recalling the past and all the good that Marcel had done, she told him that, "he had been, was a saint." Marcel was moved to tears, but quickly reassured her saying: "Ich weine vor Freude" [I weep for joy].[119]

Had a biography been written of Marcel Fleischmann when those who knew him and Elsa could have borne witness, readers would have been able to appreciate, to a much greater extent, what unique human beings they actually were. Given the dearth of information available now, the correspondence with Silone and Marcel's letters to his grandson will help in part to fill the void while also inspiring all those who are willing to believe, like Marcel and Elsa, that goodness begets goodness and carries intrinsic redeeming power.

Figure 1. Ignazio Silone and Gabriella Seidenfeld, circa 1925–7, place unknown. Courtesy of the Centro Studi Ignazio Silone

Figure 2. Ignazio Silone and Aline Valangin, “La Barca,” Comologno, 1931. Courtesy of Maria Moscardelli

Figure 3. Ignazio and Darina Silone. Switzerland, circa 1943. Courtesy of Maria Moscardelli

Figure 4. The Kleine Pension, 53 Germaniastrasse, as it also was when Fleischmann owned it. Zurich, August 2012. Courtesy of Donald Paynter

Figure 5. Ignazio Silone and Darina Silone in the Kleine Pension's studio, circa 1944–5. Courtesy of the Centro Studi Ignazio Silone

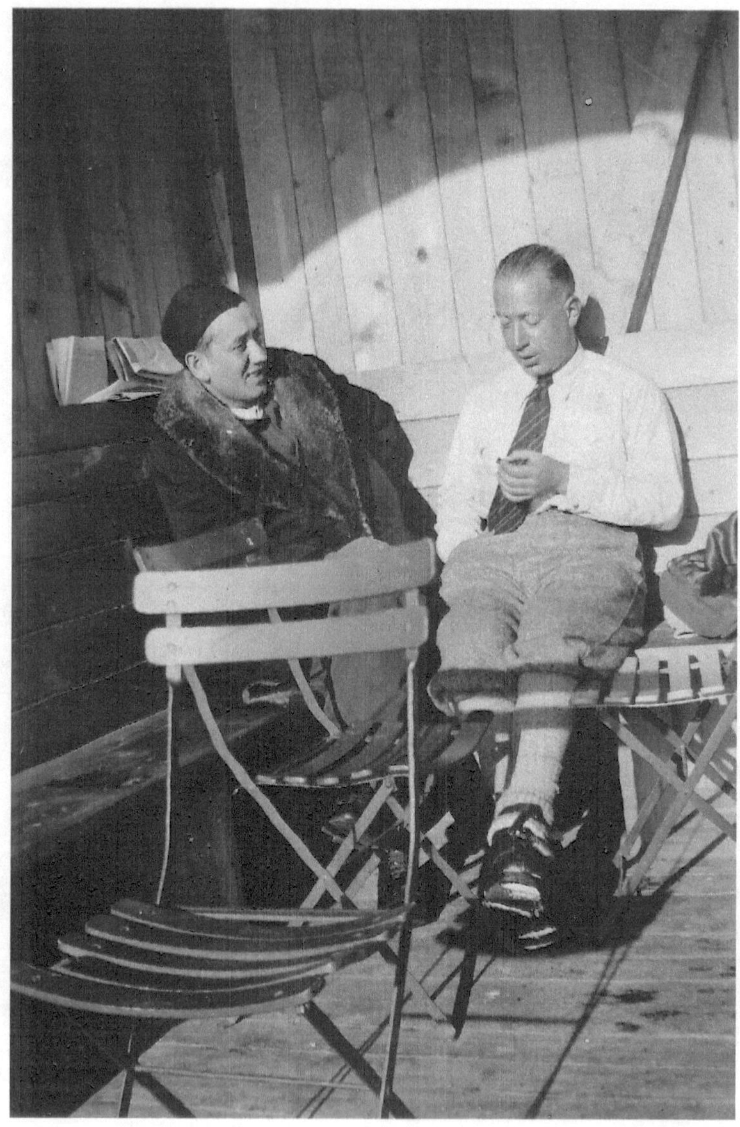

Figure 6. Ignazio Silone and Marcel Fleischmann, Switzerland, circa 1943. On the back Silone writes: "A sinistra Rebe Tranquillowitch; a destra Marcel Fleischmann." Courtesy of Maria Moscardelli

Figure 7. Marcel Fleischmann and Elsa Schiess in their apartment at 78 Plattenstrasse, Zurich, circa 1950. Courtesy of Anthony Fleischmann

Figure 8. Ignazio and Darina Silone, going to the meeting of the Congress for Cultural Freedom, [Venice?], 1957. Courtesy of the Centro Studi Ignazio Silone

Figure 9. Darina Silone's donation of Silone's archives to his home town on the centenary of his birth. Pescina dei Marsi, 2000. Courtesy of the Centro Studi Ignazio Silone

Figure 10. Ignazio Silone's tomb, as he envisaged it when writing his will. Pescina dei Marsi, 2015. Courtesy of Diocleziano Giardini

Figure 11. Marcel Fleischmann's family tomb. Friedhof Manegg, Zurich, 2012. Courtesy of Donald Paynter

The Correspondence

TRANSLATED BY MARIA NICOLAI PAYNTER AND AINE ZIMMERMAN

The Swiss Years: 1934–1944

SILONE

1

Sils Maria
12 January 1934

Dear Mr. Fleischmann,

January 13 is your birthday? January 13 is also the anniversary of the Abruzzo earthquake. Thus are connected, in life, bereavement and birth, sorrow and joy. "A door closes and a window opens." Birthdays would only be banal conventions if they did not enable meditative souls to reassess their own spiritual lives. During these sad times, when not only the balance sheets of publicly held companies, but also the spiritual balances of individuals so often end in disastrous "deficits" and failures, it must be no small consolation for you to record such a great "positive balance" and such great "profits." It will soon be a year that I have been living in your home: the material aid that this represents for me (and indirectly for Serena) is great, but it is very small when compared with the spiritual aid; even if this manifests itself through the invisible paths that lead to the soul, and they don't consist of moralizing speeches and sermons, but of the example of a life that humanizes and harmonizes itself ever more each day. For many things, you are, in my eyes, the man that I would like to be and perhaps will be at the end of my life.

You who know me, Mr. Fleischmann, know how hard it is for me to write letters to friends and so you will forgive me if I send this letter to the post office at once, together with my best wishes for the New Year.

S. Tranquilli

SILONE

2

(Postcard)
Panorama of Chateau d'Oex
5 April, no year. [Possibly 1934 since Gabriella became Mrs. Meyer in June 1933.]
Addressed to: Fleischmann Family, Germaniastrasse 53, Zurich
From: Chateau d'Oex (Vaud) Pension Borgeaud

Message, in French: "Dear Mr. Fleischmann, the place here is beautiful but the weather is mostly rainy; very little snow. Save for some old British, it is empty and calm. Cordial greetings to the whole family.

Your Tranquilli
Friendly regards, G. Meyer" [Added by Gabriella Seidenfeld].

FLEISCHMANN

3

Poveromo
9 October 1934

Dear friend,

I can, in good conscience, send you my correspondence with Mühlenstein[1] along with his manuscript. We are, after all, both good friends of his, and this concerns his existence – perhaps even his life, if Mrs. Cavin is to be believed – and Anita's life is just as important to me as well. I can't fulfil M's wish that I critique his work, because I am not a critic, but what I read, I enjoyed. Or I set it aside and didn't concern myself with the how and the why of it. It is the same way for me with images, and this is both my strength and my weakness – although I do find it easier to judge paintings.

However, I would like to tell you my impressions, in order to then hear yours so that I can not only analyse this text, but also learn how one judges a book.

The subject that M. is dealing with is the same as the one I recently asked you to cut out of the feuilleton for me, isn't it? You told me that Ms. Meier[2] either got to know the mother or the daughter. How did M. learn about this? The idea to expand this into a novel and research all of the background information seems to hold great possibility. But at the same time, I am not sure that M. is the man to do this, and I am almost sorry that this text didn't end up in more able and experienced hands. I think his treatment of the subject is too romantic, not deep or analytical enough. It's always the same problem: an apotheosis of himself and complaint about all that stands in his way. He really should get to the bottom of that before trying to rise to new heights.

I also wonder whether it's a good idea for this book to be so socialist. That means that from the start a large part of society will completely disregard it. By the same token I would have left out any mention of Trotsky in Nettie's epilogue;[3] I have heard from many others that although it is well written, it doesn't make sense as part of this book. I also don't understand why M. uses so many foreign words.

I still think that there are two kinds of artists: those who possess creative intuition and follow it while they are writing, and those who need some distance from the divine spark in order to create a real masterpiece. Both you and Wassermann[4] seem like the latter to me. Doesn't M. always write his novels in six weeks, while others take years?

I assume that, as a friend of M's, you will read his book with interest and am looking forward to speaking to you about it when I return – and also about how M. is doing.

Yesterday the Stöcklin's [sic][5] arrived; we had been looking forward to their visit. There is just so much more warmth and real feeling that issues forth from someone who works with his hands, than from someone of high society. Stöcklin told us that there was a sudden change of weather in Zurich, and we all hope that Anne turned on the heat in time to make it bearable. If everything goes well, we hope to head back on the 17th, via Ravenna, Ferrara, Verona, Padua, Mantua, Brescia and Milan, and then arrive in Zurich on the 21st.[6]

SILONE

4

Thursday, 11 October [1934][7]

Dear Mr. Fleischmann,

Thank you for your letter of October 9, to which I want to answer at once.

On the topic of Mühlestein.

After your departure, I saw Madame Cavin who was waiting for a reply after approaching you. I told her, vaguely, what you told me and advised her to ask Anita[8] to send you a copy of the manuscript of her husband's novel. Madame Cavin then spoke to me of this manuscript as a masterpiece, and informed me that Mr. Muschg was entrusted with having the manuscript accepted by a good publisher, who would immediately give an advance on the copyrights. Soon upon receiving the foreseen sum, Madame Cavin intended to leave immediately for Maloja. The following day, the dramatic act! Madame Cavin phoned me to run to her. I went to Zollikerstr. And found a four-page letter by Mr. Muschg on the topic of Mühlestein's novel. The content of the letter was catastrophic: according to Mr. Muschg, "the publication of this novel will be the definitive liquidation, literary and moral, of Mr. Mühlestein"; "it is impossible to propose such a manuscript to a publisher"; "the manuscript does not have any artistic and literary quality, any proportion, any elaboration"; " the tirades against Germany and Switzerland are excessive and grotesque"; "the manuscript reveals a state of mind of self-divinization which is already pathologic"; etc. According to Mr. Muschg, the only advice to be given Mr. Mühlestein would be that "he should abstain from writing one word for two years"; "that he give up, once and for all, drawing his means of livelihood amongst millionaires," and "that he try to earn a living with his work (not literary)." The tone of Mr. Muschg's letter was that of a friend who had to make a great effort to tell the truth. I then asked Madame Cavin to give me the manuscript that Mr. Muschg had returned to her and read it entirely that same evening.

My opinion of the manuscript.

a) *As to content:*

I found some raw documents in this novel, devoid of all artistic elaboration and without any internal connection: the killing of Hildegart by Aurora, the scientific work of Prof. Heller, the discussions between

Heller and Mühlestein at Celerina, etc. in a manner that is supported only in some small provincial newspapers. Next to this, some fantastic, absolutely arbitrary elements, such as the research of Hildegart's paternity, that Mr. Mühlestein attributes to himself! It is undoubtedly acceptable to mix, in a novel, real and fantastic elements, but on the condition that they result in verisimilitude and the first precaution to be taken is to change the names of the characters that one borrows from reality and to modify their milieu. (For instance as Toller did with Reiedel-Guala in his piece *Die blinde Göttin.*) Even as in *Menschen ohne Gott* Mühlestein has created a Russia and a Stalin that he never saw and that are absolutely false, in this novel he put real characters with their names and surnames, in strange kinship relations, in a milieu that he does not know and in a town about which he didn't even take the precaution of informing himself from a Baedeker (so, for instance, he puts Aurora in the Carcel Modelo, which is a male prison in Madrid). Mühlestein does not know anything about Spain, or Madrid, or the Spanish youth. The little documentation that he has been able to gather, he has reproduced in the novel in its raw state.

b) *As to form*:
Mühlestein proves with this book that he will never be able to write a novel. The form is so emphatic, rhetorical, filled with moral digressions, political allusions and other things that are totally foreign to the dramatic process, that reading becomes very painful. If one removed all the useless sentences from the manuscript, the volume would be reduced from 150 to 50 pages.

c) *As to the eventual utilization of the material for a play*:
This is also an idea that came to me, but I discarded it when I got to the end of the reading, to the discussion between Aurora and Mühlestein on ... Antigone and Creon! This discussion (that Mr. Muschg found to be the only beautiful thing in the manuscript!) I found to be false, ridiculous, and funny. Mühlestein knows ancient Greece like he knows Spain, that is, badly. If one wanted to do a parody of Greek tragedy, one would have to really put on the stage Madame Aurora who explains that she killed her daughter because of ... Antigone. On the passing from patriarchy to matriarchy in antiquity and on uneasy and mysterious relationships between mother and daughter, and between father and son, in the last twenty years, we have had such discoveries that it is no longer permitted to treat these topics without having studied Freud, Jung, Adler and others who have dealt with it. After studying these, it will be

necessary to go live some years with an old Catholic Spanish family. And then, perhaps, one could attempt to write the drama of Aurora and her daughter. If it were a matter of details, one could of course propose to Mühlestein that he make some modifications to his work, but in my opinion, it is the very basis of his work that is false, the basis above all. In other respects, no more false than in *Menschen ohne Gott.*

Hodler forever!

Finally, we will speak about it again upon your return. I am sending you, this very day, the notebooks and the photos concerning the towns that you will cross on your way back, but I have found little. Meanwhile, best regards to you and the rest of the company.

Your Sanser

For Miss Schiess.

I cannot send you the address you requested because I forgot it.

Saluti.

S.T.

SILONE

5

Ascona
Casa Bellaria
31 January 1935

Dear Mr. Fleischmann,

Forgive me if I have delayed in returning Miss Degen's[9] manuscripts that you gave me before your departure. I have taken the liberty of having them also read by two writers who live here, *clearly without giving them any indication regarding the author.* I have done so because when one knows the author himself, one always believes that he is not objective. But in this case, the opinion was unanimous: even as one cannot judge the talent of a young person only on the basis of some written pages, all the same it is evident that Miss Degen possesses real qualities of expression and literary construction. I do not know if she should publish what she has written so far; possibly, from the point of view of her further development (not only intellectual, but as a woman as well), it is always best to wait, it is always better not to be too hasty and not to age too soon. To publish, in literature, means to produce, to bear fruit, and to bear fruit before all the energies are worn out; it means, most frequently, to soon become exhausted. Miss Degen (and, with her, a number of young women and young men of our time, including Jürg) went on, by her intensive rhythm, to burn the stages of life. It may be that one does not have the right to influence someone, but in this particular case, it is necessary to be very careful not to influence her in the sense of accelerating her vital rhythm. Possibly, her physical malaises are due to this and she has already exhausted the resources that at her age should still be almost intact, rendering her life interesting to her. She is naturally launched in fourth gear; if possible (I am speaking of her studies) she will have to proceed at the speed of her peers. If possible. As to literature, she possesses an evident talent. It isn't clear that philology will be the most appropriate [means] to develop this talent. It isn't the study of poets that makes one a poet, but rather, life (Life itself). I have here a young Italian who is writing a novel and asked my advice on what he should do to learn to write well. Since he is strong enough, I advised him to learn carpentry, but he took it as a joke. (This is the luck of free advice.) In contemporary literature, there are many writers who are doctors and practice medicine and find in their profession the contact with the world and society that feeds their books. But, naturally, one cannot generalize; I have only wanted to say that medicine is not an obstacle to the further maturation of Miss Degen's literary talent. Dear Mr. Fleischmann, forgive me for the length of this letter, and even more for my writing: I am writing to you while lying in the sun, on a chaise longue. Best regards to you and all the members of your family.

S. Tranquilli

FLEISCHMANN

6

5 February 1935

My dear Tranquilli,

Thank you again for your kind letter, and especially for the interest you have taken not only in Miss Degen's literary experiments, but also in her life.[10]

I am certain your detailed feedback not only is accurate but that you hit the nail on the head in all regards. It happens quite often in life that you feel something is not working but you can't fix it when you are directly involved and so can't get the necessary distance from it.

For me personally this is especially the case when people I love to spoil are involved. This has been proved to me again and again, both with men and women. It is possible that many things would have turned out differently for and with my late wife if I could have combined my goodness with more mindfulness. I also think many unpleasant things in my relationship with Tscharner[11] could have been avoided if I had been able to temper my impulsivity with more self-reflection. To be sure, we all have our flaws and I do not have to be ashamed of mine when I compare them to others.

Once you are back I would like to discuss this topic with you more broadly. Until then, thank you for your efforts.

Elsa worried us a lot last week. She was in a great deal of pain, suggesting complications that might make treatment in the hospital necessary. Luckily everything subsided and it now seems it was just a passing symptom of the usual troubles. If she can sustain the long-term effects of the treatment I think that all can finally reach a good end.

Weather-wise you seem to be the lucky one this time. What we have here cannot even be called weather any more – it is simply awful. It is always snowing in Davos, but no one resents it since it is the only sunny spot in Switzerland.

At the end of this week Mr. Gerl from Ascona is coming to Zurich for a few days and we expect several other visits. One young man in particular whom I managed to track down – a militant communist from Germany but a very talented guy – is sure to amuse you. The first night he was here he almost started an altercation with Weigert, whose father starts his lectures in Germany with "Heil Hitler!" Such things greatly entertain me and give vent to my suppressed [urge] to have a fight.

I currently have some business worries because of the strong dollar, which could destroy my plans should anything go wrong with the gold standard debate in America. At my brother's in Küsnacht I met a certain Mr. Solomon, a journalist of the *Vossichen Zeitung* who praises *Fontamara* not only as the best book since the emigration but as the best book of the past few years. I always have the feeling that one of these numerous rays that shine down on you will also shine on my house. When you are back I would like to have you over along with him. Is your book coming along? What about our trip to the monastery? I'm already practising fasting, which will be easier for me than abstinence. Do they have nuns there or are you allowed to bring one? Please let us hear from you from time to time and accept a cordial handshake from me, and the whole Germaniastrasse.

Yours,

SILONE

7

3 June [1935][12]

My dear Mr. Fleischmann,

I am leaving today for Ascona and want to say, at least in writing, "au revoir," in Ascona or Zurich. I think that I will remain there two months: if the environment bothers me I'll go to the mountain. Meanwhile I would like to introduce another subject that is very painful for me and speak to you about another departure, and I would like to do it with words that come from my heart: certainly, nothing will ever spoil our friendship and if today I decide, for the first time, to speak to you of my need to leave your house, you can trust that I have not been influenced by any cooling of my friendship for you. The objective reasons that have convinced me to do so are of another order altogether: to begin with, I have always been worried about all the harm that could come to you from the fact that you shelter a revolutionary writer; until now this has not caused you serious trouble, but this could happen in the future, especially since, upon finishing my novel, I intend to intensify my activity, always within the intellectual domain. I intend to do it, not in Zurich, where the police are more circumspect, but rather in some nearby place where it is easier to influence the local authorities. Next, and a great merit for this is yours, during the time that I lived at your house my health and my economic situation, without becoming brilliant, have at least sensibly improved. In an epoch when so many needs remain unanswered, I feel some remorse at continuing to enjoy your generosity and to take from you the aid that should go to others. I do not need to repeat with many words that this will change absolutely nothing about the feelings that I have for you. You have often been deceived: although I am certain that you did not help me to have my gratitude, all the same, I can assure you that you will always have it. Concerning my definitive departure, the date and the new address, we will undoubtedly have the occasion to speak about it in person.

Your,

S. Tranquilli

SILONE

8

Ascona
1 January 1936

Dear friends,

Only a few words to wish you a happy New Year! At the house all is as usual: Anna is sick, Finny telephones, Wuli looks at me and asks himself: "After all, who is this funny stranger who acts as the boss around the house?" and he does not find an answer to this question. Myself, I don't help him find an answer. Must one always find an answer? Allora, ciao e buone cose![13]

S. Tranquilli

FLEISCHMANN

9

28 December 1936

My dear Trankus,

I just got off the phone with you – I was, and still am, so excited about your success, and was so blinded by those rays of sunshine shining on me (please, not going down [on me]) that I completely forgot to thank you for the photographic book. I looked through it very closely while lying in bed yesterday morning, picked out my favourite pictures, and then passed it on to Tscharner. There are a number of pictures in it that border on the fantastic, especially the ones of the peppers on the chair, the apple on the wood, the gothic church windows, the baroque wall, and both of the male busts. Thank you again very much.

Do continue to recuperate, and try to keep up the pace of recovery I have observed over the last few years, because then it truly won't be long until you are back in good health.

I am enclosing a letter from Raphael,[14] with a request for your advice. It involves a sum of approx. 1,500 Swiss francs and I am absolutely free to say yes or no. I believe that I would be willing to take on such a relatively large sum if you think that I can do something worthwhile with it.

I press your hand fondly

SILONE
10

I. Silone
Curhouse Clavadel
29 December 1936

My dear Mr. Fleischmann,

Thank you, thank you very much for the beautiful Christmas gifts and for your affectionate letter. Your congratulations for my literary "successes" have the effect of redoubling my satisfaction, since one likes to be alone when one is sad, but a true joy is nothing if it is not shared. I write to you lying on a chaise longue under the sun, in an inner calm that I have not known for a long time and for which my stay with your family was the ideal prelude. I am also very glad to understand that the news of my "dollars" did not suggest to you the idea of kicking me out …

I hope to see you here in the New Year and thank you once more.
I. Silone

I just got your letter with M. Raphael's letter; I will answer as soon as I have been able to decipher the latter.

SILONE

11

Davos
12 January 1937

My dear Mr. Fleischmann,

Many sincere congratulations for your birthday. Here is a man, I tell myself, for whom time is not a source of sadness, nor of aging, but of consolation and youth. Here is a man who goes against the current and becomes always more human, optimistic and liberal – youthful qualities, while other men, even the best ones, begin to harden and become embittered, pessimistic and intolerant. Here is a man who has discovered the secret pill against aging, the "pill against wickedness." Naturally, I congratulate you, but I also congratulate *us; us,* that is, the Germaniastrasse family.

Cordially,
Your

S. Tranquilli
Herr Tranquilli, Clavadel, Curhaus[15]

FLEISCHMANN
12

13 January 1937

My dear Mr. Tranquilli,

I recently wanted to reread something in *Der Faschismus* and I found some notes you had left inside it. I am sending them to you as I imagine you may be looking for them.

Elsa tells me that you are doing well health-wise and I am happy to hear it. Apparently you now live like turtledoves in a pretty apartment. Do you have a guest room too?[16]

My women are taking a vacation, and Nettie is also in Davos, so Erich and I have to accept our male lot in life of having to work at home.[17]

I have been talking about your success in America and I hope that doesn't bother you – it just makes me so happy to talk about it.

Jürg is doing well right now, he is in good health and I believe he'll be able to hang on till school is over. Then we will see that he finds something good in England. I still believe in his good character and that he was born under a good star. I shake your hand and your Mrs. Serena's.[18]

Yours

FLEISCHMANN
13

15 January 1937

My dear Trankus,

The police have phoned twice. The first time they didn't reach me, but both times they said that you are late with some kind of payment; something about bail.

They asked me if you are earning money yet. I said no, but that I had the feeling that as soon as the new book comes out, you would surely be receiving something from that. They replied that they thought you might receive a literary prize, and I said while I wasn't sure, I thought you might, one of these days. Then they asked me if you were in Davos at my expense. I said yes, and they asked why. My answer: "Just so that Mr. Tranquilli does not get into any kind of debt."

Then I asked if I should tell you about any of this, and they emphatically said not to, that the matter was already taken care of and that you should not be bothered. Did you leave something unpaid on purpose? I believe more and more that you will need an accountant very soon, Mr. Capitalist![19]

With cordial regards.

Your,

SILONE

14

Davos Platz
16 January 1937

My dear Mr. Fleischmann,

Thank you very much for your letter of the 15 c.m. regarding my residence permit. Generally speaking, allow me to tell you that I do not fear any investigation on the part of the authorities and if in the future they should still bother you because of me, the best and surest [thing to do] will be to simply tell the truth and nothing but the truth. My residence permit expired October 31 and even though I have enough highly located friends who could easily have informed themselves and informed me about the causes of the delay of the new residence permit, I have avoided all these steps. The delay means that there was an inquiry and that does not worry me at all. Even in the case that the inquiry should lead to an unfavourable conclusion in my regard, I will always have the possibility to prove that I don't do anything that is contrary to the obligations I undertook as a political refugee. The late deposits to my account only prove the lack of order in my bookkeeping. In fact, I thought that I was up to date, but since I do not make the deposits each month on a regular basis, but every 3 or 4 months, it is quite probable that I still have two or three monthly payments due for 1936. Had I been warned in time, I would have already deposited the rest, as I will do today. Finally, forgive me if, among all the worries that you have, I cause you additional needless ones. Won't you come once to Davos while I am here with Mrs. Meyer? We will not be able to host you since we only have two rooms, but we will be able to "nourish" you. Miss Schiess is well and she helps us a lot with all sorts of things. She belongs to the number of people who forget their own worries when friends need help.

Very cordially,
Your

S. Tranquilli[20]

FLEISCHMANN

15

1 February 1937

Dear Mr. Tranquilli,

I had and still have a genuine desire to spend one or two days with you alone somewhere, but it can't be in Davos because skiing there is for me what soccer is for you. That's why I didn't say anything else the other day, because there was still the possibility of a little drive around 10 o'clock. Maybe some time in Ascona or during the season somewhere else? We should really look for a special place for our first meeting alone.

I asked Miss Degen to give you two articles to read from the *Zürcher Zeitung* that I would have liked to talk to you about, since at the moment I am quite interested in the Russian affair.[21] I also read the Gide article but don't understand the trial or the different articles.[22] By the way, I was very happy to see you so completely content in Davos and wish you and Miss Serena[23] all the best.

Yours

Mr. S. Tranquilli, Promenade 51, Davos-Platz

SILONE

16

4 February 1937

Davos Pl., Promenade 51

My dear Mr. Fleischmann,

Thank you for your letter that I received yesterday and for the one that arrived today. I rejoice very much at the idea of spending a little time with you; but meanwhile I hope that you will now not begin to consider it like a "promise that must be kept," like a "duty" and a "chore" because, then, if it is realized, it will no longer be a pleasure but a fatigue. Also, the travels that one talks about a lot in advance always fail to live up to expectations. Once we are in good humour, instead of going home, we will go the station and leave. Nightgown, toothbrush, toilet paper, etc. we will buy where the train takes us. That's one idea for the departure. For the place of destination, I think that what matters must be that it has a good climate and some of the attractions one can find in the picture books. I will certainly be pleased to spend a few days, in a tranquil place, with you. I truly believe that after a few hours we will begin to be silent and will only exchange a few brief words; this is, for me, the highest point that a friendship could reach. As long as one chats, gets agitated, asks and answers, that is not yet the highest point; sometimes it is the path towards the summit; sometimes it is the opposite path. I speak to you almost like a Pastor; but a banal Pastor, because the majority of the Pastors are preachers and "men-who-have-the-profession-of teaching-others" through words. I don't know if your fears about M. Raphael's books are justified.[24] The books that are forbidden by Swiss law are: 1. Those that have been printed illegally, not having, therefore, the name of the publisher and the printer, 2.Those whose sale is forbidden in Switzerland by order of the "Procure Fédérale." I do not believe that in Raphael's boxes there is a single book that pertains to these categories. The books of Marx and Lenin, which are in his cases, anyone can buy in any Swiss bookstore, and they are also found in the public libraries at the disposal of the whole world, and in the private libraries of all who are interested in sociological issues. – The same considerations are also valid for my books: I believe that in my little library there are some Communist or Socialist books, some Fascist books, others that are Catholic, all permitted by the law. The mail brings every day Socialist newspapers (to which I never subscribed, nor requested and that I receive by initiative of the publishers), Fascist newspapers and Catholic newspapers. I suppose that the mail of any writer, even bourgeois and reactionary, must carry the same variety. I don't believe that a writer was ever criticized for reading certain books. It would be different if you had some hundred or thousand copies of a book by Marx or Mussolini, that would then be a propaganda depot, and as such the police would have the right of control. – This, as long as there is a legal regime in Switzerland, as long as the law must be respected not only by the citizens but also by the authorities; because, under another regime, it is not absolutely necessary to have books by Marx in order to have one's house pillaged and set on fire. Now I have spoken to you like a lawyer. Actually, just as through diseases one can become a doctor even without a diploma, through the troubles with men one can become a lawyer. But I do not pretend to be a good lawyer. (Have you noticed how in my books the most ridiculous people are the lawyers, such as don Circostanza, don Zabaglione, etc.?) What renders the lawyers' role a bit uncertain in our time is the arbitrary police. It is not enough to respect the law; it is also necessary to keep the good will of the police. But in order to attract some of their chicanery, it is not indispensable to be surprised with some books of Marx and Lenin belonging to M. Raphael, or me; it may suffice having offered us hospitality. Basically these are thoughts that I express against my temperament. I believe that in life one must not be concerned about pleasing or displeasing others; but one must act according to one's own conscience and always be ready to face the consequences. (This letter has become ridiculously long, and I do not want to add anything else.)

Very cordial regards to the whole family and to you in particular.

Your

S. Tranquilli

SILONE

17

12 February 1937
Davos Pl.

Dear Mr. Fleischmann,

Thank you for the newspaper *Neue Zürcher Nachrichten* with this dreadful picture of yours truly. One morning at the beginning of February, while I was still in bed, a reporter from the Zurich Agence Photo-Press (a Catholic agency), who said that he had gotten my address from "Consul Fleischmann,"[25] begged me to allow him to photograph me. While I was putting on my socks, my pants and my shirt and while I was shaving, he kept calling me "Mr. Literature Laureate!" something to really make one burst out laughing. He took a dozen pictures. Among these, the one that appeared in Zurich is, unquestionably, the most Catholic; some others have appeared in the other periodicals of Swiss priests. If the unlucky readers of this press will buy *Bread and Wine*,[26] they will be astonished that the devil has such a power to be able to even influence the Catholic press. This will be the fun ending of a banal story.

Cordially,

Your

S. Tranquilli

FLEISCHMANN

18

13 February 1937

My dear Mr. Tranquilli,

I have your letters of February 4th and 12th in front of me right now, and am quite proud that you have taken such an interest in me.

I could have written back sooner, but decided to handle this the way I am approaching our next meeting: everything should just happen spontaneously. But you needn't worry that I now somehow feel obligated – after all, there was plenty of opportunity for me to have felt that way in the past.

But I do need more time than you do to gather the necessities. When you ran through your list you forgot some things: notepads, pipes and tobacco, a phone book. I am as excited as a kid about our meeting!

I hope you did not misunderstand me regarding Raphael's boxes. I hope and believe that I possess a decent amount of civil courage, but I am saving it for the moment when it will really matter and pay off. I took this up because of Elsa's lack of space; I didn't want to cause you any inconvenience, but I also didn't know if that would be the case because I am not knowledgeable about it all. Just as I am happy to provide you with information about stocks and taxes, I also think I should ask you when it comes to these things. I just don't want you to judge me as "fearful for myself."

I did not give your address to the photographer, Miss Schiess did. How does it feel to have your picture sent around the whole world?

It is with great interest that I have learned about the possibility of an operation and I am of course happy to talk this over with you in Zurich as a doctor, although not as a medical doctor but as a doctor interitio.[27] It's "a hell of a thing" as Jürg would say.

I have decided to send 100 Swiss francs to Polgar.[28] Schmid alone advised me not to, saying that he doesn't deserve it. I am practically speechless about the massive conceit with which this parasite sits in such judgment.

I also wanted to quickly mention that my early morning walks in the forest are so beautiful that, although I enjoy the solitude, I still have the urge to share this pleasure with someone. Sometime I will wake you up and together we will listen to the morning concert of the birds, especially the call of the little Strix owls.

About other news: we had a very nice person stay with us, a Dr. Rosenthal, the famous Munich antiquarian. You really have to meet him; you will like him.

Please thank Mrs. Meier for her words and to both of you a warm handshake from your

SILONE

19

Le Cannet
24 January [1938][29]

My dear Mr. Fleischmann,

Thank you very much for your letter from Vienna. Your description of the "burial grounds" is worthy of a great writer. You know that, of a great writer of French literature, Mme. de Sévigné,[30] we only have some letters written to family members; perhaps one day we can also edit your letters. I am returning (pardon my delay) Mr. Reich's letter.[31] Even though I am in correspondence with Toscanini,[32] I do not believe that he will give any importance to my musical opinions. He is an "old man" terrible and admirable, an "old man" who, in his profession has never shown indulgence toward anyone. That is also why he has a good orchestra. As for Stefan Zweig,[33] he is: 1st an anti-Semite, 2nd serious enough to never recommend a musician that he never heard, based only on the request of a writer to whom said musician was in turn recommended by a friend. This said, I find your desire to help Mr. Reich touching and admirable. But even as you understand that a banker does not hire as a cashier a person who has no other references than those provided by casual acquaintances who are alien to the world of finance, you will admit that a conductor does not even listen with one ear to a recommendation he receives from a painter. Actually, everyone is "strict" within *his domain*. I also think, for instance, that I *never* recommended anyone to you for your firm. Once, I introduced you to Dr. Heker, only to give you the possibility of correcting a rudeness he had suffered in your office – an involuntary rudeness, but one that left him with an unfavourable impression. – In the letter to Miss Schiess you will find some details about this delicious place that some time you will have to know.

Cordially,
Your

S. Tranquilli

SILONE

20

4 February 1938

My dear Mr. Fleischmann,

I'm sending this letter for Miss Schiess to you, in case she has already left and because in my letter I answer some practical questions (my mail, etc.). I hope that you are well.

Cordially,
Your

S. Tranquilli

Dear Miss Schiess,

How are you? Let me hear from you. – Serena wrote you something separately about my cure. I now begin to think that perhaps Dr. Kartager [sic][34] has been a bit too passive: on the very basis of his diagnosis (congenital bronchiectasis of the top left lung), Dr. Hüberlin sees that one can be cured through an operation. Only, it is necessary to first check the basic conditions of the two lungs. If they are in relatively good condition, I will have the surgery. Only, I am so accustomed to being sick that when I am cured it will seem impossible to me.

Affectionately,
Your

S.T.

SILONE

21

Le Cannet A.M.
Hotel Astoria
17 February 1938

My dear Mr. Fleischmann,

I heard from Miss Hegnauer that you are bedridden, but I hope that it is because you only need some rest. Here as well, for some days, it rains

and it's cold. In short, I have not benefited much health-wise, but I have worked a lot. In case you should find it interesting, I send you the initial dialogues of my new book, *The School for Dictators*.[35]
I think that you know Italian sufficiently well to give these pages a glance. Maybe you will feel the call to take advantage of my advice and become a dictator.

I don't want to stay here much longer. I plan to leave toward the end of the month. Possibly (depending on my health) I will go to Paris for a few days where I have some pending matters before returning to Zurich. But I will write to you again. I wish you good health and send you friendly greetings,

Your

S. Tranquilli

I am enclosing the receipt for 1000 francs.[36]

FLEISCHMANN
22

26 February 1938

My dear Tranquilli,

I regard it as dear proof of your affectionate friendship that you sent me the manuscript of your new book, or that is, a few parts of it. I believe that I know enough Italian to read it, and will start on it with Miss Degen very soon – not only because I am curious, but also because I am excited about it. Since I read *Bread and Wine* for the second time and believe that I have understood its contents, I am extremely interested in what occupies your mind.

I believe that I haven't responded to your last letter, and regret that you are not as happy with your stay as you had hoped. But none of us is, currently, and that certainly has to do with other factors. How can we be happy and content when everything that we reject is triumphing?

I had imagined the time when Elsa is away to be calm and introspective; the opposite has occurred. There is a lot going on business-wise, and at home Miss Sachs hangs above me like a demon, having extended her initial three days to almost fourteen. When I am in the house, I tiptoe along the walls to get upstairs to avoid the tiger that seeks to strangle me with her paws. She gives orders around the house as if she had actually experienced what is in your new book, *The School for Dictators.* Once she leaves, I will feel young at heart again.

A postcard of Werner Lewerenz arrived today: “after a long illness, I am once again well, and send my dearest friends the most heartfelt regards.” It seems that the poor guy really was in a concentration camp. He probably won’t be allowed to leave Germany, or I would invite him here right away, but I haven’t even replied yet out of fear of harming him.

If I understand you correctly, you are thinking of coming home soon. Thus I will keep this short, and wait until I can sit in your room and tell you everything myself. Give Mrs. Meyer my dear regards and accept a warm handshake for yourself, from your

Mr. S. Tranquilli, Hotel Astoria, Le Cannet

I look forward to your being with us again and think that you are never as well taken care of as here in the G’str [Germaniastrasse], which I hope you have come to see as your “first home” by now. Come soon, it is lonely without you.[37]

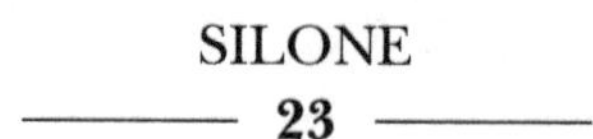

SILONE
23

24 January 1939

Dear Mr. Fleischmann,

I received the requested amount and thank you cordially. I am enclosing the receipt. In Davos, I have just visited Dr. Eric Fromm[38] of New York, a learned man, well regarded in the field of psychology. He needs the address of Dr. Deutsch[39] in Australia for a relative who is still in Germany. Tomorrow or the day after tomorrow Dr. Fromm will be passing through Zurich and he will phone you in my name to ask you for this address. I would be very grateful if you could give it to him.

It has been snowing here since yesterday and we have relapsed from spring into winter.

Best regards to Miss Schiess, Jürg and you.

Your

I. Silone

SILONE
24

2 December [1940][40]

Dear Friends,

The naval war renders me mad. In order not to miss the morning paper and the midday edition, I find myself obliged to return home late in the evening and get up early in the morning; the rest of the time I am at the radio – yesterday I met Mrs. Paryla in town: she seemed very worried about Michael who is still at Klosters (Kinderheim Soldanella)[41] and, dissatisfied with the environment, is on a hunger strike with unfortunate consequences for his health. I believe that she will be happy if, going down from Parsenn towards Klosters, you will go check how he is (his mother does not know if the people in charge of the Kinderheim are telling all the truth). Enclosed are some letters in arrears. At home all is in perfect order. In Zurich it rains.

Cordially,
Your

Tranquilli

SILONE
25

13 January 1941

My dear friend,

It often happens, and this is easily explainable, that those who, with the least merit receive the most, can hardly express their joy and gratitude. On holidays they remain by the stairway or at the edge of the table, silent, because words cannot express the inexpressible, only glad if their embarrassment doesn't attract attention. If, even so, I am writing you, my dear Friend, it's not to try to express the inexpressible, but to hide behind a sheet of paper the words that emotion would prevent me from saying. I don't know if you know that January 13 was a day of mourning for me until my arrival at your home: the day when, at the age of 15, I lost my family and my home. When, as an orphan, I was leaving my native village, my grandmother said some words which at the time I thought were dictated by pity: "Often" she said to me, "the good Lord closes a window and opens a balcony." I could not have known then, that on that same fatal day on

January 13, a man was already born at whose home I was later to find again a home and interrupt my nomadic life; I could not have known that the good Lord, in place of the window that he had just shut, already kept in reserve a magnificent balcony. And since I can't say that any merit on my part, any other external reason, any racial bond or political solidarity – nothing that is usual is enough to explain the hospitality that I enjoy in your home, your goodness towards me has the same character of "gratuity" that is normally attributed to saints and whose highest praise was written by the apostle Paul. I will copy for you the verses of the apostle who is [sic] a hymn to pure, sure, patient, gratuitous love.[42] I beg you to find in it the invisible signatures of all the other friends that you have also helped and who are now scattered all over the world; the signatures of all those to whom, as to myself, you have given at the same time the bread of your table and the courage to continue to live.

Your

S. Tranquilli

SILONE

26

Tuesday [April 1942][43]

Dear Mr. Fleischmann,

No news, good news. During the days of Easter Zurich was empty of Zurichians but full of Tessinians among which are a family of my acquaintance. I also received a visitor from Basel and another from Davos, all at the same time! … Some complications about the Italian that you also know will probably force me to run to Bern toward the end of the week. How long will you still remain there? We (Lina and I) don't know if Miss Schiess will come back tomorrow or later; this is the answer we gave her sister who just phoned. From this morning the new chambermaid is here; I have not yet seen her, but heard her steps down the hallway. I believe that our plan to spend some days together in Ascona risks failing, unless you remain there next week as well. With Miss Schiess will probably come some decisions as well.

Cordially,

Your

Tranquilli

Bruillon [Draft][44]
His Excellency the Apostolic Nuncio, Dean of the Diplomatic Corps, to Mr. Dr. Carlo Fleischmann, Ancien Consul, Küsnacht (Zurich).

Sir, it is with inexpressible emotion that we have learned that the 28 of April of this year you celebrate your 50th birthday. We cannot help discerning a providential coincidence between this event and the one the Holy Mother Church is preparing, this same year, to honour your great fellow citizen, the blessed Nicholas of Flue,[45] for his elevation to the glory of the altars. Because after all in both cases we exalt the same virtues: asceticism, humility and poverty and a filial attachment to the native land. On this solemn occasion, our memory also evokes the remembrance of your father, the much mourned Consul General Michael Fleischmann, whose historic merit is directly akin to that of Christopher Columbus. In fact, even as Columbus discovered America and connected her with Spain, your unforgettable father discovered Romania and connected her to the Swiss Confederation.[46] Alas, gratitude is not always the reward of idealistic men; you know, Mr. Ancien Consul, that Columbus ended his days in prison, and we pray the almighty God that you will be spared such an end. I can assure you that the Holy Father, His Holiness Pius XIII,[47] has deigned to join our prayers and together with his wishes asked me to convey to you his apostolic blessing.

Ad multos annos, Mr. Ancien Consul, et ad majora.

SILONE

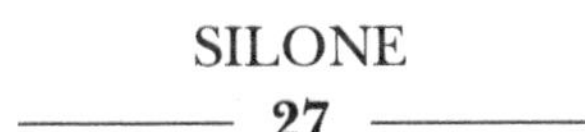

27

Zurich
21 July 1942

Dear Miss Schiess – Dear Mr. Fleischmann![48]

Thank you for the two cards you sent. Enclosed you will find the rest of the wool. This is all I found. No mail has come for you and nobody called. Nothing new here – it has been raining every day so I have to sweep water off the garage roof. Lina wrote that it's beautiful in the Ticino. I guess it will stop raining here some day and the sun will shine. Wooly is doing well so far, and I haven't had any surprises in the morning, but I don't want to praise him too loudly. I myself am doing better every day and will soon walk without limping. Besides wishing that you get better, I send you my best regards.

Your Friedel Kinstetter

Since you want to stay in Sils, I am guessing that you are finding it relaxing, despite the cold and solitude. Mrs. Friedel is using Lina's absence to demonstrate her culinary art. She is responsible for me gaining a few pounds. Yesterday I was sick from drinking too much coffee; besides the normal black coffee I drink at home, I had to drink four cups of coffee in the city and I felt quite sick (1 cup at the train station with a friend who was leaving, 1 cup with Serena, and 2 cups at 4 pm with an Italian family who didn't have any other refreshment to offer). I tell you this in such detail as a way of repenting! … Otherwise, despite the rain and the work, I am doing well. Miss Walker is convinced that it's because of her. She can endure dentist's pain without injection. She says that, "pain comes from resistance. If you don't resist, the pain spreads itself out throughout the entire body and then stops being painful." She says that is what the Indians discovered. The theory itself is convincing, but trying to put it into practice is hard because you resist without wanting to. I am telling you about this method so you can use it during your vacation if there is an emergency. It is cheap and painless and Miss Schiess is the ideal subject in all experiments where thought is involved. It seems that a warm front is coming in from the south; as of yesterday it has been quite nice in the Ticino and here it has been very warm since this morning. I hope a part of it will reach you and make the rest of your vacation more beautiful.

Heartfelt regards,

Tranquilli

FLEISCHMANN

28

18 December 1942

My dear friend Tranquilli,

I hope that you are doing as well as possible under the circumstances, and that justice and humanity will prevail.

I was very sorry that you weren't allowed to have the mineral water, as I know how much you need it.

Numerous friends are inquiring about you and I know that you can feel their good wishes, which culminate in the hope that you may be with us again very soon.

If I or someone else will be allowed to visit you at some point, please let me know.

If possible, please let me use your textile coupons, which will expire at the end of the year, to buy you some warm things.

I cordially shake your hand.

Yours

Mr. Secondo Tranquilli, Polizeikaserne, Kantonpolizei, Zurich

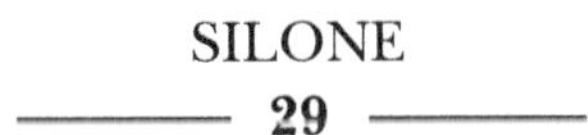

Secondo Tranquilli
Kantonspolizci Scfangnis[49]
Zürich
21 December 1942

My dear friend,

The days flow peaceful, quiet, thoughtful. I am well. Thank you so much for the exquisite fruit. I am sorry to give you so many worries of the kind so foreign to your ordinary concerns. And now, forgive me if I talk business.

1) First, here is the answer to the cable from New York, but I beg you to verify the address: NLT Harper Brothers Publishers

45 [corrected by hand to 49] East 33d [sic] Street New York

I agree tentative settlement with Fles for eight hundred seventy-five dollars.

Ignazio Silone

2) Then, since time is short, some small Christmas commissions for Miss Schiess or Friedel: a) Please send Gabrielle [sic] the coffee package that I received from Mrs. Rupprecht.

b) To Mrs. Oprecht,[50] a coloured cardboard box with the title: "La fantasia degli italiani" which is in my room's linen closet.

c) To Mr. Dr. Kurt Dübi, the paper cutter in pyrographed wood that is on my desk.

d) To Miss Darina Laracy, Pension Schmelanberg, a fruit basket and a big picture of a Greek temple of Syracuse that is on top of my armoire.

For you and Miss Schiess: you will each receive from Oprecht a bound copy of "Il Seme [sic] sotto la neve."

I thank you once more for all and everything and send you very cordial regards.

Your

Secondo Tranquilli

SILONE

30

12 Jan. 1943
Pension Strela

My dear friend,

It is not the first time that I am far from "home" on your birthday, but it is the first time that my departure was forced upon me.[51] You might as well tell yourself that I am more present than ever. If I think that next month it will be ten years since my arrival at your home, and if I give a quick glance at the road travelled during those ten years, the quantity and quality of things to tell you on this occasion would by far exceed the framework of a letter of congratulations and would turn into a confession of a series of events, interior, poignant and pathetic: it would be almost a resurrection narrative. Bureaucratic incidents cannot, therefore, separate me from you and your home, nor weaken the bonds of friendship that meanwhile developed between us. And the decisive proof, the proof positive, if one can say so, I had last month during my involuntary stay at the Kasermenstrasse: that was the proof that imprisonment becomes almost a holiday when it does not bring detachment, indifference and hostility on the part of one's friends but offers their solidarity and affection new possibilities of manifesting themselves. I do not believe that there is, in this life, a more precious reality. And I do not believe that I could formulate a greater wish for you than this: that you may live the second half of your life in the loving company of your friends, among whom you will always number me.

Your

S. Tranquilli

SILONE

31

12 March 1943
Pension Strela

My dear friend, The season is now so advanced that, if you have some free days, it would be best for you to go to Ticino rather than here. The snow is almost all gone, except for the peaks, and springtime in the mountains is not very pleasant, especially if one is affected by the föhn wind. Naturally, from a selfish viewpoint, I will rejoice greatly if you come; if I suggested that you go for the moment to Ticino, it is also because of another thought: the two days that you would like to spend in Davos now, could become two weeks in the month of June. June here is one of the most beautiful months. Also, on April 5th I will have to hold a literary conference at the Lyceum Club in Zurich, and Madame Prof. Gäumann-Wild has requested the authorities' permission. It is a series of lectures involving writers of all tendencies and since they will give permission to some Nazi, I hope that they will give it to me as well, in honour of the balance game, which is the symbol of neutrality. Would you be kind enough to inquire from this lady as to the outcome of her efforts? Thank you, then! It is possible that I will spend a weekend at Germaniastrasse! The mere idea renders me quite sentimental.

Good and affectionate greetings to you and Miss Schiess.

Your

S. Tranquilli
Regards to Miss Rachel and Miss Lina

FLEISCHMANN

32

15 March 1943

My dear friend,

Over the past few weeks I have been busy with a number of things (war profits taxes and the Witting affair, etc.) that have not allowed me to rest. That's probably also the real reason why I couldn't bring myself to take a few days off to see you, and why I am going to remain business-like today, and write to you on the typewriter. But please don't take it to mean that I'm not truly looking forward to the time we can see each other again and talk. In any case I thank you for the information about the snow and southerly winds; it is not much better here – that is to say, it's so warm that it makes you tired.[52]

You probably heard from Mrs. Meyer that I have invited Mr. Witting here, and that as long as my brother and sister-in-law are staying here, he has taken over your room, but this should only be for a few days. Afterwards he will move upstairs. This gives me the chance to tell you something you should know: no matter what, your room will always be waiting for you as you have left it. I have the urge from time to time to put some flowers in it even when you are not here.

I recently asked Professor Gäumann what she had heard – she also received a negative answer, but she emphasized that she did not consider this the last word on the matter. I advised her to get in touch with Dr. Oprecht or Dr. Huber.[53]

Elsa is not doing as well as I hoped. Tomorrow I am taking her to Professor Traugott and I have high hopes, as he has an excellent reputation.

"Good things come to those who wait," as they say, which I think applies especially to our next meeting. Until then I remain

Yours

PS I am enclosing the 500 Swiss francs you requested in bills. Please confirm receipt.

Fr.500-insured.

SILONE

33

Friday [Davos, 9 April 1943][54]

Dear friend,

Now I understand the pleasure of waking up in the morning and, as my first concern, plugging in the electric kettle to warm the water needed to shave; then, go to gather the news about the war. I engage in my old bachelor's apprenticeship and try to imitate you. At the beginning there was a certain disorder in my drawers, but now even the order gives me pleasure. Also in the eyes of the sister who makes up my room, I put myself out too much if the disorder is too great. But the purpose of this letter is to tell you that on Davos' roofs there are already 70 centimetres of snow and it continues to fall day and night. So, if you want to ski, there is plenty of snow.

Friendly regards to you and Elsa,

Your

Tranq.

SILONE

34

Baden
8 July [1943][55]
"Schweizerhof"

My dear friend,

Here I am, from one hotel to another in my new "Zwangsaufentalt" [forced residence]. If in Davos, all along the Hohe-promenade one meets people of excessively romantic paleness, here, on the banks of the Limmat, everybody hobbles and one could think of being in Lourdes, to such a degree the people around the fountains have a serious, meditative and pious air. If you were here, in our dining room, you would be, with Gabriella and myself, among the youngest people. You would feel like Napoleon at the pyramids (when he exclaimed: "40 centuries of history look down on us!"). Gabrielle [sic] is happy because she is the thinnest woman. All this aside, this life [moving] from one hotel to another is far from pleasing me. But I repeat to myself: this will pass. – Your last letter (which I am sorry for answering late, having received it at the moment I began to pack my luggage) was very sad. I am not one of those who believe that one must flee sadness; when it is well-founded, one must accept it and face it like a man. But maybe your state of mind, at that moment, was too sad, and the very facts that are at the bottom of your sadness, when looked upon with serenity, can be for you some source of inner satisfaction. There is the loneliness of wicked men, and that of good men. There is the evening of lazy, useless men, and that of men who did their duty. And from father to grandfather is a melancholic step,[56] above all when something as important as this happens under the absurd conditions imposed by the war. In such times, only entirely superficial people can be cheerful. – I hope that the mountain will do you good. I will send you a little book by Fr. Brupbacher[57] that will interest you without fatiguing you.

Very cordially,
Your

Tranquilli

FLEISCHMANN

35

Zurich
8 September, 1943

My dear friend Tranquilli,

I've had the urge to write to you for a while now, but haven't done so because I knew you would be too busy with current events. – And now it seems no coincidence that I have found out from Mrs. Serena, to whom I resorted [to speak] by telephone, that you were expecting news and you often think about the Germaniastrasse.

I myself "still and still" – as Jürgli used to say – yearn for the days when you had your room with us and gave the Kleine Pension its character. – As you know, not a day went by when I didn't ask at noon if you were there and if you would join us for lunch and – even though we didn't speak much – there was a quiet kind of mutual understanding between us. – Your inner calm and composure, and your aplomb affected all of us so much – especially me – and it is only now that we (and I) recognize how we miss you here. – You surely know that feeling when one has lost something in life and one keeps constantly looking for it, and that sense of emptiness and pain. –

And so I often go into your room and see if everything is still in its place – that all is ready and waiting for you, just as we are.

Yesterday all three brothers Weintraub were with me – Elsa guarded Männedorf – and we had serious discussions about Jürg and about you until midnight (!). And I said that it could very well be that you will continue to make your home with us and that you will always come back to the Kleine Pension from Italy in order to show the people, through your books, what they are missing. Just as you did before, in *The Seed beneath the Snow*, which I am currently rereading and which now moves me twice as much. I go so far as to judge people by how this confession affects them – I also judge them by whether the book shakes them up, and whether they agree with the ending – the most beautiful of all sacrifices.

Human beings could be good … –

Tranqus! I've just gotten the news that the hostilities in Italy have come to an end! Now every word is too much! We are expecting you. Let us know [when].

In loyal friendship,
Yours,

Marcel Fleischmann

FLEISCHMANN

36

Zurich
30 September 1943

My dear friend Tranquilli,

I was very pleased to get your message yesterday.

The quieter it gets around quiet people, the more intense and stable they seem. Conversely, when all is quiet, those who are loud appear fake and shallow.

Elsa is going to Schwellbrunn for about 8 days with her mother, and I am supposed to meet an acquaintance in Teufen. If you plan to go to St. Gallen alone, it would be nice to go together. I would not bother you while reading, as I will also bring along a book. By the way, Elsa and I have promised Mrs. Huber[58] a visit. This may turn out to be possible, and I'll take the chance to speak to Huber briefly about a female acquaintance whom he represents.

In case you'll be spending the night in Zurich, we assume that you will stay with us in Jürg's room. And if this happens more often in the future, Mr. Witting will certainly move to Jürg's room and Silone's will be at your disposal.

With cordial regards,

Mr. Secondo Tranquilli, Hotel Schweizerhof, Baden.

SILONE

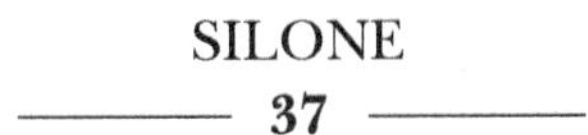

37

Baden
19 July [1944][59]

My dear friend,

I just sent a telegram to Jürg. Thank you for the address. If I had received the news that you or I were at the point of concluding a marriage in America, this would have surely worried me; but ... for Jürg, I don't worry at all. I have never seen him being *carried away* by a woman and I believe him incapable of entering into an "unreasonable" marriage; I therefore imagine Jane Cook to be pretty, bright, of good character, and rich. Next year the Mediterranean will be cleansed of all fascist control, and Mr. and Mrs. Fleischmann-Cook will probably come to spend their vacations in Switzerland; you will accompany them to Sils, Ascona and Venice, and you will behave like a mother-in-law. Therefore, still a little patience. I hope you are well; here it is terribly hot. Best regards to Elsa and to you,

Cordially,

Tr.
Regards and best wishes to M. Witting[60]

FLEISCHMANN
38

28 September 1944

My dear friend Silone,

You may be surprised that I am writing you again about my razor, but I am not sure if you need it or not. If you do, I will gladly leave it for you, but there's no point in doing so if it would just end up lying around somewhere unused (after you have not been using it for months) – and I would have to buy a new one for myself. I do hope you understand my asking.

I hope to hear from you before you leave, and send you best wishes as always.

FLEISCHMANN
39

Added to Mr. Fl.'s letter to Mr. Tranquilli[61]
3 October 1944

My dear, we are supposed to talk to each other so that these kinds of grave misunderstandings don't happen. The innocent razor sharpener has the following history:

A few years ago, it came to our house as a gift from Kurt to Marcel or Jürg – I don't remember exactly. Then for a while it lay despised in our cupboard (there are witnesses to this). In November 1942, Mr. Grünberg stayed at our house for ten days before going to the refugee camp in Gyrenbad, and I gave him the sharpener to take with him.

When you were sent to Davos, I asked Mr. Grünberg to return it if he could (there are witnesses to this). I knew that in this small humble pension razor blades sharpened themselves, but I presumed that there were no such gnomes in Davos doing that work. – And that is how this tool came into your hands. There is supposedly a law (seriously) that after a certain period of time the things that are borrowed change hands and automatically become the property of the other person. We should discuss this time period at the court in The Hague. It would be nice if you and Miss Laracy would come for a "cosy" visit with us. Although we don't have much planned, we would appreciate a note from you beforehand.

With affection,

SILONE

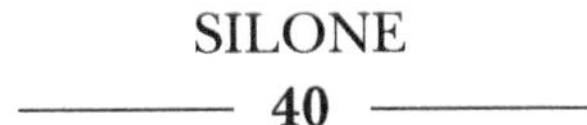

40

Rome
28 October 1944[62]
Hotel Plaza
M. Marcel Fleischmann.

My dear friend,

I take advantage of an opportunity to send you a nostalgic greeting. We arrived in Rome only last week and little by little we are "re-accustoming" ourselves to the Italian disorder, dirt, and bad smells. This means that we often think about the Kleine Pension and its people. The only advantage here is the climate: we take walks like in the summer. Happily, communication with abroad is rapidly improving, both for the mail and transportation. The *Weltwoche* and the *NZZ* have reappeared in the newspaper stands, and we no longer have the impression of being confined to the end of the world.

Waiting to see you again, I send you and Miss Schiess, Mr. Witting and Miss Friedel my most cordial regards.

Your Tranq

Bridging the Distance: 1945–1976

FLEISCHMANN

41

Zurich
27 July 45
M. Fleischmann
Germaniastrasse 53

My dear friend Silone,

You must think that a letter from us got lost, as you haven't heard from us and especially since you haven't received any thanks for your short, but pleasant note. This is due in part to all the personal and business matters that we postponed over the past six years with the excuse that we would get to them "after the end of the war" – and in part because of the depressed state everyone is in. We were all looking forward to a fresh start after the war and are now disappointed. You writers and politicians have it better: you can at least try to be active. We have to sit back and watch how all of our hopes are being buried.

There is little news to report from the Kleine Pension. Things are going on about the same way they did before. Our summer vacation will be problematic, as it will be difficult for me to get away from my business. My brother Kurt is in the USA with Jürg to try to build something new. He'll be gone for six months and will return via South America and Africa, where the Schmids have a coffee plantation. Maybe, Elsa and I will be able to take some time off at the beginning of September; a little late, but better late than never – that is what you used to say.

Lina left us after things became too difficult for her here. She is currently at Zuans in Sils Maria and they are all getting along very well together. We have a new cook who can only stay on temporarily and I fear this will be a problem for a while.

Klaus Witting might be leaving us soon to go to Frankfurt for the time being. Degen will return in a few days from Brest where she has been in charge of the entire mission for the past few months. After that she may work for a hospital in Paris.

And now you know everything, except that we are very much looking forward to your visit, which has been announced many times and which we hope will happen some day soon. I will leave the back page blank for Elsa and sincerely shake your hand.

Your

ELSA SCHIESS

42

[July 1945][63]

My dear friend,

No, no letter got lost as none was written. Why? If all it took were simply going to the mail box with it, maybe I would have written. There are people who do it, but I have yet to receive a confirmation that these letters really arrive. Now when I look at the dates of your two letters I am dismayed that many thoughts to be with you were never put into a letter. But this is now how things are and nothing can be done about it.

My family has also been absorbing me both time-wise and mentally in the last weeks and months. First, my brother seriously injured his knee when he was returning home from his birthday party. Then, my brother-in-law Mr. Bolleter passed away, then my older nephew had a serious eye burn in a chemistry lab, luckily without lasting consequences, then my widowed sister underwent a stomach operation, and then my younger nephew has been suffering from recurring allergic reactions to protein. Also, eight weeks ago my elderly mother had an accident; she broke her hip and has been in the hospital ever since. She lost her hearing and almost her memory due to a cerebral haemorrhage and I often ask myself why she was not spared all of this suffering by dying; the doctor told us that mother has literally been brought back from death. All this has worn me out and has depressed me.

I have always taken care of your different requests and "we" do not have anything to object to your application. It is unfortunately very badly worded, since it makes it seem that I personally advocated for you in Bern. I would have done it and made a case for you needing to arrive as soon as possible, but I was not asked to do it. I can only assure you that we all can't wait for the day when we can see you again. The Kleine Pension has barely changed; the guests come and go. We are expecting Mrs. Frisch tomorrow; brother Klaus[64] is also still here and will write to you as well.

Jürgly recently called, but in the middle of all the commotion we did not know what to say to each other and the censor interrupted just as I was going to talk to him. We were probably supposed to apply for the call beforehand. We think that Jürg will come to visit for Christmas and are looking forward to it. You must remember him only as a little boy; now he is president of his own company. He seems to be business-minded and hard working. Kurt writes that he has kept his good character and he has a very nice wife.

When you have the time and the chance, drop us a line. Sincere greetings to you and Darina.

Your [feminine form]

FLEISCHMANN

43

19 October 1945

My dear friend Silone,

Just a quick note to say that the suitcase and the key which we had given you for Mr. Tauber[65] don't belong to him, but rather to an acquaintance here in Zurich. I therefore ask you not to take the suitcase with the key to Florence, but rather to Zurich together with Mr. Witting's one. – Elsa and I had a great vacation in Maloya [sic]. Elsa is staying there a little longer, while I try to chip away at the mountain of work that has accumulated on my desk. Hence, only this short note today. Many cordial greetings to you and your lovely wife Darina.

Yours

FLEISCHMANN

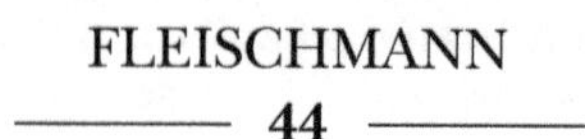

44

14 November 1945

Dear friend Tranquilli and dear Mrs. Darina,

Thank you very much for your friendly letter that my brother brought me from you, while I was out taking the other letters to the post office. I was very touched at how wonderfully you welcomed my brother Kurt.

Everything here is following its normal routine. At some point I am sure Elsa will tell you about the major and minor changes.

Regarding your message concerning Mr. Biddle, please warmly recommend him to Prof. Dr. Friedrich Ebrard, the brother of Dr. Hans Ebrard,[66] just as you did brother Klaus.[67] As you know, Dr. Hans Ebrard is a good friend of my brother Carlo. I also had the opportunity to get together more often than usual with Dr. and Mrs. Ebrard during my summer vacation, and would very much appreciate anything you can do in this matter and regard it as a personal favour.

Prof. Dr. Friedrich Ebrard, born in Basel May 5, 1891, and currently residing in Meggen (Luzern), is a Swiss *and* German citizen, and a Professor of Roman Law, Civil Law, and Modern Law. He is undoubtedly one of the few completely moral and politically upstanding people that there are, and is entirely qualified to meet Mr. Biddle's professional needs.

Should Mr. Biddle be already out of town, I would be very grateful if you could bring Prof. Dr. Friedrich Ebrard to his attention.

I end this letter today by promising to write you a more detailed one as soon as I have a bit more time. Sincere wishes to both of you and thank you in advance for your assistance on Prof. Ebrard's behalf.

I shake your hands warmly,

Your old

Marcel Fleischmann[68]
Mr. and Mrs. Secondo Tranquilli, Albergo Plaza, Rome.

FLEISCHMANN
45

27 December 1945

My dearest friend Silone and Mrs. Darina,

Your dear telegram quite delighted us and I thank you kindly for it – also on behalf of Elsa, Klaus, Kurt, and Nelli. We too have thought and talked a lot about you, especially since we have been enjoying Mrs. Serena while she has been staying with us the last few days. Originally we had been thinking about spending Christmas in Ticino, but the weather was too bad. Perhaps we will go for the New Year.

We were very interested to hear on the radio and see in the papers that you are the new director of *Avanti!* As I understand, it involves much work, particularly at night, which I was sorry to hear. As soon as I can confirm that you will be writing the editorials yourself, I will become a subscriber (and we will finally learn Italian).

Last night, an Italian refugee from Paris suddenly appeared at our door. He has survived several German concentration camps, is very ill and came to see Mrs. Serena. He will stay with us for the time being and we will see what happens next.

In general, we are very tired from all the various work to be done around the house and for our business, as well as from the mostly unpleasant news that reaches us from around the world. It would do us good if you came to Zurich and brought us some of your optimism if you could.

We sincerely wish you few disappointments and much success with all of your plans in the coming year. With love from the whole house to both of you.

Yours

FLEISCHMANN

46

Zurich
12 February 1946

My dear friend Silone,

I just received a letter from our acquaintance, Gino,[69] asking me to write him a letter inviting him to Switzerland. Please let me know *as soon as possible* if that is a good idea. Send me a short telegram if you can.

I'm sorry that I wasn't able to catch up with you on your way back from London, but hope that you and Mrs. Silone are doing well.

We've received word from Gabriella Meyer that Witting's suitcase has been sent from Lausanne to Zurich. In her telegram she wrote that she labelled the suitcase "Priority mail to Bern Station." We do not have any receipt; our inquiry at both stations was without results. Please clarify what is going on as soon as you can, and if possible, send us the receipt.

As always, very heartfelt regards,

Mr. Ignazio Silone, Albergo Plaza, Rome[70]
[Note] Originally sent to Rome, carbon copy via Mrs.Gabriella Meyer.

FLEISCHMANN

47

28 March 1946
Mr. Secondo Tranquilli
Albergo Plaza
Rome

Dear friend Silone,

I wrote to you on February 12th through two different means and telegraphed on the 4th. I still need to know if you think I should send Gino an invitation to come to Switzerland as he is requesting, or if it is better not to respond.

I really don't understand why you aren't getting back to me about this, and I would like to ask you again to do so.

Yours,

Certified mail
Express

DARINA AND IGNAZIO SILONE

48

Rome, Albergo Plaza
4 June 1946

Dear Elsa and dear Marcel,

We are, admittedly, true barbarians, who have become incapable of writing a letter, lost among congresses, electoral lists, referenda, preferential votes, away from all human interaction. We must cover our heads with ashes and humbly ask our friends for forgiveness. But things have gotten to the point that we want to react get out of this caravanserai, where one is easy prey of journalists and lice and find a peaceful, quiet spot, with a bit of green. But Rome's population has nearly doubled after the war and it is almost impossible to find a house. We will need an immense effort to settle down. Nevertheless, one cannot live forever in the provisional. When we have a house, I hope you will come to visit us. Since they brought back the Rome-Milan wagon-lits, it is no longer necessary to have an adventurous spirit when visiting Italy. As for us, we have travelled very often of late. First, to London, last January.

Rome-Paris two days and two nights in wagon-lit! It was a sort of vacation. The English do nothing but repeat that London is depressing, fatiguing, abysmal, boring, but we received a wonderful impression of [its] life, order, will, progress, freedom. Unfortunately, it was only a very short visit. But I was also in Ireland for the first time in ten years. It is a country that would like to teach neutrality to the Swiss and Catholicism to the Vatican. It is the reign of the blackest obscurantism. Naturally, that does not prevent a very pronounced respect for the goods of this world. The word socialism is anathema; Franco and Salazar are the heroes of the daily press; I often heard them say that Belsen and Buchenwald were inventions of British propaganda. People are capable of complaining because it seems that there seems to be a certain lack of raisins. For the great majority of the people, the problems troubling Europe don't exist. However, despite these rather repulsive aspects, it is easy, in Ireland, to let oneself be lulled into a sweet carelessness, with the sensation of being a bit outside time and place. For vacations, it is a country to recommend. In April we spent two weeks in Florence on the occasion of the National Congress of the Socialist Party. We barely had the time to notice that Tuscany was in bloom and springlike, and Florence, despite her wounds that can never be healed, has retained all of her beauty. On the way back, on Easter day, we stopped in Arezzo and Borgo San Sepolcro to see the frescoes by Piero della Francesca. Borgo San Sepolcro, Piero della Francesca's native village, is one hour's driving distance from Arezzo on a road that leads nowhere. Buried in this village, in a room of the little town hall, there is this unforgettable fresco of the Resurrection. To continue our touristic chronicle, we have also been in Umbria, in Perugia and Assisi. I don't know if you are familiar with this region. Giotto's frescoes in Assisi were very badly restored. These last weeks we have been in Abruzzo, which is a bit in the Middle Ages. The spouse, as candidate in Abruzzo for the Assemblea Costituente, had to conduct his electoral campaign.

The elections caused great emotion. On that day one could see the progress made by the Italians after the fall of fascism. I remembered Rome in 1941, the whispering, the servility and the fear. Last Sunday one truly breathed an air of freedom. People cared a lot about casting their votes, they were proud of it; they realized that it was a very serious matter, everyone felt like a citizen. They had to wait in line for hours under a scorching sun, but they were very patient, and calm, and courteous and good humoured. It would obviously be to expect too much [if one thought] that all were aware of the reasons that inspired their votes. They haven't yet come that far. Too many of them, quite too many, voted with the priests who used the church, the confessionals, heaven and hell to convince their parishioners to vote for the Catholic party ("Democrazia Cristiana"). But finally, if barely, there is the Republic.

He is very tired from the work at the newspaper; he often comes home at 3:00 a.m. I hope that this will not be for much longer. The heat has already arrived, the great heat and exhaustion of the Roman summer. And you? If you can forgive our silence, write us your news. This will please very much the "Zurichian in exile." How is Klaus doing? I yield the place. Many affectionate regards

Darina

Dear friends,

This letter, that Darina gave me to complete, remained unattended in a drawer for ten days. During that time I was in Milan and had a visa to come to Zurich to commemorate Matteotti on June 11 at the Volkshaus; but at the last moment I had to return to Rome because of the political situation. You must have read in the newspapers all that's happened in the recent weeks; my life is still so tied to public events that you can easily imagine what it has been. Day and night in turmoil. The king[71] left and the situation is calm enough for the moment, but I believe that I will be given new responsibilities and will not be able to enjoy a bit of rest. For some time now, it is possible to buy Zurich's newspapers at the local newsstands: you can well imagine that I read them regularly and I know what is going on at Schauspielhaus and at the Banhofstrasse, as if I were still living at the Kleine Pension. But what we are missing is your personal news. Darina and I often ask ourselves questions about your life, but we are not sure that we make the right guesses. Write us, then, a long letter!

Very affectionate regards from your

Tranqu

For Marcel:

I tried to gather information on the Snia Viscosa project; but it is a complicated story, and not entirely clean, heavily criticized by my party.

FLEISCHMANN
49

Zurich
6 August 1946

Dear friends,

We can see that you barbarians have punished yourselves with sackcloth and ashes, and will forgive you this time – but not in the future.

No doubt you have incredibly much to do, but we do as well, and even though we cannot compare the quality of the work, the commitment to one's friends should at least remain the same. With your detailed letter you did make up for a lot, though, and we thank you for that. It gave us a good idea of what life is currently like for you, and what your plans are for the future.

In return, we will now provide you with an exhaustive overview about our life and everything that is going on here.

No. 1. Jürg and his wife are going to arrive in Zurich in mid-August (the evening of the 17th) and you can just imagine what a party we will have until they leave six weeks later! We heard only good things about them from everyone, even disinterested parties, and so we have high hopes for a lovely time together with them.

Elsa, on the contrary, is very worried about her brother and his latest business crisis – things don't look good for him, and may even be catastrophic. This is really weighing on Elsa because she has always been very close to him in spite of everything. We have been trying to help him for weeks now, but unfortunately without results. On the other hand, we have found new friends in the Hunzikers,[72] with whom we are spending much time and whose company we enjoy. We were not aware that they both are such remarkable people. We already have 3 paintings by him and will show them to you on your next visit.

My friend Tscharner[73] died an agonizing death and everything connected to it is rather unpleasant and unbelievable. But we'd prefer to tell you more about this in person. It has really affected me deeply, and I had so wished that he would be able to have a better death, a nicer end to his life.

You will probably already know that Dr. Düby was made a federal judge. No comment.

While the rest of the world's household staff is either inadequate or non-existent, we have been blessed with two absolute angels. I have always believed in justice and regard this blessing at our Kleine Pension as such. The cook is Elsa's cousin and the chambermaid is Baron Rothschild's cousin.

Tony Degen is marrying an American navy officer (or I should say, civilian captain) and I believe that she's made the right choice this time.

Klaus Witting is between Munich and Zurich with much going on and I have the impression that he is not at all satisfied with his present career.

Our business is finally beginning to take off again, but requires unending effort, work and worries, and my brother Carlo and I, at our age, often ask ourselves: Why do this?

And now back to you. Do you already have your own apartment or are you still living at the hotel? Once you get established, we expect a formal invitation with a special train from Chiasso onward. We would do the same for you.

We hear repeatedly that you are coming through Zurich on your travels, but every time it isn't true. An architect named Hubacher[74] recently called us about you but he turned out to be completely misinformed.

Your reports of your travels to Paris and London, and your impression of Ireland were all very interesting. It seems to me that the latter has a lot in common with Switzerland, where the people also think they know everything. Our next vacation will therefore be to Ireland, in order to learn to take this [presumption] to the next level.

We aren't more jealous than usual of your time in Florence, but we are envious of your stays in Arezzo and San Sepolcro. We love both places, partly because Piero della Francesca is the Italian painter I am most fond of and admire. We know Perugia and Assisi well, and they are favourites of ours, especially Assisi. I still had a car back then, and drove over hills and dales to the most unlikely places, and we spent a whole day at the grove of St Francis of Assisi. Back then my late wife was still with us, along with Ernst Toller[75] and other friends.

What you told us about the local elections and people there was very interesting and informative. It is a shame that the Republic didn't get voted in by a larger margin, but at least it passed. Are you, dear Silone, Abruzzo's representative in the Assemblea Costituente? It's really too bad that Catholicism exerts such a strong influence on politics in so many countries. There's just no peace to be had, and again I have to ask: Why?

Should you, dear friend Silone, want to come to Zurich again, on such occasions as the anniversary of Matteotti's death,[76] please let us know.

You owe us that much. How is your health doing, given all of the various demands on you? We don't know how you do it! You did regain so much strength while staying with us.

And now we come to the end, dear friends. We've been continuing to have so many overnight visitors and often look forward to a little reprieve. But if you were to disturb our quiet, we would throw a party. Come visit soon. Until then, best wishes from our house to yours.

Yours

DARINA SILONE

50

(Postcard)
20 August 1946

Panorama: Isola di San Giulio, Lago d'Orta

To: Marcel Fleischmann and Miss Elsa Schiess, Germaniastrasse 53, Zurich

From Lago D'Orta

Message: illegible. Signed: Darina Silone

FLEISCHMANN

51

4 November 1946
Mrs. Darina Silone
Albergo Plaza
Rome

Dear Mrs. Darina,

I haven't heard from you for quite some time and hope that this means that all is well. Gabriella Meyer stayed with us for a week and told me a lot about Italy.

In order not to bother my friend Silone personally, I am turning to you with the following question: Do you think that the Italian currency has stabilized sufficiently to determine the amount of lire necessary for travelling and vacationing in Italy? I believe that your husband has sufficient resources to be able to oversee this complex matter well.

There is not much new with us. The Kleine Pension is always busy and there is often a fantastic cacophony of languages, especially during the past two months, when our children were visiting from the USA. It was very enjoyable and Jürg is very satisfied with how his business is doing.

Elsa's concerns about her brother have decreased, but it will take some time for her to recover from the scare. She is considering going to stay with Jürg for two months once she gets transportation.

With best wishes, for both of you.

Yours

FLEISCHMANN

52

25 November 1946
Mr. Ignazio Silone
Albergo Plaza
Rome

Dear friend Silone,

I am enclosing a letter from my son Jürg that I ask you read immediately. I am asking you this favour because it is of utmost importance to me.

My brother Carlo returned from New York a few days ago, where, among other things, he checked up on Jürg's family as well as his business. My brother, who is generally quite a sceptic, reported that everything seemed to be going extremely well for Jürg. For this reason I am convinced that after you read the letter and honour its request, you will be very pleased with the successful results.

You will see from Jürg's letter that this is a very urgent matter, and I would be grateful if you would respond as soon as possible.

May I ask you to briefly confirm receipt of this letter via postcard, so that I know that it has reached you? As a precaution I will send you a copy of this letter again tomorrow.

At home everything is fine. Witting returned from Germany yesterday and will stay in Zurich for a while. He is no longer at Bavaria-Film.

With best regards also to Mrs. Darina, I am

Your old

Registered
Original copy sent by registered mail. [Handwritten]

FLEISCHMANN

53

Rome
2 December [1946][77]

My dear friend,

For the advertisement of the Italian edition of *Fontamara* I need a copy of each translation of this book: these [copies] are in the armoire or on the bookshelf of "my" room at the "petite pension." Please give them to the person who will call for them, and who will be either Mrs. or Mr. Comencini.[78]

Very cordially,

Your

Trankus
Mr. Marcel Fleischmann
Germaniastrasse 53,
Zurich

FLEISCHMANN

54

19 December 1946
Mr. Ignazio Silone
Montecitorio
Rome

Dear friend Silone,

Thank you for your friendly note concerning my son Jürg, which I immediately passed on to him in the original. Here is his address for your records: Werner Jürg Fleischmann, 10 Park Ave, New York City.

After considerable effort, I have managed to free your assets from the house and the Schweizerischen Kreditanstalt in the amount of £200 as well as the monies from your book sales. The last thing to be done is for you to contact the Schweizerischen Kreditanstalt, Rigiplatz branch *without delay* (so that the matter will not be held up further) and provide them with a written request to pay out the £200 to me. I kindly ask you to take care of this matter at your earliest convenience.

There is nothing new at the Kleine Pension. Mrs. Frisch from Ascona and Witting are here. We are leading an eventful but also quiet life and are doing well.

Hopefully, you will be able to spend the holidays, as you desire. I send my best regards to Mrs. Darina, and press your hand in old solidarity.[79]

FLEISCHMANN

55

27 December 1946
Mr. and Mrs. Ignazio & Darina Silone,
Montecitorio,
Rome

Dear friends,

Sincere heartfelt thanks for your lovely telegram. We at the Kleine Pension this year celebrated Christmas with only a few close friends, but very happily. We thank you for your good wishes and hope that they will come true. We also truly hope that by moving into your new apartment, you will be able to do many things that are only possible in the intimate environment of one's own private home. We are now even more excited to come visit you, and one day one or two representatives of the Kleine Pension will arrive at your door.

Elsa and the two maids from Zofingen have flight tickets to New York for February 10th. We are trying to move back the departure a little, so that Elsa doesn't have to travel in the winter, but rather in the spring. Hopefully that will be possible. Mrs. Frisch and Klaus Witting are currently staying with us and Uhde[80] from Paris and Jürgen Fehling[81] from Berlin are expected to arrive. You can see that the Kleine Pension has remained true to its tradition.

My son just goes from success to success[82] both in his personal life and in his business. I am very happy for him, for there is nothing that fires up a young person more than success.

I warmly shake your hand also on behalf of all in our household and remain as always,

Your old

FLEISCHMANN

56

16 January 1947
Mrs. Darina Silone,
Casella postale 355,
Rome

Dear Mrs. Darina,[83]

Sincere thanks in the name of the entire Kleine Pension for your kind letter of December 30th. As always, I completely understand your silence. As long as we get a detailed letter once or twice a year, that's sufficient.

You, dear Mrs. Darina, have described the atmosphere of your house in such detail that we can picture it all as if it were right in front of us: we see you, and breathe in the scent of the magnolias, hear the donkey braying, and hear your and Silone's laughter by the fireplace. It is really very kind of you to take the time to write to us in such detail. It is always a great comfort to know how people with whom one spent so many years together are now living their lives.

Your description also tempts us to come visit you this summer. Elsa will definitely go to see Jürg at the end of February and stay for about two or three months. Once she comes back, and if I keep my trip to New York scheduled for the end of autumn, I might go to Poveromo for a while, and then it's not too far for you. But the picture you paint of your poor country is much darker. We completely understand, and everybody is happy to hear that Silone continues to withdraw from the public eye and returns to his previous life as a writer. The lack of character that one needs these days to engage in politics is appalling, and we are sure that it must be very beneficial to have left Rome, and leave that ugly profession to someone else.

We of course followed the Socialist Congress and the party's fragmentation, and were delighted that Silone's name was never mentioned in connection to these events.

If you should travel to Germany in the spring, please let us know in a timely manner. The Kleine Pension is always ready to receive you, regardless.

I also wish to dutifully report that the Schweizerische Kreditanstalt matters are finally all in order.

I would also like to inform you that I got two copies of *Der Samen unter dem Schnee* from Oprecht in Silone's name. I hope he doesn't mind.

We will have to settle this later. You know my penchant for saving on small things whenever I can.

I probably shouldn't have written today because I am under a lot of pressure and my thoughts are not flowing the way I would like. Well, I will make up for it next time.

We hear nothing but good news from Jürg and I sincerely thank you for your intervention in New York on his behalf although I don't exactly know the outcome.

In closing, everyone here at the Germaniastrasse (which will soon be changing its name!)[84] offers you a sincere handshake and wishes you all the best.

Your

P.S. Klaus is currently in Germany, he doesn't have it easy right now either.

Elsa is doing very well and is looking forward to her trip to the US. Baroness Guttry may get in touch with you – please help her.

FLEISCHMANN

57

Zurich
31 Jan. 1947
Signor Ignazio Silone,
Montecitorio,
Rome.

Dear friend,

I was at Dr. Kartagener's yesterday and he asked about you. He took such an interest in how you are doing, and asked that you contact him now that you are in your new place. He did all this so sincerely that I feel compelled to put his request in writing in this letter, and do hope you will get in touch with him. Please remember to do so the next time you are in Zurich.

Elsa is travelling to the U.S.A. on February 20th – that's the big news around here at the Kleine Pension.

I hope that you and Mrs. Darina are doing well and I sincerely shake your hands.

FLEISCHMANN

58

28 March 1947
Signor [sic]
Ignazio Silone,
Montecitorio
Rome

My dear friend Silone,

My brother Carlo is in the US and is very taken up with that right now. Elsa has also been there with my son for the last four weeks and rarely writes, as she is busy setting up his household. She took two good maids along with her.[85]

Mrs. Ritter's son had no sooner been released from the mental hospital with a diagnosis of incurable schizophrenia, when I had to take her to Dr. Brunner[86] in Küsnacht for the guardianship. You can imagine how difficult it was. Lia Ritter has been in St. Moritz for the past 14 weeks with a complicated fracture of her hip and had to be operated on for a second time because the bone callous was not forming properly. In addition, she is showing symptoms of leukemia.*

At home all is well except for Baroness Maria, who is in very poor health and I don't know what to do about it.

The purpose of this letter is to accompany the enclosure, with the request that you inform me by return mail if you have heard anything new and whether caution is necessary.

I absolutely need to know in order to determine how I should proceed.

Dr. Keese-Degen[87] is going to visit her husband in New York on April 8th and will be looking after my picture collection.

I sincerely hope that you and Mrs. Darina are doing well and that we will see you again soon. Once Carlo returns, I may fly to Florence or Rome.

I hope to hear from you very soon and remain

Sincerely yours

P.S. What does the first sentence in Gino's letter mean? Should I send him money?

* It is so sad to see her in such a state of physical collapse.[88]

SILONE

59

ASSEMBLEA COSTITUENTE[89]
9 April '47

My dear friend,

I hasten to answer your letter. Judging from the copy of his letter that you sent me, Mr. G.S. evidently wants some money. Personally, I do not know his current position, I have never met him here, and this is somewhat extraordinary, because, due to my social obligations, I meet almost everyone. At any rate, he never showed up and never tried to see me, although he very often reads my name in the newspapers and knows that I know you and at times still come to Switzerland. In short, he is a rather bizarre man.

I end here, so that the letter can leave right away; but Darina will write you more at length to invite you to visit us.

Very cordially
Your

Silone

FLEISCHMANN

60

6 June 1947.
Mr. and Mrs. Ignazio Silone
Hotel Baur au Lac
Zurich

Dear friends,

I just now discovered a telegram in the office, stating that I have to work Sunday afternoons and evenings. That's too bad – I would have liked to go to the theatre with you. Thank you for your good will.

Sincerely

Achim's address is:
Achim Wilkens
79, 3rd Avenue,
Linden,
Johannesburg (South Africa)

DARINA SILONE

61

Casella postale 355
Roma Centro
20 July 1947

Dear Mr. Fleischmann,

There wasn't enough time in Zurich, and I am sorry that it wasn't possible to see you a bit more while I was there. We haven't heard from you since then and hope that you haven't changed your mind about coming to Italy on vacation. Remember that you are invited to come stay with us and we are looking forward to seeing you. If possible, let us known a little beforehand when you are thinking of coming since we may have to be away from Rome for a short while. And, if I am not mistaken, you also have some credit with us.[90] Send us a short postcard and let us know your plans.

Love,

Darina Silone[91]

FLEISCHMANN

62

29 July 1947
Mrs. Darina Silone,
Casella postale 355,
Roma Centro

Dear Mrs. Darina,

You are right, your visit was short and it was hot, and so we didn't see each other much. I also know how busy the two of you are professionally and otherwise, so I fully understand.

In the meanwhile, both my brother and Elsa have returned from the US almost at the same time after being there for a number of months. They have lots of news to report from there about Jürg and business in general. It has been very interesting to hear how Jürg's business and personal life have been going, and to learn more about the economic and political mentality in the U.S.A. In any case it has strengthened my conviction not to go to America, but visit Naples instead.

Due to my brother's recent absence while in France and Belgium, and his upcoming trip to the US, I have set my own vacation plans aside, and you shouldn't think about me for the time being. It might not be until September that I can find some free time and then I will decide between going to Poveromo or Maloja. Of course, if I go to Poveromo that will also include a trip to Rome.

Elsa asks me to send you her love. It's never been easy for her to travel, and so she's still very tired from her big trip and all the new experiences. She will most likely write to you herself very soon.

Until then I ask you to make do with this letter and accept my sincere handshake

Your

DARINA AND IGNAZIO SILONE

63

(Postcard)
4 August 1947
Woman in folkloristic garb working at the pillow lace
To: Mr. Marcel Fleischmann, Germaniastrasse 53, Zurich 6, Switzerland
From: Scanno, L'Aquila, Abruzzo

Message, in German: "Here the women wear these beautiful costumes. One more reason to come to Italy."

Darina.

In French: "Waiting for you, a cordial remembrance" I. Silone

FLEISCHMANN

64

6 September 1947
Mr. Ignazio Silone
Casella Postale 355
Roma Centro

My dear friend Silone,

My brother Dr. Carlo asked me to reach out to you about the following matter. My brother is interested in meeting Professor Lombardi,[92] in order to make some business contacts through him.

They say that Professor Lombardi works for the Italian government and for the Vatican in New York and also deals in agricultural crops, which is of interest to both my brother and our business.

I don't know if Professor Lombardi is the same person as Mr. Jvan [sic] Matteo Lombardo, director of the "Delegazione tecnica italiana" [sic] in Washington, to whom you introduced my son when he was there. My brother would be very grateful if you would introduce him to Professor Lombardi. If that's possible, my brother would contact him in writing now, rather than waiting until he is there in person in the fall.

We are aware that Professor Lombardi has business connections to Dr. Rosenstein, President of the bank La Roche Lombard Odier Inc. in New York.[93] You could do Professor Lombardi a favour by suggesting he exercise the utmost caution when dealing with Dr. Rosenstein. We can tell you this from personal experiences as well as information we've recently received, but please do keep this just between us.

I hope that your travels went well and would be thankful if you could send us a quick note about the above matter soon.

With sincere regards from our house to yours. [94]

SILONE

65

ASSEMBLEA COSTITUENTE
9 September 1947

My dear friend,

[In answer] to your letter of the 6 c.m., as you suspected, the Prof. Lombardi is not the same person as my friend Jvan [sic] Matteo Lombardo.[95] I do not personally know Prof. Lombardi. On the other hand, J.M.L. is no longer in America, but in Rome, head of the Italian delegation for the treaty with the U.S.A. I suppose that the letter of reference by J.M.L. for Jürg remained in the archive of the "Delegazione tecnica italiana a Washington." If Jürg thinks that it is useful to offer whatever products he represents, he can mention, in his letter, that there is a character reference [letter] by J.M.L. (and, to facilitate the research, he should mention the date.)

Cordial regards, also for Dr. Carlo,

Ignazio Silone[96]

FLEISCHMANN

66

Marcel Fleischmann
Stockerstr. 31
Zurich
26 Sept. 1947

My dear friend Silone,

Thanks for your letter of September 9th.

My brother Carlo, not Jürg, would be grateful if he could somehow get in touch with both Mr. Ivan Matteo Lombardo and Prof. Lombardi. If I understand correctly, both gentlemen are conducting business with the Italian government. Maybe it would be possible for you to provide me with two recommendation letters for my brother.

My brother anticipates travelling to Italy in the near future. Jürg is coming during the second half of October and I am looking forward to his visit.

I hope these requests aren't too much of a burden on you. Sending you my best wishes.

Yours[97]

SILONE

67

ASSEMBLEA COSTITUENTE
30 September [1947][98]

Jvan [sic] Matteo Lombardo is at present in Rome. His (provisional) responsibilities concern the treaty of friendship and trade with the USA; but they will probably change in the next few weeks, at the end of the political debate in progress before the Constituent Assembly and the ministerial crisis that may result from it. In any case, if your brother, Dr. Carlo, comes to Rome, I will be delighted to arrange a meeting with my friend Lombardo. (All things considered, a letter of introduction would not be as effective!) I don't know if I should add that J.M. Lombardo is no longer in any business from the date of his entry into politics (previously he was in the printed textile business).

As far as Prof. Lombardi, I regret to have to correct a statement I made in my previous letter: in Italy there are as many Professor Lombardis as there are Dr. Meyers in Switzerland; but no Prof. Lombardi has been charged with any mission in the USA (at least not recently) and it is possible, therefore, that he is the same as J.M. Lombardo, despite the fact that this one does not hold any academic title. In fact, having questioned him about the banker of whom you have written to me, *he told me that he knows him.*[99]

Darina and I regret that your letter does not say anything about your coming to Italy. Is Jürg's imminent arrival holding you back? Friendly regards for you, Elsa and your brothers, from my wife as well.

Your

I. Silone

SILONE
68

ASSEMBLEA COSTITUENTE
8 October[100]

Dear Elsa,

I write to you quickly to ask you to tell Mr. Witting (and to be kind enough to phone Mr. Samson[101] who is in the same situation) that I have immediately taken action for the visas; but until this morning the questionnaires had not yet arrived. Let's hope that they are on their way!

Cordially
Your

Silone

SILONE
69

ASSEMBLEA COSTITUENTE
15 November [1947][102]

My dear friend,

I should have left last night for Milan-Basel with a one-day stop in Zurich; but the unrest in various Italian cities (in Rome today we have a general strike) keeps me here, in order not to leave Darina by herself and also not to give the impression of saving myself alone. I must, therefore, delay my trip.

Yesterday I received your letter regarding the accounting for the year 1946–1947: I believe that there is no longer the same reason for this as before, but you can follow the same method of the previous year, at least as long as Gabriella is not in Switzerland and there are no consequences for her. I don't know if this letter will arrive quickly, because

I don't have the news regarding the strike in the North. I would be grateful to you if you could phone Mr. Samson (whom I had notified of my arrival) that the situation here prevents me from leaving.

Cordially
Your

Silone

My best regards to Elsa.

FLEISCHMANN

70

20 November 1947
Mr. Ignazio Silone
Montecitorio
Rome

My dear friend,

Thank you for your letter from the 15th of this month. All sorts of people had told me that you would be coming, and it is a shame that it didn't come to pass.

The Kleine Pension will be very full the next few months. So please do let me know in advance if you are planning to visit so that we can make the necessary arrangements. We have been looking very much forward to having you with us by now.

I will take care of the accounting matter as you have advised me to, but we should discuss this at the next opportunity.

Elsa informed Mr. Samson.

I have been asked to take in Bert Brecht,[103] but I don't think that we will be able to. It's a shame.

Jürg will be staying with us for another eight days. You can imagine how happy we are to have him here. He goes back on the 28th.

I think that the international situation is coming to a head rather than settling down, bearing a disturbing resemblance to the way things were right before the last world war. What an uplifting prospect!

I have been asked to pass on best wishes from everyone and remain to you and Mrs. Darina

Always sincerely yours

My brother Carlo is travelling to Rome for 8 days on the 24th of this month. – He will contact you. – Accommodation would be greatly appreciated. Jürg sends his best wishes.[104]

FLEISCHMANN
71

19 Jan. 1948.
Mr. Ignazio Silone,
Casella postale 355,
Roma Centro

Dear friend Silone,

As a special favour to me, could you please put out your feelers to help me locate a

Marchesa Julia Santasilia, nèe Ginsberg.[105]

I unfortunately don't know in which city she lives in Italy, but maybe some of your acquaintances might by chance know or have heard of her.

I should emphasize that this is an *urgent* matter for me; otherwise I would not ask you to spend the time or go through the trouble.

I thank you in advance for all that you can do for me in this matter and remain

much obliged to you,

Yours

FLEISCHMANN
72

Marcel Fleischmann
Zurich
23 Jan. 1948
Signor Ignazio Silone,
Casella postale 355,
Roma Centro

My dear friend Silone,

We are so excited to see you again on the 2nd/3rd of February at the Kleine Pension.

You chose an excellent time to come, because Mr. and Mrs. Guttry will be joining us on the 5th/6th, and with the Grillinos (Carry and Lisely) also staying with us, space would otherwise have been scarce.

The only thing you need to bring with you is your friendship, which – as always – is the thing we value the most.

It's high season at home and at work, but otherwise there's nothing new going on.

Best wishes to Darina and you from Elsa and me,

Yours

Their new place will be at the "Casa Grilliano" [sic] Brione Kt. in Ticino.[106]

DARINA SILONE

73

(Postcard)
31 May 1948
A reproduction of "Roma Ponte Molle" by Giovan Battista Piranesi, featuring three arches on the Tiber River, with Castel Sant'Angelo in the distant right background.
To: Mr. Marcel Fleischmann, Albergo Bellavista, Casamicciola, Isola d'Ischia (Naples).
From: Palazzo Caetani, Via delle Botteghe Oscure 32, Rome.
Tel.54617.54717.53231. Monday [sic].

Message, in German: "Dear friends – We waited until now to write to you because we were hoping to be able to come to you in a few days, but unfortunately, that is not going to be possible. It could work for us to come in two or three weeks, but you probably won't be there any longer. At the very least, please get in touch with us, and if possible stop by on the way back. We can recommend the Albergo Milano, Piazza di Montecitorio, and then we can perhaps show you Abruzzo. Please don't go back without seeing us. Love, Darina"

DARINA SILONE

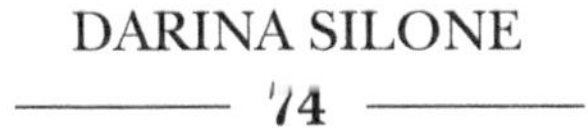

74

(Postcard)

9 June 1948

A reproduction of "41-Roma sparita – Prati di Castello (Museo di Roma)" from the series *Roma sparita* by Ettore Roesler Franz, featuring a boy rowing on the Tiber River, with Castel Sant'Angelo in the background.

To: Miss Elsa Schiess, Germaniastrasse 53, Zurich 6, Switzerland.
From: Casella postale 355, Rome

Message, in French: "Dear Friends, so you have not received our postcard we sent to Ischia? We were a bit sad that you passed by Rome without even telephoning us. To our great regret it was not possible for us to come to Ischia at the time, but wanted to show you a bit of Abruzzo. Write us soon a few words to give us your news; [and tell us] how were the rest of the stay and the trip and why you did not get in touch with us. Affectionate regards, Darina."

FLEISCHMANN

75

16 July 1948
Mr. Ignazio Silone
c/o Mrs. Irene von Guttry
Villa Irene
Ronchi Apuania

Dear friend Silone,

Through Irene Guttry[107] I heard that you have been in Ronchi Apuania from July 12th, and since my son sent you a letter to your Rome address on the 11th of the same month, I am taking the liberty of mailing you a copy to Ronchi, with the hope of not troubling you too much with it.

My son is returning from Paris tomorrow and plans to stay here for another ten to fourteen days. I would therefore appreciate a timely response.

With best wishes also to Mrs. Darina for a lovely vacation, I remain

Always yours

Add

This is an important and pressing matter.[108]

SILONE
76

Gènes
27 June 1948

My dear Fleischmann,

What a pity that we didn't see each other upon your return from Ischia. But I understand what Elsa wrote us; and besides, for us to go to Abruzzo half a day would not have been sufficient. The plan is therefore postponed. During some weeks in July and August Darina will go to Dublin and I to Poveromo. So I will know the place I heard so much about when I was in your home. I already wrote to Mrs. Gutry [sic][110] and I expect to find myself in the very middle of a very Swiss setting. What a pity that you will not be there!

After Poveromo we thought about going to Engadine, and to secure the necessary means, I have made arrangements with some foreign publishers that owe me money, and they will send it to me at your address. Be kind enough to do me this favour again.

Friendly regards to you and Elsa.

Your

Silone

SILONE
77

Sorrento
11 August 1948
Villa la Rufola

My dear friend,

I didn't write anything about Jürg's question, because truthfully, I haven't found anyone, among my acquaintances, in the position he indicated in his letter. I truly hope to be able to assist him at another time. In the last weeks I had to travel a lot, to Milan, [and] to Gènes on Lake Garda and I had to postpone my stay at Poveromo, perhaps to the beginning of September. I now am in Sorrento for two weeks; I will spend the rest of the month in Pescina, at my cousin's place. It is possible that sometime in September I will rejoin Darina who will be coming back from Ireland and we will spend a few days in the mountains. This can give you the impression of a life completely dedicated to leisure, but I take advantage of the distance from Rome to work more seriously than I could do there. And you? I can't imagine you in Ascona now that the road to Italy is free. Give me news of yourself and Elsa.

Cordially
Your

Silone

FLEISCHMANN

78

19 August 1948
Mr. Ignazio Silone
La Rufola
Sorrento
Italy

My dear friend Silone,

Thank you for your letter of the 11th of this month and for your news regarding Jürg. We are now trying to get the access we need through other channels.

I was interested to hear about your many travels and that Darina is currently in Ireland. I can imagine that it is better for her to be away from Rome and all of the politics and noise.

The time we spent in Ischia did me and Elsa good, and we feel refreshed and ready to take things on again – which is good, since we are expecting a number of guests to arrive soon: friends from Italy, friends of my son from the US, Jürgen Fehling and Johanna Gorvin[109] from Germany, etc. etc.

Despite much work and a lot of rain, we are trying to swim in Küsnacht during the midday hours; I walk to my office in the morning, and Elsa often plays tennis. Everything is running very smoothly at the house.

The Grillinos are doing well in Brione. Mrs. Fleischer is going to come visit us for a few weeks soon.

Ali Ritter is back at the Burghölzli[110] and there is no way to prevent the family from falling apart completely.

Elisabeth was here with us recently. She has now found a second home at the Rothschilds in Paris and she's doing great.

Now you have a brief overview of what's going on at the Kleine Pension. The Hardekopfs[111] will return to us in the near future. When will you come to visit us again?

Please tell Mrs. Darina I say hello. We are waiting very anxiously for a new book from you – I sincerely shake your hand, also on Elsa's behalf.

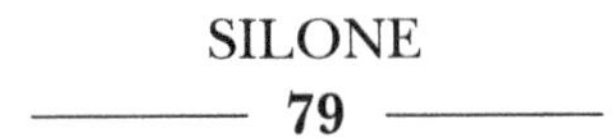

SILONE
79

Pescina (Aquila)
29 August [1948][112]

My dear friend,

I have to come to Switzerland around the 10–15 of September where I will rejoin Darina coming back from Dublin. I will probably accept an old invitation of the Italian Minister, my friend Reale.[113] But for the additional costs I have recently asked some publishers who owe me money to send it to your address. In particular the publisher of the *Schweizer Rundschau* (Einsiedeln) and a Miss Karin Alin of Stockholm should have already sent some payments for me. I would be grateful if Miss Hegnauer could write me a short confirmation about it.

Tomorrow I return to Rome.

Best regards to Elsa and you.

Your

Silone

P.S. If I am not mistaken, before leaving Zurich I gave you a sealed envelope with my last will.[114] Since I recently modified it, when I am in Zurich I will ask you to return me this old copy.

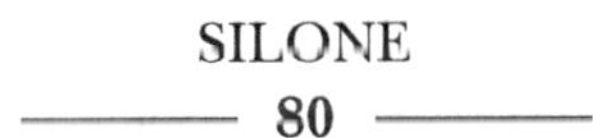

SILONE
80

CAMERA DEI DEPUTATI
Rome, 6 September 1948

My dear friend,

Thank you for your letter. I'll sign the Swedish cheque when I am in Zurich. This will be, I think, towards the 15th of this month. Please do not worry about hosting me; my stay is so short that I can go to a hotel without difficulty.

Best regards, and au revoir

Silone

SILONE

81

Bern
2 October 1948
Italian Delegation

My dear Fleischmann,

Regarding the degree of trust that this Mr. Oscar deserves, they were unable to tell me much. People here dealt with him personally. Please tell Elsa that starting tomorrow, Monday, she can keep the correspondence addressed to Germaniastrasse. I hoped to be able to work here, but there are always people around me. Since I have to absolutely finish a big job in 3–4 days, I am thinking of going to a small, unknown place for the time needed to do my work.

Cordialities to you and Elsa,

Your

Silone

FLEISCHMANN

82

Zurich
17 Nov. 1948

Dear friend Silone,

Two days ago I received the following telegram from Darina: "Impossible arriver Zurich avant debut Decembre prie Mademoiselle Senn attendre mon passage pour etablir [sic] date son depart." [Impossible to arrive in Zurich before the beginning of December, please ask Miss Senn to wait for my arrival to establish the date of her departure.] Unfortunately, I don't have Darina's address anymore and had been expecting to hear from you about this. I don't know whether Darina plans to take responsibility for the fact that Miss Senn resigned from her position on November 1st. Since then, she has continued to work, but under very unpleasant conditions. Her boss has been quite nasty since her resignation, and Miss Senn really wants to leave. She has all her things together and is ready to travel, since she had been planning to leave on November 1st until it was pushed back to the 26th. I have now advised her that it might turn out to be as late as December 1st, and she said she was expecting that. But I can't keep putting her off with further delays, although it seems that Darina may not arrive until December – and maybe even that is not certain – and wants to wait until she is here to set a date then.

I have not yet informed Miss Senn of the most recent delay, because as I said, I had assumed that you would have been in touch with me by now or would have written directly to Miss Senn.

What should I do? I am in a hurry, but greet you.

Sincerely yours

FROM FLEISCHMANN'S OFFICE

83

16 December 1948
Mr. Ignazio Silone
Albergo Milano, Piazza Montecitorio
Rome

Dear Mr. Silone,

You will receive L.87,500 through a good acquaintance of Marcel, which you will be able to use in accordance with your discussion with him. Briefly confirm receipt to me.

With best wishes for the coming holidays,

Your devoted

May I ask you to convey my sincere wishes from the entire office to Miss Senn.

SILONE

84

ASSEMBLEA COSTITUENTE
20 December [1948][115]

My dear friend,

All of my and Darina's good wishes to you and Elsa for Christmas and the New Year. The mail will bring you (or has already brought you) a volume on Abruzzo, with my preface. I hope that the photos will make you desire to know my native region. Probably Darina and I will spend the holidays in Capri. Should your brother Kurt and his wife come to Rome, we would hope to find them here upon our return.

Cordially,
Your
Silone

FROM FLEISCHMANN'S OFFICE

85

21 December 1948
Mr. Ignazio Silone
Albergo Milano, Piazza Montecitorio
Rome

Dear Mr. Silone,

In connection with my letter of the 15th, I need to inform you that the balance of the concerned account is Fr.572.9 from which we deducted Fr.12.99 for commission, so that Fr.560. – remained. I hope you will agree with this.

Sincere greetings

Your devoted

FLEISCHMANN

86

2 March 1949
Mrs. Darina Silone,
Casella postale 355
Roma Centro

Dear Mrs. Darina,

Sincere thanks for your letter of February 24th and for telling us about all the interesting things that are going on. Under the current circumstances, we are by no means unwilling to appear at your home one of these days. At the moment it's impossible though, since Carlo is leaving for Abyssinia in ten days and Jürg is due to arrive here in fourteen days. When I do come to visit though, I will have to tell you all about the impression the US made on me – although it may be vastly different from what you have heard from other friends. In my opinion, America, or rather New York is a disaster. I am pleased that your "consort" is writing again. "On revient toujours à ses premiers amours" [One always returns to one's first loves]. Or did his politics exist before he wrote books? I am glad that things are working out well with Miss Senn. I am surprised that you worry she may leave soon. Maybe we can think of a replacement for her.

Regarding your friends the Smiths, I have been able to find some interesting information, and my only regret is that more people haven't gotten in touch with me about them.

I have located the best pediatric lung specialist, Dr. H. Wissler, the head physician of the children's sanatorium PRO JUVENTUTE, in Davos, phone number 083/3.61.32. Besides him, there are also Mr. and Mrs. Spiro, pediatricians, Pravigan, Davos-Platz (phone number 083/3.51.30), Alpine Children's Clinic.

Finally, I should also mention Dr. Fanconi, the head physician of the Children's Hospital in Zurich, who is treating tuberculosis in an entirely new way (not using streptomycin). Fanconi is quite well known outside of Switzerland, but his methods are completely different from Dr. Wissler's, the doctor I personally prefer out of them all. The children's home Pro Juventute is a private institution and is not connected with "Pro Juventute" in general.

It would be best if you contacted these doctors personally concerning their rates. However, if they end up calling me, I will tell them everything you've told me. Unfortunately, I don't know their addresses.

Strangely enough, my brother's three-year-old son has TB too. That's why I am so up to date on all of this.

More another time – with kind regards, from Elsa and myself, I remain,

Yours

Also for Louise Senn[116]

FLEISCHMANN

87

Zurich
12 March 1949

My dear friend Silone,

We asked Nettie Sutro to have you call Jürg, if he hasn't reached you already. You may have tried to make a person-to-person call to Zurich, only to have us not accept it – that was because Jürg had to return to America sooner than anticipated. He would have liked to ask you several business-related questions, and maybe would have travelled to Rome, but then had to change his plans. It's quite likely that Jürg will return to Europe within the next two or three months and throw himself into his work here; he wants to leave no stone unturned. We are extremely pleased with Jürg. He is hardworking and, as it seems, also very successful. He also promised me that despite all of the "millions" buzzing around his mind, he still sees the flowers in our garden. I consider that very important.

We've received a bill in the amount of Fr. 100 from Prof. Rüedi.[117] Would you like us to pay it for you?

I'm sure you remember that you have some boxes stored at our place and it would be great if you were able to "remove" them one of these days. I would very much appreciate it since there isn't much space at the office and I need to move some items from there to the house – even though there's not all that much room here either! And above all, aren't your empty walls crying for paintings? If I didn't know that you probably want to go through the boxes and get rid of some things, I would just suggest sending them to you. I am sure that only you or Darina can decide about the contents. Besides, it would be great if you would come here so that we could see you again. The Kleine Pension has been cleared out; Hardekopf's[118] negative reaction to our request to move out taught us to only invite friends to stay in the future – friends for whom we haven't had room for some time! Of course you know that you two have absolute first priority in this regard.

We've been out of touch, and it saddens me that business-related matters are the reason we write to each other these days. Actually, let me change that: I think we have a close friendship even without exchanging letters.

Sincerely yours

DARINA SILONE

88

36 Via di Villa Ricotti
Rome
25 April 1949

Dear Elsa,

As always I must begin by apologizing for my sins of omission. But if I was able to get to the end of the maze with the basic organization of the apartment under rather poor financial conditions, dedicating myself to some overdue translations, this has been only by living a very secluded life, without telephoning, without writing, hardly seeing friends. I must smile at Silone's optimism when he invited you for Christmas: Easter has come and I have not yet dared to renew the invitation since we still don't have enough beds; but I hope we will have them toward the month of June, after which, you and Marcel will be welcomed any time. Are you going to Ischia again? We have been gardening on our balcony; there are climbing vines and I believe that it will be cool enough even in summer. I hope that you are well. Miss Senn will remain with us until the fall: at that time I hope to find an Austrian or German [helper]. Can you by chance recommend anyone? The day after tomorrow we leave for Paris where, on April 30, Silone will speak at the "Journée de la Résistance à la Dictature et à la Guerre." They will cover all expenses for both of us. It was an occasion not to be missed. I hope we find a way to stay for about ten days, but they say that it will only be a week. At any rate, our address, beginning April 28, will be Hotel Royal-Condé, VI a. I give it to you because, on our way back, we are thinking of stopping in Zurich for two or three days, to see you and to relieve you of our belongings and our books at the Germaniastrasse. But we want to be sure that you'll be there. Can you send us a word to Paris in this regard? I am not writing much more because I hope to see you soon; the last time it wasn't too gemütlich [comfortable], but this time we hope not to go up to Ziegelbrücke. The spouse complains all the time about the madness of setting up an apartment without having millions, and in theory he may be right, but somehow we will pull through this, and even if he does not realize it, this is enormously beneficial for his nerves, having this little place of peace, rest and order.

Very fond regards to all of you.

Darina

P.S. He says that *he has already paid* Ruedi through the Büchergilde.

DARINA SILONE

89

36 Via di Villa Ricotti
Rome
26 June 1949

Dear Marcel:

Your second letter arrived just after I sent you mine: I hope it arrived and you have forgiven me. Meanwhile I thought of someone else who could eventually be useful to Miss Frisch.[119] Her name is Miss Tylia PERLMUTER [sic][120] and her address is 8 Villa de Ségur, Paris 7e. She is very poor and has to work a lot (translations) to earn a living, but she knows quite a few people and she may have an idea for Miss Frisch. Since I have to write to her today, anyway, I will tell her in my letter about Miss Frisch's situation, without giving you a separate letter of introduction: she will have been informed by the time Miss Frisch contacts her (by mail, since she cannot be reached by telephone).

It may be that Miss Perlmuter [sic] will be able to suggest something about the housing. [And] maybe even the other people to whom I introduced her in my last letter. With these, I do believe that I have exhausted the list of people I know in Paris who could be helpful to her in any way. You know that it is no use to give addresses and letters of introduction when one knows full well that the people in question will not do anything, either because they are too busy, or because they don't have connections, or because they live a different lifestyle; or only because regarding simple acquaintances they don't feel connected enough to the person asking the favour to want to bother. I repeat that these four people may also be able to give some indications about housing. I must say, however, that regarding housing for young people who don't have a lot of money, Paris is very well organized: there are a number of small hotels where one can rent a room by the month at a price not found elsewhere. I think that this is more practical than renting a room with a family. If one is "au pair" that is, of course, a different matter. A younger sister of mine, nineteen years old, arrived in Paris last year without announcing her intention in advance. (I was then in Ireland.) She didn't know Paris at all, had no advice or introductions, and had almost no money. On the same morning of her arrival, she found a hotel room for 100 francs per day; the owner and his wife were very kind to her, took care of her, and at times invited her to have supper with them. Maybe that was a fortunate coincidence. But one can try.

In Paris there are also a number of "Foyers de la Jeune Fille" of all kinds. But I only know the ones for students. If I get another idea, I will write to you at once. Let me know if she gets some results with the addresses I gave. I think that it will be rather difficult to find an au pair position in Paris during the time when people go on vacation and she should not discard in advance the possibility of going outside of Paris during the summer.

I will soon write to Elsa. Has she come back? It is hot already. Miss Senn is still in Ischia with her parents. They were not enthusiastic at all about Rome and she was very disappointed. When will you come? And Jürg?

All our love,

Darina

FLEISCHMANN

90

7 July 1949
Mrs. Darina Silone
Via di Villa Ricotti 36
Rome

Dear Mrs. Darina,

Thank you very sincerely for the great effort you have made regarding Miss Frisch's[121] apartment search in Paris. I have taken the liberty of forwarding your letters to her, and as far as I know she is actively looking for a place. I am sure she will let you know once she has found something. Again, thank you for your help.

Thanks also for your letter with the news about you and your husband. I've heard indirectly about how active Silone is and how very well regarded he is in all of the most influential circles. As I am sure you can imagine, we are very pleased about it.

Mr. Senn phoned me yesterday and sometime wants to tell me all the reasons why he was disappointed with Italy; such people simply have too narrow a view to be able to understand that heavenly land. When you come to Zurich, we'll tell you all about what's been going on at the Kleine Pension – quite a lot – but we will wait for the time when we can talk in person.

Until then, I warmly shake your and Silone's hand in Elsa's name as well.

Yours

DARINA SILONE

91

36 Via di Villa Ricotti
Rome
9 November 1949

Dear friends:

We haven't heard from you for a long time. Here the pace of life is such that we hardly have the time to answer the urgent letters that we receive and besides, everything is so depressing that one has nothing to say. Is there, by chance, any possibility to get together, and *se retrouver*? We would like it very much. What would you say about the two of you, Elsa and Marcel, coming to spend the Christmas holidays with us? There are many things still lacking in the apartment, but I believe that we have the essentials and there is room for both of you. Maybe you have already made plans, but if you haven't, we hope you will think about our offer. The Holy Year will have already begun, and there will be even more choreography in the ecclesiastical ceremonies, but I don't know if this would be an attraction for you. In any case, we will have central heating. I had better clarify what I mean by "room for both of you." First, the room where I work is also the guest room and when friends visit us, I move elsewhere. There is a big sofa bed, some tables, a typewriter, books, lamps, and there will soon be an armoire for the guests. In another room, where Silone works, there is a Louis XIV bed (but with new mattress and box-spring!). I feel like an innkeeper who advertises her place. I will add that Mrs. Dr. Müller's nice Austrian [girl] did not come, despite her promises, having found something during the summer with an American family in London. This is quite understandable, but she never informed me and I waited for two months, with Miss Senn leaving in early September, having to do the chores myself with an occasional maid. Finally, the day before yesterday, I solved the situation by hiring a Hungarian refugee who arrived three weeks ago from Budapest (with her husband and daughter, but these do not live with us), who doesn't know a word of Italian but answers the phone in Russian: she says they seem to understand her. What can I tell you about us? Nothing much. I try to remind Silone that he is a writer. Politics continue to be his daily illusion. He returns tonight from a Paris federalist conference. As for myself, I do translations and give private lessons. It is far from an ideal existence, but I always hope that I will eventually be able to control the circumstances a little more brilliantly. My fondest thoughts to both of you. I repeat that we would be very happy if you decided to come. Maybe you felt that there was some detachment on Silone's part, but you know his difficult character: I can assure you that for him you remain and will always remain, I believe, his real family, and he will never forget you. If you can forgive him his rudeness, come.

Until Christmas?

I hope so.

Darina

DARINA SILONE

92

Rome
23 November 1949

Dear friends:

Marcel's letter with its atrocious news affected us deeply.[122] Silone will write to you to express all of our sorrow and solidarity, but I am eager to send a few words to assure you that our invitation for Christmas stands for the whole year and for as often as you would like. Naturally, later on, the weather will be better, and it will still be a happy occasion to have you with us.

We strongly hope that things can be worked out, at least partially, that Carlo will be assailed by remorse and act accordingly, and that you will be able to keep your house. It would be too sad if you no longer had Germaniastrasse. We did not know anything about it and your letter was a sad surprise. So, please don't forget that you have a standing invitation from us, and that, without planning a big trip, when you feel the need for a bit of sun and "south" that is not Ticino, all you have to do is send us a telegram announcing your arrival: as often as you please.

Hoping to see you soon, I send affectionate greetings to both of you.

Darina

FLEISCHMANN

93

Phone 34.15.64
Platterstrasse 78
9 February 1950

Dear Mrs. Darina,

I've received two bank transfers for Silone in the amounts of Fr. 573.60 and Fr. 15.20 from the Gutenberg Book Guild, which I am holding for S[ilone]. As I am no longer going in to the office and am not on the best terms[123] with them, I recommend that you have the Book Guild keep such remittances in the future until one of you can pick them up or make other arrangements. Normally, I would have said that you could have them sent to my home address, but we will often be away travelling, so that wouldn't be practical. I am, however, at your disposal for any commissions or withdrawals. Please let the Book Guild know about this change.

We are so pleased with our new apartment that neither of us has been missing the Germaniastrasse even for a minute. – So it has all worked out fine, it just should have been under different circumstances. – My brother Carlo continues to ruin all of his personal relationships, and ours is no exception – things with him are tenser than ever. – I never knew how much talent Elsa had for organization and how much untiring effort and endurance she possesses! You will see for yourselves someday.

Elsa is going to Germany next week for about one month and after that we both want to go away for a while to Brione to see Carry and Lisely, and then to Poveromo to see Irene.[124] We don't know yet when we will make it to Rome, but you will definitely not be spared! But before then we would like a report on your conditions.

Elsa and I send you cordial greetings.

Your

Since you didn't tell us what to do with the plates [?] we went ahead and destroyed them

FLEISCHMANN

94

4 May 1950

Dear Mrs. Silone,

In my letter of February 9th I had asked you to inform the Book Guild that they should no longer send your husband's remittances to my former office at Stockerstrasse, but, if possible, to keep them at the Guild. I informed them that I no longer work there and did not leave on good terms, and that it causes difficulties for me when amounts are sent there for my friends. The office is no longer willing, as it did before, to provide favours for me without compensation.

Recently, two credit notes in the amounts of Fr. 22, and Fr. 97.80 were sent to the Stockerstrasse besides the bank transfers. I will have the money sent to me and keep it for now, but I ask you again to please make other arrangements with the Book Guild so that this will not reoccur.

I have also notified the Book Guild twice of my new address, Plattenstrasse 78, to no avail.

I hope that you are doing well. It might be of interest to you – or perhaps more so to Silone – that Mrs. Irene von Guttry has died of cancer. She tried to recover twice while staying with us at our old house. In general, there isn't much pleasant news here to report.

With heartfelt greetings

Your

SILONE

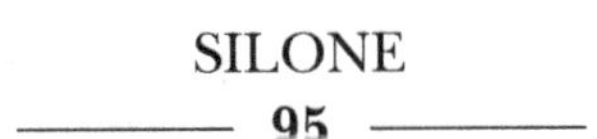

95

Rome
2 June 1950

My dear friend,

Darina is in Florence for a month as translator at the UNESCO conference and I will join her Sunday and remain there for about ten days. On the 24th we will have to be in Berlin for a writers' conference, and we plan to remain (in Germany, not Berlin) at least two weeks. It is quite possible that we will make our return trip via Switzerland, if we can have the chance of meeting you somewhere, you and Miss Schiess. Be kind enough to let us know where you will be during the time I mentioned. Only by speaking "a viva voce" will it be possible to tell each other all that life has brought us in these recent times. But I also want to add this: later, in full summer, we will again be away from Rome; it is not the best season to stay here, but since you didn't come in the spring, if you feel like coming in the summer, the apartment is at your complete disposal, with the maid; otherwise we will wait for you in the fall.

I send you and also Elsa my cordial regards.

Silone[125]

I have written to the Büchergilde not to send money for me to the Stockerstr any longer.[126]

SILONE
96

Zurich
4 July 1950
20 Hirschengraben

My dear friend,

I arrived here yesterday from Berlin after spending a day in Frankfurt with Darina and Witting. Darina went to see some ruins in Fribourg, B. [Breisgau] and will return directly to Rome. I will remain a few days in Zurich. We had planned to come to Zurich, but Witting told us that you and Elsa will stay at Poveromo until the 8th of the month and then will go to Brione. What a pity! We had consoled ourselves for not meeting you in Florence (I had to suddenly go back to Rome) with our plan to stop in Zurich. The week I spent in Berlin cannot be summarized in a few words. I saw again many friends from all countries; and also, this city whose reality surpasses all imagination. The news from Korea has not caused the impression I expected in Berlin. If the Parisians or the Romans were subjected to such a regime, they would already have gone crazy. I must apologize to you for a small blunder of mine: I remember full well that you wrote to me that I should have all mailings to my account at Stockerstrasse suspended; but I thought that the remittances that were already made were still with Miss Hegnauer. So, I phoned her and she explained the matter to me. Believing that I was in distress, she kindly offered me an advance on your behalf, but I thanked her. In reality here I don't need it, I already have about one hundred francs at my disposal, but I will need this money in Italy and I am counting on bringing it back with me. What should be done? If it's possible for you to write to someone (or send me a letter that I can present to someone), you would do me a favour. I can remain here, for this, until next Monday or Tuesday. Yesterday, some people who knew about our friendship were talking to me about you with great sympathy and admiration.

All my best, also to Elsa.

Cordially

Your Silone

SILONE

97

Rome
10 January 1951

My dear friend Marcel Fleischmann,

This January 13th you will be 60 years old. This is something that, in itself and for the circumstances under which it arrives, touches me deeply and, I am sure, all of your friends; those who these days are near you and those who are very far. Darina and I thought of coming to Zurich for the occasion, at least for a day, and only the thought that you might possibly prefer to be alone and, on that day, to be outside Zurich and your usual surroundings, kept us from coming.

My dear friend, we met in 1931, when you celebrated your 40th birthday, and I was at your house on your fiftieth; we have, therefore, known each other for twenty years. Never have private lives been so influenced and disrupted by public calamities as they have been during these twenty years. And, despite the changes, we find ourselves facing the same dangers and anxieties. How often, these days, when I am in company and I hear what everybody says, I am struck by the resemblance to our thoughts and problems of the years preceding the war. I always found cruel and wicked an Italian saying that goes: "common misfortune is half good fortune"; but, on the whole, how can we complain about our individual misfortunes before the horrors of these last years and the horrors that are expected? Me, I lost many illusions; I persist in doing what I perceive to be my duty as a citizen, but deep down, I feel quite sure that the only thing that matters, that one never regrets, and that gives courage, is the sincere affection between friends. I am

sure that you also feel the same. We will talk about it again on your 70th birthday, and to get there well, we express our most affectionate wishes.
Silone

FLEISCHMANN

98

Ronchi
4 June 1951

Dear Darina,

We've just returned from our trip to Florence – Arezzo – Cortona – Perugia – Assisi – Siena – and found your letter awaiting.

Unfortunately, we have to leave Thursday morning – for several good reasons – and it wouldn't be enjoyable for either of us to only see each other so briefly. We also wouldn't want you to make the trip under these circumstances, no matter how much we would like to see you again.

We were touched that you were so readily willing to come and I am sure we would have had so much to talk about. – But as I have mentioned, we are not completely in charge of our schedule, and our friends are pressuring us to come home.

Normally we would have returned a little earlier and left a little later, but our rental car caused us some delays along the way. The mail has been en route for eight days now and still hasn't gotten to us! I've heard that letters to Zurich arrive in half the time, and practically as fast as the mail from here to Forte or Florence!

We should have informed you earlier (from Zurich) about our planned arrival in Ronchi, but we all needed a few days of complete rest when we got here and then forgot to alter our plans accordingly. We made our decision to go to Assisi at the very last minute for our friends' sake – we had already been to most of the places, but our friends hadn't and couldn't have gotten there without our car. We seriously considered continuing on and driving all the way to Rome, but then we wouldn't have had a day of rest between all of our strenuous enjoyment of the arts and our having to return home.

Are you not coming to Zurich? In that case, we will definitely come here ourselves next year and make Rome our first stop. We've now reached the age that we prefer the south over the mountains, and if all goes well, we will get a Fiat so if something goes wrong we can always be on the spot at a moment's notice.

Please say hello for us to your "master and lord," and thanks again for making the effort to see us – we truly regret that yet again it wasn't possible to get together.

Sincerely

IGNAZIO AND DARINA SILONE

99

(Postcard)
8 August 1951
A beach panorama: "10- Forte dei Marmi – La spiaggia"
To: Mr. Marcel Fleischmann, Plattenstr. 78, Zurich
From: Villa Irene

Message, in French: "We are here from the 1st of August. What a pity that you and Elsa are not here as well. We are thinking of staying for the whole month. The weather is beautiful – variable. The official language of the pension [is] Swiss-German. What will you do this summer? Cordially, Silone and Darina"

FLEISCHMANN

100

14 August 1951
Mr. and Mrs. Ignazio Silone,
Pensione Villa Irene
Ronchi/Massa-Carrara

Dear friends,

I forwarded a business-related letter to you in Rome. In the meantime, I also received your card for which we thank you. We just keep missing each other while travelling in the last two years.

Our plans:

Elsa is leaving tomorrow for Germany and I'm leaving for America on the 30th of this month. Since I want to stay there until the end of October and Maria still has vacation time left once she returns from Ronchi, Elsa will most likely not return before the end of October. So, until then Plattenstrasse 78: huis clos [sic].[127]

By the way, Elsa sent Darina a card, which has hopefully arrived by now.

As you can tell from our plans, we are doing well.

Please say hello to everyone and accept a sincere handshake from Elsa and myself.[128]

IGNAZIO AND DARINA SILONE

101

(Postcard)
3 June 1952
Aerial view of Paris: The River Seine, the left bank of the Île de la Cité and the church of Notre Dame.
To: Mr. Marcel Fleischmann, Plattenstr. 78, Zurich, Switzerland.
From: Paris

Message, in French: "After two weeks in Paris we are still hoping to see you again, with Elsa, in Rome or Poveromo (where we will be in the month of August). Cordially, Silone [and] Darina [by Darina]."

SILONE

102

Via Villa Ricotti, 36
Rome, 8 July 1952

My dear Friend,

Papini's book,[129] from which the passage that you have cut out was extracted, only contains imaginary interviews, as in the saying: "it isn't true but it's a good story." On the other hand, the statement that appeared on AUFBAU, regarding your brother Carlo, contains this detail concerning me about which one can say: "it isn't true and it's a bad story." It is obviously a paid insert, therefore an advertising by-product that does not deserve the honour of a correction. The correction would be needed if it were a biographical dictionary or another serious publication. Despite it all (I mean: despite the scant liking I have for your brother Carlo, despite all my dislike of the regimes behind the iron curtain) I think that *DIE NATION* did not have any right to publish private letters. Very cordial regards to you and Elsa, from Darina and myself.

Your

Silone

SILONE

103

Rome
21 December 1952

My dear friend,

How are you? And Elsa? I don't know if this letter will arrive by Christmas, but it is the only means that I have to express some greetings. Also, I gave Mrs. Oprecht your address so they will send you my new book.[130] The last news I had from you dating back to Poveromo came with some details by Mrs. Sachs which gave the impression that you would establish yourself in America and Elsa in Germany; but I do not know if these personal events took place. About us: Darina is in New York (545 West 112th St., New York 25 [sic]) and I will have to rejoin her there in the spring, to return to Europe in June, first to Ireland and then to Rome. Meanwhile, I have worked enough. My health has improved thanks to new therapies that have been found for bronchiectasis. But age leaves its mark upon my spirit and I am quieter than usual. I would have come to Zurich in the next few days, if I had known that you were there, but it is quite possible that I will come, in any case, during the month of January. I hope that you, Elsa and Jürg are in good health and I send all of you my most affectionate greetings.

Your

Ignazio Silone

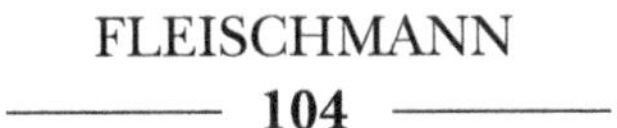

FLEISCHMANN

104

26 December, 1952

My dear friend Silone,

Sorry that I am typing this, but my handwriting is somewhat unsteady.

Your letter and your *Hand voll Brombeeren* [sic][131] came at the right time. When everyone around us was talking about your book and Oprecht even offered it to us, we knew that you had forgotten about us. And this made us very sad.

We are going through a difficult time. Elsa has been seriously ill for some time now and neither medical attendance nor the sympathy of our friends has so far brought any improvement.

As you had heard, we had been planning to make some major changes in our lives, but since then I have come to realize that this violation of destiny was wrong. So I reversed course, but this has been very hard on Elsa and has taken a toll on her mind as well as her body.

You lived with us long enough to empathize with our current distress. Even though the external situation has remained the same, the internal needs more time to find its way back. We are taking things month by month, waiting for Elsa's condition to improve. I know my guilt, but I also have the strength to carry out my atonement.

It's a shame that you and I keep missing each other these last few years. Please let us know via postcard approximately when you are planning to visit. I will be away in January from time to time but would still like to see you. We are also expecting Jürg and his wife. Our living room is too primitive to offer it to you.

I am glad to hear that your health has improved even more and that you are again finding full satisfaction in your work. I'd be happy to send a note to Darina while she is in New York.

I am not adding any thanks or wishes to these lines, as I would rather do this in person – and can only do so if you do come, so I hope this guarantees us a visit, and one which we are very much looking forward to.

DARINA SILONE

105

(Postcard)
20 May [1954 postmark]
Reproduction of: Still Life by Candle-Light, by Pablo Picasso.
To: Miss Elsa Schiess, Pension Villa Irene, Pover'Uomo [sic] vicino Forte dei Marmi (Lucca) [crossed out in purple pencil. Unreadable word in black pencil follows].
From: Rome

Message, in German: "I lost the letter. [Until] when you will be there? If you do not want to make it over to us, we'll come to you, but we would be happy to have you here. Let us know as soon as possible. We don't want to miss you this time! Darina."

FLEISCHMANN

106

13 February 1955

Dear Mrs. Darina and Ignazio Silone,

Elsa is doing wonderfully again, and she and I are spending the entire month of May in Ischia where we have already reserved rooms. Carry Streuli and Lisely Sidler will be accompanying us. They don't know Rome at all. We plan on driving in our car and being there *around* April 30th – May 1st, and maybe even until May 2nd, so for approximately two days.

You have invited us so often that we are now hoping to take you up on it, and are wondering if Elsa could stay with you. Our friends will be staying at a guesthouse or a hotel, and I will stay with them, so as not to be of additional burden to you.

I heard that Rome will be very busy at that time and that one needs to have booked the rooms already, although this doesn't make much sense to me. The following hotels and guesthouses were mentioned to us. It would be nice if you could recommend one that you like and is near you.

Pensione Helvetica, Via Marche 48 (the owner is Swiss. Also owns our hotel in Ischia).

Pensione Bellavista-Milton, 16 Via Porta Pinciana

Pensione Gerber, Via Lombardia 31

Albergo dell' Opera, Via Firenze

I assume that you know more about these places than we do. Hopefully you are going to be there when we come. We'd love to see you again and you will be delighted by Elsa's health. She is currently travelling through Germany with Jürg and is buying toys. – Please get back to us *very soon.*

Sincerely

SILONE

107

Rome
15 February 1955

My dear Marcel,

Thank you very much for your letter. Darina is presently in Dublin where she will stay until the month of June. Therefore, our apartment is easily available to you. If by chance I too will be away from Rome, you should know that the apartment has two bedrooms: one of them, Darina's with one bed, the other with two beds. Even if I am there, which is probable, there are always two available beds. But you can tell me, even at the last moment, if you will use one or two. As far as the pensions, the most popular is Bellavista, whose name is not misleading as it is located in front of Villa Borghese; then comes the Helvetica; the Gerber is frankly bad; the fourth one is a mediocre hotel near the station. If Miss Streuli[132] and Mrs. Sidler who don't know Rome want to stay with us longer, I hope they will take advantage of it; or else Miss Streuli and Elsa. About you I don't dare to hope because you prefer i fanghi di Ischia.[133] So then, goodbye for now.

Many friendly regards from your

Silone[134]

Passing through Geneva, a month ago, I learned the news concerning your brother Carlo, but I don't dare to report it because nobody confirmed it to me.

FLEISCHMANN

108

24 February 1955

Dear friend Silone,

Sincere thanks for your letter and your kind invitation, which we accept with pleasure. The "Grillino's" [sic] also love the idea and may take you up on your offer. We will inform you about definite plans and dates by mid-April.

It is a shame that Mrs. Darina will not be there. Maybe we will be able to see her briefly on our return trip.

Elsa returned with Jürg yesterday with much good news. For the first time since Jürg has been in America, it finally looks like he will really be able to make it. But as they say: "if it brought delight, it took effort and hard work." Even Witting,[135] our very helpful "business consultant," is confident that it will work out.

We can't get your comment about my brother Carlo out of our heads,[136] and we need you to clear this matter up for us. I haven't read an obituary or an engagement notice in the newspapers, nor anything about bankruptcy or ennoblement. Remember, neither Kurt nor I, or anyone in the family, have any contact with him. Because of his guilty conscience he has even forbidden (!) his friends to have any contact with us! The rumour, therefore, interests us very much and we will treat it with the necessary discretion.

The Etruscan exhibition in the art gallery is unbelievably beautiful and is a good preparation for our journey, – and if you should have any particular suggestions, please let us know.

Much love from all of us, many thanks, and do drop us a line about Carlo.

Your

SILONE

109

Rome
15 April 1955

My dear friend,

I have reserved two single rooms for you at the Hotel San Giusto, 58 Piazza Bologna, one hundred metres from my home; at the same time I confirm that on May 4 and 5, and also in the following days, if you want, you can have two beds in a room of my apartment. The solution of the Hotel San Giusto is the best one, because the other hotels that I spoke to you about only have double rooms and are very far from my home, so that it would cause you an unnecessary loss of time whenever the four of you (for the meals, the excursions, etc.) want to be together. It goes without saying that you will let the people who will stay at the hotel also be my guests and have their meals at my house. So, upon arriving in Rome with your car, ask first in which direction is Piazza Bologna; at one of its corners, the left corner, where Via Livorno begins, you will find the Hotel San Giusto; you will ask the doorman about the Via di Villa Ricotti. My telephone number is: 830.858. All that remains is to wish you bon voyage.

Cordially,

Silone[137]

SILONE
110

Wednesday morning, 4 [May 1955][138]

My dear friend,

I regret that I was not at home at the time of your arrival in Rome, but I expect to return tomorrow night, before you leave for Ischia. I have given instructions to my maid to receive Miss Streuli and her friend; they are free to do as they like, or can ask the maid for instructions (the use of the bathroom, breakfast, the other meals). It goes without saying that I'll be happy if when I return, I'll learn that my apartment was truly useful to you. You must only bear in mind that the maid is off Thursday afternoon. She is a fairly good cook and I have forewarned her that, unless she is told otherwise, she has to prepare dinner for four on Wednesday night and lunch on Thursday. I will also phone home tomorrow morning to make sure that you arrived all right.

So, welcome, and until tomorrow.

Your Silone

SILONE
111

[1955][139]

My dear friend,

From your letter, it is evident that the news concerning your brother is false. As I have already written to you, I got it in Geneva, from Prof. Jadasson.[140] I was there for a writers' meeting when I thought of stopping by for a check-up of a skin condition I have had since 1937. After a few minutes of conversation, by his own initiative, he began to speak about you and your brother Carlo, "the one who lived in Kusnacht and recently died." Since I told him that I had not heard the news, he confirmed it to me; and I did not insist on knowing where, how and due to what illness, because, I will admit it to you, the matter did not interest me. That's all. Evidently Jadasson had him confused with somebody else.

Very cordially,

Your Silone

IGNAZIO AND DARINA SILONE

112

(Postcard)
1 May 1956
Five views of Paris with Montmartre at the centre. [The upper right corner, where the stamp was, has been cut off].
To: Mr. Marcel Fleischmann, Plattenstr. 78, Zurich, Switzerland.
From: Paris

Message, in French: "It is cold, but people get hot and excited for other reasons. Best regards to you and Elsa, your I.Silone. Fond regards, Darina" [By Darina, in Italian].

IGNAZIO AND DARINA SILONE

113

IGNAZIO SILONE
Via Villa Ricotti, 36
Rome
23 December 1956[141]

My dear friend:

My most affectionate greetings to you and Elsa and best wishes for the New Year.

Silone
Darina

IGNAZIO AND DARINA SILONE

114

(Postcard)
4 May 1958
Panorama: Paris, with the Eiffel Tower in the foreground.
To: Mr. Marcel Fleischmann, Plattenstr. 78, Zurich, Switzerland
From: Paris

Message, in French: "Dear friend, are you still in Ticino? Have you reached absolute calm and wisdom? If Italy still attracts you give us a hint. We would be very happy to finally see you again. Your I. Silone [and] Darina [By Darina].

SILONE

115

Rome
7 June 1958
Via di Villa Ricotti, 36

My dear friend,

I thank you very much for your letter, to which I want to reply with the same candour and friendship. You are entirely right on the topic of "correspondence"; among my many faults, the one of not externalizing my feelings and rarely writing to friends is not the least. (I believe that on several occasions, at the time of Germaniastr., I even talked about this with Elsa). I write letters painfully and unwillingly. I am so aware of this flaw that I have attributed it to a character of "The Seed beneath the Snow" (Simone la faina, who, on principle, never wrote letters and only communicated verbally). But I don't say this to justify myself or lessen the feeling of remorse that I experienced reading that you ask yourself if I still have a memory of the life we lived together. On the contrary, I think about it, and speak about it very often with Darina. My life, you know, has not changed a lot. Aside from the turmoil of the immediate post-war, I now live like I did in Zurich, at least in the sense that I lead a very secluded life, and that the things to which I give the most importance are my memories and my personal relationships. I do not know what the "Frankfurter Allgemeine" could have published about me; I have not seen it; but I am accustomed to the newspapers' fanciful inventions. I no longer recall who told me that you had settled in Brione sur Locarno (maybe Paulette Brupbacher),[142] but I don't think that believing in such a possibility meant lack of respect for you. You have always loved nature and the simple life. But these are not things that are worth our arguing about. During the last years, I went through some difficult moments; many times I had to choose between pride and honesty, and I felt very strong nostalgia for our life in common, not in the sense of being able to speak with you, but simply being together. At the time when I had the impression that the hardships had been overcome and I was again in harmony with myself, I told Darina: what if we went to Switzerland to spend a little time with Marcel Fleischmann and Elsa? (It was then that I wrote you the postcard from Paris to ask about your whereabouts.) In January I finally got my driver's licence, and now have a small Fiat 600; on that day I wanted to write to

Elsa to remind her of the first driving lesson she gave me on the road to Dohen. But, I am just an awful letter writer. I find it a compliment on Elsa's part when she says that my Christmas wishes resemble those of your "Lieferanten" [suppliers] because mine are normally more banal. I am ashamed that I have not learned more civilized manners. But for the rest, I assure you that the affection that I feel for you is too great to be defined with words of gratitude, etc. Finally, I hope that before long we will have the occasion of being a few days together.

Amicably, your

I Silone

I was happy to hear the good news about Jürg.[143]

IGNAZIO AND DARINA SILONE

116

(Postcard)
18 [?] 1958
Knossos: The Throne of Minos
To: [Addresses missing due to cut to remove the stamp] Plattenstr. 78, Zurich, Switzerland.
From: Crete

Message, in French: "We are tired and dazzled by so many beautiful things. But the ruins of the last war remind us of today's reality. In fond friendship from your Silone. Darina [By Darina].

SILONE

117

27 September, 1958

My dear friend:

I have been in Vienna for a week and I intended to return to Rome via Zurich but at the last moment I had to change my plans because on October 4th I have to go with Darina to the island of Rhodes for a meeting with some personalities from Africa and the Middle East. This leaves me too little time for Rome, where I will be tomorrow and where I always have a lot to do, especially between two trips. Meanwhile, here in Vienna, I saw some names and things (for instance some store names) that reminded me of your travels here before the war. What distant times! Since then the city has changed a lot: it is like an impoverished old lady who lives on memories.

I hope you returned well from America and that you and Elsa are well.

Cordially,
Your

Sil

FLEISCHMANN
118

Brione sopra Minusio, Casa Grillino
5 October 1958

My dear friend Silone,

Elsa and I were very happy to receive your remembrance from Vienna and it evoked our own past memories.[144] By coincidence, the Kuffners[145] are also originally from Vienna (but now are [living] in the US), and are currently in Zürich where one of the brothers is having an operation. You probably still remember them. Fortunately, we are in Ticino at our friends' house right now and so I don't have to see them; I'm not interested in keeping up that superficial connection.

It is too bad that your time did not allow a side trip to Zurich. We would have been pleased to see you and Darina. We spent five months with Jürg in the USA and have much to report. We experienced the entire recession and learned quite a lot from it. It wasn't difficult to predict the progress, as the parameters were obviously predetermined.

Jürg is doing well in his business and in his private life. In addition to Steiff, he's taken on sole agency of Märklin in Göppingen and Britain, and Corgi in London, all of which are first-class businesses with good reputations. His six-year-old daughter is receiving the same miserable upbringing as all American children, while his young son, on the other hand, is a little angel; Elputzeli gets along marvellously with all of them. He bought the house he was previously renting and it has an enormous yard, and you would most definitely enjoy spending a few days there.

We also met Dr. Toni [sic] Kesse[146] who is now practising in the university town of Ann Arbor, Mich., and has finally found the intellectual milieu she was always looking for.

Old Epstein has died and Fred, along with his wife and children, are all seeing a psychiatrist. I am telling you this assuming that you still remember all these people, at least by name. We also saw the Dickinsons[147] again, who are now head of the UN's film department. Martin Rich[148] has made quite a career for himself and has given concerts in Florence, Milan, and Rome (at the latter on the radio station). There are many other names we could mention from the past, but we will save that for a reunion.

Carry and Lisely send their best regards. We cordially join them.

Your old[149]

IGNAZIO AND DARINA SILONE

119

CARD-SIZE PHOTO
Silone standing, looks at Darina holding a small lion.
To: [No addressee, evidently sent in an envelope]
From: [Unknown]

Message, in French: "Dear friends, we wish you happy holidays in Montegrotto and a good start of 1959; we wish you good health! Where will you be toward mid-January? It is possible that I will cross Switzerland. Cordially, your Sil. [And by Darina] Here you can witness my debut as a lion tamer … very affectionate regards, Darina."

SILONE

120

IGNAZIO SILONE
Via Villa Ricotti, 36
Rome
13 January 1959

My dear friend,

I have just finished a narrative piece of about 70 pages, which will be 100 printed pages, based on the short story "The Fox" from the collection *The Journey to Paris,* but I expanded the subject and deepened the characters, so that this work now seems to me to be an integral part of the rest of my works. And since this is the only narrative set in Switzerland and since the core of the narrative is the theme of friendship and solidarity among men, in a totally natural manner, I got the idea of dedicating it to you. I hope you will not object. Waiting for the book to be published and translated, I sent you, separately, a copy of the original. Next Tuesday, January 20th, I'll leave for Paris, where I'll probably remain for a week; then, before returning to Rome, I'm counting on coming to Switzerland for two or three days. This time Darina will not accompany me. I'll phone you from Zurich and I hope to find you in good health and good humour, and also Elsa.

Very cordially,
Your

Ignazio Silone

By happy coincidence today is January 13th. Be assured of our fondest best wishes.

FLEISCHMANN

121

16 January 1959

My dear friend Silone,

Along with your lovely letter I received a copy of your new book,[150] which you dedicated to me out of friendship and in remembrance of old times. Please accept my sincere thanks for this proof of your devotion. I have no objections to make, and I now must prove myself worthy of it.

I am so glad to hear that Switzerland and a natural friendship between people triggered your thoughts of me. It is those human characteristics that connect us the most. To be able to understand this, one has to have experienced many disappointments as you and I did, but also to have such an unshakeable belief in human goodness as we do – even if things occurred in different ways for us, the result remains the same.

I have made much progress with my Italian and I will try to read the original, which will make me twice as happy.

Jürg arrives here tomorrow, the 17th of this month, but has to leave again on the 29th for 14 days. It would be great if we could arrange for him to speak with you while here and we are looking forward to seeing you soon. Unfortunately, we are unable to offer you accommodation, as there is no room. But you will be more comfortable somewhere else than in our small apartment.

I also thank you for your birthday wishes, and I send love from Elsa and me to Mrs. Darina and you.

Your old

FLEISCHMANN

122

21 March 1959

Dear friend Silone,

I have been wanting to write to you for the past few weeks to tell you that your new book prompted us to reread the story of the fox in *The Journey to Paris.*[151] To our surprise, we discovered the part about the trout, which had also remained deep in our memory even though we couldn't remember where it was written. It is quite moving and full of classical poignancy.

I would like to thank you for sending the newspaper and join in with Goethe: "It is too great an honour, Master!" But as you might imagine, I find it very flattering to be reminded of the wonderful decade we spent together under the same roof and which was filled with such important inner and outer experiences for me.

The newspaper encouraged me to try reading the story in the original Italian and I am enjoying it. I hope to see you soon here or there. In the meantime please accept Elsa's and my best wishes, also for Darina. (Did she reconsider her plans to visit Zurich? We are still expecting her.)

Your old

FLEISCHMANN

123

17 April 1959

Dear friend Silone,

Did you know that there is a cemetery in Nuremberg where famous men such as Albrecht Dürer, Veit Stoos, Feuerbach, and many other immortal men rest in peace? The part of your book about the *Journey to Paris*[152] reminds me of this place: there is a chasm between man's destiny and what society makes of him. Everyone may travel in a separate car but we are all on the same train.

It is not the names that impressed me, but rather what separates the old part of the cemetery from the new one. There's a whole world between them.

The old gravestones are without exception flat, sunken plaques made out of sandstone, marble or bronze. Laid out in long horizontal lines, they transmit a great calm and quiet. The dead are sequestered, as if they had accepted their death and made peace with their fate.

In the new part of the cemetery there is the usual inelegance – nothing but erected tomb-stones that loudly project themselves into the world of the living. It seems as though the dead are not at peace yet and want to continue to be active in this life, even if it is only by their tombstones interrupting the solitude. The sight of them is embarrassing. "Everybody has their own grave, but they all lie buried in the same ground." The similarities between your thoughts and mine caused me to write to you. I hope that you do not find it presumptuous of me to draw this comparison. There is so much shallowness these days that we try to escape it by taking refuge in more substantial realms.

The fact that Darina hasn't written but is coming is proof, we assume, that she is doing well. We will be spending June at the sea in Ronchi (Poveromo) at our friend Tauber's place. Will we see each other then? There's enough space for you!

I have arranged for a second copy of Mondo [sic][153] to be sent to my son in the USA so that he can be at least a little proud of his father. You and I and he all know how much Elsa is part of this honour too.

Take care, and love to Darina and you from us all.

Your old

SILONE

124

IGNAZIO SILONE
Via Villa Ricotti, 36
Rome
28 April 1959

My dear friend,

What you quote from *The Journey to Paris*[154] is not in the last version of "The Fox." Also, you will read it soon in French and German and you will see that it is all a different work. Darina's health is very variable; as soon as one speaks about going to a clinic she feels perfectly well. So, it does not depend on the blood, but on nerves. On the 11th of May I will have to be in Geneva; on the 15th, in Paris with Darina; then she will go to Dublin because one of her sisters is expecting a baby; on the 21st of June we will meet again in Paris; on the 26th we will go to Berlin since I am on the jury of the international film festival. All this doesn't amuse me at all; moreover, nobody forces me to do it, but I do it anyway, because if I didn't do that I would do something else and it would be the same.

Friendly regards to you and Elsa,

Your

Silone

FLEISCHMANN

125

Zurich
20 May 1959

Dear friend Silone,

Mrs. Funk called me and since we are always more or less in contact with Kartagener,[155] I called him about Darina.

He would much prefer the time *after* your return from Germany, that is, after July 7th, as he is quite busy right now and will soon be going on vacation for 14 days.

He will only be able to determine if it is necessary for her to be hospitalized after meeting with her, and possibly even later if he decides to do ambulatory surgery first. He works at both the Hirsladen Clinic and the Red Cross. The rates are about the same, approximately Fr.60. – with lab and x-rays, etc. He noted that at the same cost one would receive better care at Hirsladen,[156] and Mrs. Funk and I agree. The rates depend on one's requirements, of course, in particular when it comes to the room and whether one wants it with or without bathroom, etc.

I informed him about your concerns, which, he says are completely superfluous. That's how it goes with tradition! But he promised to provide a bill for Darina.

Since we won't be returning from Italy until around mid-July, it would be kind if Darina would not come until then. As an alternative, she could live with Mrs. Funk first and then move in with us after the hospitalization. Otherwise, we and Mrs. Funk would quarrel [over her]!

I believe that this is all you wanted to know. Kartagener sends his kindest regards and we cordially join his wishes.

Your old

Copy to Mrs. Funk.

SILONE

126

Castello, Island of Corfu
10 September 1959

Dear friend,

We have had very beautiful holidays here. The island of Corfu is one of the world's most beautiful places because it combines qualities that one rarely finds together: the clarity of the sky, very rich vegetation, friendly people and … few tourists. Unfortunately for us, but fortunately for the people who were born poor, the tourists will come: from next year Lufthansa and Air France will have flights to Corfu and it will be possible to take the cars by ferryboat from Brindisi (from 10 to 20 dollars according to the weight of the vehicle and 5 dollars per person). All of these details are for you, to exhort you to come here next year. We have already reserved our room. But I hope that we will have the opportunity to speak about that beforehand, in Rome or Switzerland. I have again worked on "our" narrative, "The Fox"; I incorporated a new chapter at the beginning, added another at the end, and some half pages here and there, so that now it is a short novel by the title *The Fox and the Camellias.*[157]

I mail this letter to Zurich, just in case, as I imagine that you are probably in Brione. I hope that you and Elsa are well.

Very cordially,
Your

I. Silone

SILONE
127

12 November '59[158]

My dear friend,

I have been three days in Geneva and one day in Zurich, where I only saw Samson (who just lost his wife, as you probably know). Sunday afternoon I phoned you twice, with no answer; then I thought that you probably were in Ticino. But your letter tells me that you are in Zurich: maybe back after a short absence? My plans: the 16th of December we will go to Tunis (for a conference at the University) and we will stay in North Africa until [Saint] Sylvester. In 1960, if I were to accept all the invitations of the Cultural Institutes, and satisfy Darina's dreams, I would travel around the world. But I will probably not go far, because I often feel very tired. *The Fox* [*and the Camellias*] abridged version, with text in Italian and German, 130 pages, has been released by Verlag Langewiesche-Brandt K.G. Hebenhausen in Munich. I am sending you a copy today. Since it is a bilingual edition and therefore, for the schools, it is quite probable that it has to be obtained by special order to receive it. The full version will only be published in the fall of 1960 by Kiepenheuer.

Friendly regards also from Darina to you and Elsa.

Silone

SILONE
128

(Postcard)
1 January 1960
Camels in the Oasis
To: [Addressee missing due to cut at right upper corner to remove stamp].
From: Djerba

Message, in French: "We have found here a colony of Jews arrived directly from Israel after Titus's destruction of the temple. They have not blended with the Arabs, but live together in perfect harmony. Summer is wonderful, the weather spring-like. Our best wishes for the New Year. Silone"

SILONE

129

11 June 1960

My dear friend,

We would have come with great pleasure to Ronchi, especially since for some weeks I have been driving a Dauphine that rides very well. But Tuesday, the 14th, we will take a plane for Berlin, where we will remain for ten days, and then we will go to Venice for three days. These are half-work half-leisure trips, but they are tiring. Will you go to Abano this year? I think that we'll be in Rome the month of July and then, like last year, we'll go to Corfu for 3–4 weeks. But we'll write you the more precise dates to see if we can possibly meet.

Good wishes for the holidays.

Cordially
Your

Ignazio

IGNAZIO AND DARINA SILONE

130

(Postcard)
25 June 1960
Berlin, Kaiser Wilhelm Memorial Church
To: Mr. Marcel Fleischmann, Villa Redena [sic], Via degli Ontani, Ronchi Apuania (Massa) Italy.
From: Berlin [Postmarked]

Message, in French: "I think that your card crossed my letter of 13 June where I spoke of your coming here. Sunday we will leave for Venice (Albergo Europa) till 2 July. Friendly regards from your Sil.
[By Darina] and from Darina."

SILONE
131

Rome
8 November 1960

Dear friend,

Albert Bolleter[159] will be able to look up the three books at the Cantonal Library; but, if he wants to have them, he must order them from an "antiquarian" bookseller and he will possibly receive them after some research. The books will be republished in Germany in two or three years.

The Fox and the Camellias has already appeared by Kiepenheuer & Witsch (Rondorferstr. 5, *Cologne, Marienburg*). I think that if you want a certain number of copies, it would be best to order them directly from the publishers; and ask them for a RABATT "discount."

Darina had to run to Dublin where her father is gravely ill and we fear his end. Because of this and other uncertainties, we do not know if we will be able to realize some travel plans to Africa.

Very cordially,
Your

I. Silone

SILONE
132

13 January 1961[160]

To explain what our long friendship has meant to me, my dear Marcel Fleischman, it may be sufficient to simply allude to the explicit sense of each of my literary works. In a few words, all that I have written thus far is nothing if not a tribute to friendship, always represented in my books as the only vital element in a landscape that is almost always arid and desolate; most often dealing with men fleeing from country, family, politics; men in danger, in jeopardy, who are saved because they meet some friends. Of course I am the first to deny that mine are *romans à clef*, in the sense that to each character represented there corresponds one in real life. However, it seems evident to me that there is a direct relationship between this vision of the human condition in our times and the author's personal experience, particularly that which he lived in Switzerland between 1930 and 1944.

Ignazio Silone

SILONE

133

IGNAZIO SILONE
Via Villa Ricotti, 36
Rome
26 June 1961

Dear Friend,

The news of the loss of Maria saddened us very much. She was an example, ever more rare and just about impossible, of an employee who, for her human qualities and honesty of character, participates in the life of a family and ends up being part of it.

Upon receiving your letter, this morning, I thought of coming to Ronchi; however, due to your decision to return to Zurich in the beginning of July, that becomes difficult for me. I will speak about it with Darina and, in case we decide to come, I'll send you a telegram to inform you and to ask you to reserve a room, for 2 or 3 days, at Villa Redenti, or in the vicinity, possibly with bath, especially since I do not go to the sea. If I come, I'll reserve the train, since I detest the Via Aurelia, especially if I am alone in the car. So, we will possibly see you soon.

Very fondly from the two of us, to you and Elsa, Lisely and Carry.

Your

Sil.

SILONE

134

8 October 1961

Dear Friend,

I waited for Martin Rich, but he did not show up. Perhaps he gave up on his trip to Italy? I remember him and would have gladly seen him, but I don't know if I could have been useful to him, since I am totally removed from the world of music, I rarely go to concerts, and the only music that I listen to is that of records that we have at home. The last Swiss doctors she[161] consulted during the recent years have always limited themselves to checking the lungs and the heart, as if there was nothing else in the body. The most distressing thing, with hypothyroid, is the lack of oxygen assimilation, which weakens and produces sleepiness. I rejoice at the good news about Jürg.

Very friendly greetings to Elsa as well, from the two of us.

Silone

SILONE

135

(Postcard)
10 January 1962
Panoramic view of Rio de Janeiro
To: Mr. Marcel Fleischmann, Plattenstr. 78, Zurich, Switzerland
From: Rio de Janeiro

Message, in French: "Here I am in this country immensely beautiful and full of contrasts.

Very cordial regards to you and Elsa. Sil."

SILONE

136

Washington D.C. 25 May [1963][162]

My dear Friend

I am writing to you from the "George Washington University Hospital" where I am being treated for a complicated condition regarding my lungs. Upon arrival with Darina in New York, April 13th, we visited several universities (Princeton, Yale, Harvard, etc.) and then we went to the South, attracted by the social question. Unfortunately, the great heat and the air conditioning quickly gave me a bronchitis that I was wrong to neglect. I carried on my active life from morning to night until the day I burned with fever. The doctors who visited me were truly alarmed: they claimed to see, in the x-rays of one lung, an abscess or something worse. After some first aid, my friends preferred that I should come here. After all, I am well accustomed to health scares. All the same, I regret having to cancel the second half of my trip (to California) and a longer stay in New York, before returning to Rome. We would have been glad to see Jürg and also Elsa, if she should still be there. But it is now very likely that as soon as I leave the hospital, we'll return directly to Rome.

During the forced inactivity imposed by illness, one easily returns to the memories of the past. You can therefore imagine, dear friend, how often and with what affection Darina and I think of you.

Your

I. Silone

FLEISCHMANN

137

Zurich
2 June 1963

My dear friend Silone,

After a short absence, I returned home to find your letter that made me very sad.

I still remember the time you spent at the Germaniastrasse when you were very fragile, but I thought that those days were long over. And now this setback!

I have forwarded your letter immediately to El [Elsa]. I am not sufficiently informed about her plans to return, but imagine that she would like to visit you if it can be arranged. I would prefer to hear from her directly how she found you and about the diagnosis and prognosis.

Getting older, we continue to believe we're still in our 40s – a big mistake! I've had to pay for this foolish belief myself several times. I am certain that you will now be more cautious, and once you are feeling better I will come to Rome to visit you. You will require a lot of rest for the time being and should not rush to get back to work right away. Maybe you could have the chance for some nice conversations.

El is much missed here. She has always been the censor of my letters and my feelings, which were often in need of her corrections. She is the calming influence here at the Plattenstrasse and when she returns, she will find some signs of my impulsiveness. I will have to straighten out many things again with her help once she is back.

Darina must be very frightened, as the lung is not easy to deal with. Hopefully yours is already well trained and recovery will occur faster than you would imagine.

You and Darina accept a warm handshake and a "see you again soon."

Your old

IGNAZIO AND DARINA SILONE

138

(Postcard)
28 August 1963
Alpine Flowers
To: [No addressee, missing envelope]
From: Zermatt

Message, in French: "Dear friend, we have come here for a convalescence, but have not had good luck with the weather. Even so, they say that the altitude always does one good. Has Elsa already returned from America? Among the discoveries of my trip there, one of the most agreeable has certainly been Jürg's transformation. I think that you can now be proud of his success. Stay healthy, and so long, your Silone.

[And by Darina] All my affectionate good wishes to you and Elsa, we'll see you soon, I hope. Darina"

SILONE

139

(Postcard)
[Undated] Postmarked 22 [illegible] 1963
Our Lady with the Child, by Giovanni Di Paolo
To: Mr. Marcel Fleischmann, Plattenstr. 78, Zurich
From: Rome

Message, in French: "Dear friend, I am no longer pressed neither for the book nor for the doctor, so I am postponing my trip indefinitely. Very cordially, Sil."

IGNAZIO AND DARINA SILONE

140

(Postcard)
3 September [No year]
Panorama of Positano
To: Mr. Marcel Fleischmann, Plattenstrasse 78, Zurich, Switzerland
From: Positano

Message, in German: "Lots of love to you and Elsa. Darina [Followed by] and S. Tranqus [by Silone].

In French: "I hope to come to Zurich in November." [By Silone].

SILONE
141

Rome
4 October '63

My dear Fleischmann,

Once more I need your advice on a delicate matter that I will briefly explain to you. You know, at least from reading the newspapers, that in Italy we are expecting a further devaluation of the currency. This is a real psychosis that has contaminated most of the people. It seems that already about two hundred billion liras have fled to Switzerland and have been converted into shares. This is partly explained by the excess of imports over exports, and partly by the capitalists' hatred of the government's leftist bent. But everyone knows that inflation means a high cost of living and the ruin of humble folks. Despite this, I did not want to touch my savings that are invested in government bonds. They have already lost some of their value and probably will lose even more. For my future material needs, I rely only on the sale of my books. Unfortunately, the Italian banks exchange the dollars and the German marks that I receive for the copyrights into liras. Therefore, to protect these fruits of my work, I was thinking that it would be advisable not to let this money come to Rome, but to leave it on deposit in a Swiss bank. I suppose that the operation is not difficult and I don't want to trouble you with it. But there are practical modalities for which I would like to hear your advice. Are you going to be in Zurich at the end of this month or during November? (I will take the opportunity to pass by Kartagener[163] for a check-up.) I hope that you are well, and also Elsa. Many greetings to both of you, also from Darina.

Your

Sil.

IGNAZIO AND DARINA SILONE

142

(Christmas card)
December 1963
Nativity Scene by Rossello di Jacopo Franchi
To: [No addressee, missing envelope]
From: Rome

Message, in French: "Dear friends, Elsa and Marcel, this year we will spend the holidays in Israel, despite the fact that the Pope has had the same idea. I have had this intention for a long time as an "honorary Jew." I am encouraged to travel by the fact that despite my 63 years, the American therapy that I am continuing is doing me a lot of good. And you? Will you be in Ticino? My visit to Zurich is postponed, for the moment, to February.

[By Darina] With all our best wishes and most affectionate regards, Darina [By Silone] and Sil."

SILONE

143

IGNAZIO SILONE
36 VIA VILLA RICOTTI
ROME
2 May '64

My 63rd birthday passed without the expected event! So much the better. It will be for another time. Until now the American therapy is very helpful to me. Darina, on the other hand, continues to have problems and I don't think that we will find a good solution. We haven't yet decided anything for our vacations, but at the end of the month we will have to run to Germany and maybe Paris. What is awful, everywhere, is the great number of tourists and cars. From this point of view Rome is already unlivable. Peaceful life is no longer a hope but a memory.

We often think about you and Elsa and wish you good health.

Cordially,
Your

I. Silone

SILONE

144

(Christmas card)
22 December 1964
Christ among the Fishermen, by George Rouault
To: [No addressee, missing envelope]
From: Rome [Based on the message]

Message, in French: "My dear friend, a short note to wish you all the good that you desire, beginning with good health, for you and Elsa. We are doing pretty well, despite the bad weather that seems to be all over, at least in Italy. We too will stay home for the holidays. And we will think about our friends. Your, Sil."

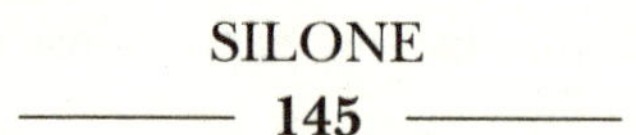

SILONE

145

IGNAZIO SILONE
VIA VILLA RICOTTI, 36
ROME
8 May 1965

My dear Fleischmann,

Thank you for your good wishes and your news. I am very sad about what you tell me of Elsa's depression. I hope that in the meanwhile she is doing better. Usually, very sensitive people suffer more during the change of seasons. I envy you for your upcoming trip to America. After being there, I have great nostalgia to return. Especially since my health is better after my stay at the hospital in Washington and my following the therapy I told you about. But, for the moment, I don't think that I will have that opportunity. Please give my regards to Jürg and his family. To you and Elsa, I wish a good trip and good health, from Darina as well.

I. Silone

IGNAZIO AND DARINA SILONE

146

(Postcard)
Christmas 1965
View of the Mazzarin Castle, Pescina (L'Aquila)
To: [No addressee, missing envelope]
From: Rome [?]

Message, in French: "Dear Marcel and Elsa, no matter where you will be spending the holidays, rest assured that my thoughts and Darina's will often be with you. We wish you all good things and especially good health and serenity. Ignazio and [by Darina] Darina."

FLEISCHMANN

147

MARCEL FLEISCHMANN
TEL. (051) 34.15.64
8032 ZURICH
PLATTENSTRASSE 78[164]
2 January 1966

My dear friend Silone,

We were very moved by your and Darina's dear message of friendship and devotion. We think of you the same way, with sincere affection. The nice card depicting your hometown made us think of many of your stories. We have been composing a letter to you both in our minds for some time, but …

After many months of being indisposed, I finally had to make the obligatory sacrifice to the gods that goes with getting older: I had an operation on my "nether regions." Dr. Wyler operated and everything went according to plan, including my weeks spent recovering at the Red Cross. The normal recovery time for a prostate operation is 2–3 months, and I am still confined to bed at times, although now luckily at home. I am dictating these lines to Elsa who is typing them up, and I don't know what I would have done without her care during this whole thing – I wouldn't have fared half as well. It's common knowledge that such procedures can affect one's mental state, but at my age, it is amazing that such positive outcomes are possible at all. During such times one thinks more about what has already happened in one's life than what is yet to come, and while I was in the hospital I had El bring me a "document" that I have carefully saved for many years. This document is the letter you wrote to me on January 13th on the occasion of my 50th birthday.[165] It is a comfort to me personally, and I also enjoy its literary qualities; I can hardly even imagine that there is another letter in all of literature that contains such warmth and artistic form. Over the years I have been both indiscreet and egotistical enough to read it aloud to friends at various occasions, and the pastor at the Red Cross, Frick, remembered meeting you. This year we are just having a small celebration for my 75th birthday, with only Kurt and Jürg, who arrives on the 7th of this month. This year as well your above-mentioned letter will be my best present.

You probably have heard that my brother Carlo died a few months ago, and you know that we were estranged. It was very difficult for me to stay true to myself and stay away from the funeral celebrations. Unfortunately, this was all happening at the same time as my operation and recovery. But I have now managed to insulate my feelings and my rational mind from one another, and this makes it possible to go on with life.

We keep hearing how excellent your new book is, and can't wait for the German translation – we are hoping to receive it from you. There are others also waiting along with us, such as the Hunzikers[166] with whom we are still very good friends.

It is terrible to watch Nettie Katzenstein's decline – she is losing her memory and is also deteriorating physically. It is now often very difficult to communicate with her – she who once was so lively. Her family and friends try to keep her occupied but she seems to be losing her will to hang on. I assume you have already heard that Fega Frisch has also died and suffered in the same way.

We recently saw Achim Wilkens and his very nice wife, after 25 years of not seeing each other. El and he heartily embraced and we spent two great days together reminiscing about old times. Achim is a Physics and Chemistry professor at the University of Cape Town. We got the impression that he would be willing to drop everything there and move back to Switzerland as soon as feasible.

Just as children leave the best for last on their plates, I have also left this news for the end: our dear El has been doing exceptionally well since the spring, and we are quite confident that her depression has been defeated. After so many unsuccessful treatments, Prof. Herbert Binswanger[167] was finally able to perform a miracle in just 14 days. His diagnosis was radically different from all of the previous ones, as was his treatment: medication instead of therapy. You can surely imagine how relieved we are.

So, I have taken up enough of your time now, but as the year draws to a close, one often has the need for intimate conversations with their nearest and dearest. And so along with this letter we send our warm and heartfelt handshake to you both.

Yours,

Marcel[168]

SILONE

148

(Postcard)
Undated [January 1966][169]
A card-size picture of the Swiss General Henri Guisan
To: *Militaire* Kdo. Ldstr. Drag. Kp 66
Hotm. Fleischmann
Bet-Restante
Zurich, 6
Germaniastrasse, 53
From: [No location given]

Message, in French: “My dear Captain, I send you my portrait so that my patriotic smile, together with your Hö.-So, can help your convalescence. Cordial but federal greetings, your Guisan.”

SILONE

149

(Postcard)
16 June 1966
United Nations Headquarters, New York City, the General Assembly Building and the Secretariat Building
To: Mr. Marcel Fleischmann, Plattenstr. 78, Zurich 32, Switzerland.
From: NYC

Message, in French: “In both weeks in N.Y. the humid heat is disagreeable. I will try to get in touch with Jürg at least by telephone. I hope you and Elsa are well. Amicably, your Sil.”

FLEISCHMANN

150

21 November 1966

My dear friend Silone,

Please excuse the typing, which is due to my age. I should have waited to thank you for the signed copy of your newest book until I was able to delve more deeply into it a second time. For now, let me just say: Elsa and I, and also Max Hunziker, to whom we gave the book as a present, are absolutely impressed by it. The honesty of your avowal – in a way, your last will and testament – shook us to the core. Every word of the 6th paragraph in the chapter "Emergency Exit"[170] has stayed with me. It is an encouragement to bear what life brings. What moves you in a universal sense touches me just as much in my small sphere.

"Due to what fateful disposition or hypersensitivity does one decide at a certain age to become a rebel!" – "Do we choose or are we chosen?" – "How is it that many people are unable to accept injustice even when it is not they but others who are affected by it?" – "Wherefrom does the sudden feeling of guilt arise when one is sitting at a table full of food while the people next door have nothing to eat?" – "And who bears the pride of persecution (or in my case, of misunderstanding) more easily than self-contempt?"

These are the kind of questions that have largely occupied my mind in the past decade. I was unable to give up my entire family in order to remain faithful to myself. Only in music do I find such things expressed the way you also express them. I wish I had the chance just once to speak to you about all of this. When we travel to Ronchi-Poveromo again next year we would like to try to visit you and Darina, even if for only one day.

In a few days we leave for Israel for several weeks. We have forgotten how to believe in miracles, but maybe there we will learn to believe again.

Elsa and I sincerely shake Darina's and your hand.

Your old

IGNAZIO AND DARINA SILONE

151

(Postcard)
End of 1966
Pompei, Villa of Mysteries, Reading of the Ritual
To: [No addressee, missing envelope]
From: Rome

Message, in French: 'My dear Friend, it did not surprise me that you enjoyed your trip to Israel. It is a wonderful country and will still remain it for a long time on the condition that they let it work in peace, and above all they allow the two or three million Jews who are still in Russia to go there, which today begins to be deemed possible, naturally not all at once. Possibly they have pointed out to you that the country's best cadres [executives, managers] are all old Russian Jews who arrived in Palestine after the 1905 pogroms. I would be happy if I could live long enough to see the Negev desert transformed into a vegetable garden (notice to what extent I am verjudet [sic]). But I have some wishes that are even more personal. For you and Elsa, dear Friends, a good 1967, a year in good health and serenity of the spirit. Your Ignazio and Darina."

FLEISCHMANN

152

Zurich
4 October 1967

My dear friend Silone,

Elsa and I are writing to you in memory of our good old friend Nettie.

Although a reporter from the NZZ [*Neue Züricher Zeitung*] was invited to Nettie's funeral, his coverage in that newspaper was quite poor and does not do justice to the amazing spirit of this woman. For this reason, Nettie's friends and colleagues from the Kinderdorf are planning to issue a small pamphlet about her and distribute it among her circle of friends. It will include contributions such as the farewell speech given by the refugees' pastor Vogt;[171] an essay by Lore Hartmann von Monakow,[172] Nettie's successor and president of the Kinderdorf, as well as notes by Dr. Wyler (vice-president) of the Israeli Wochenblatt.

All of these contributions emphasize Nettie's fine qualities as a caregiver of the refugees, and refugee children in particular. What is missing is the portrayal of Nettie's real being, her fight against all that is unjust in the world, her devotion to her distinguished husband, as well as the spiritual atmosphere she created in the Mühlebachstrasse.

When Dr. Hartmann and Georges Bloch,[173] who came up with this initiative, asked my advice about who could best take on this task, I named you, and both liked the idea. So I have taken it upon myself to contact you and ask if you would do it. Death has taken many from our circle of friends and this gives us pause.

We hold your and Darina's hands in ours from across the miles.

Yours,

Marcel Fleischmann[174]

FLEISCHMANN

153

My dear friend Silone,[175]

You of course supplied exactly what we needed [for the pamphlet]. Many, many thanks. It is so nice to know that you have such dear memories of Nettie.

Elsa's nephew, Professor Bolleter, who is currently the principal of a high school, began the translation with us last night; we are including it in the original for you, and we ask that you make any needed corrections and then approve it.

Until we hear back from you, we will be working our way through the carbon copies of the whole pamphlet with its initiators, who are due to return from abroad today.

At the moment I have nothing else to add, except to thank you again and send affectionate regards from myself and El.

Yours,

M. F.
6032 Zurich. 13 October 1967

SILONE
154

ASSEMBLEA COSTITUENTE
Rome, 20 January 1968

My dear Friend,

Darina and I have very much regretted that we were in Capri during your brother Kurt's stay in Rome. When we got home, our first concern was to phone his hotel; but unfortunately it was too late. Also, although life in Capri during winter is much more pleasant because there are very few people, we suffered a bit due to the wind and the rain. To your very friendly Christmas letter I must answer that the volume on the Abruzzi has just come out and I couldn't have given it to you sooner because it had not been published. The only news that I can tell you now is that on February 2 or 3, I will be in Zurich for one day: the next day I have to hold a conference in St. Gall (at the Museumsgesellschaft) and then in Bern. So, I hope that we'll see each other again shortly. If you need anything from Italy, write to me at once. Goodbye and lots of friendship to you and Elsa.

Tranq.

SILONE
155

Ignazio Silone
36 Via Villa Ricotti
Rome
12 March '68

My dear Friend,

Thank you very much for your letter. Although the tidings aren't happy ones, it is always preferable to know them. I am above all saddened by what you tell me about Elsa's health; but also by the rest concerning Jürg and yourself. To tell the truth, my life as well, most of the time is spent discussing doctors and tests, not so much concerning me, but Darina. She is a little better, she is calmer, she is almost sober, but weakness keeps her lying down almost all of the time; she eats very little and yet weighs twice as much as before; as a result, she avoids seeing friends and dressing appropriately; her room is in an inconceivable disorder, piles of newspapers, books, boxes of all kinds, never opened packages and letters … I don't know where I will be April 17th, but I would love to know, a few days in advance, where you and Elsa will be. I regret that the brochure about Nettie[176] hasn't yet been published. It is then very probable that it will remain only a project. In regard to my little text, I suggest that you offer it to Dr. Jakob Ragaz (Prof. Ragaz's[177] son) who is the editor of *Aufbau* (Gartenhofstrasse 7). The readership of this little weekly newspaper founded by Pastor Gerber[178] is quite different from that which will receive the brochure that Madame Dr. Hartman is handling, if it ever comes out. I hope that our future letters will be less sad.

With all my affection for you and Elsa,

Your

Sil.[179]

Ignazio Silone
36 Via Villa Ricotti
Rome
28 October 1968

My dear Friend,

What you wrote us about Elsa's health condition[180] has painfully stricken Darina and me. Here, in such cases, people think that they must look elsewhere for more capable doctors; but I suppose that in Zurich, if the illness drags on and recurs, one cannot blame the doctors. It is really the saddest thing when one doesn't precisely know what to expect. We are, of course, wholeheartedly "with you."

I have received the brochure on Nettie. It's rather slim and they could have completed the documentary part and adopted another format. That could have been a contribution to Zurich's contemporary history (a small, but valuable contribution). As it is, it's an expanded obituary.

I don't know if I wrote to you about the incident that occurred to me in August. I was on vacation, in a small mountain place in Abruzzo, and I felt well, possibly too well. One morning, I woke up at 7 o'clock and I realized that I could no longer use my left arm and leg. I didn't panic, and I myself phoned the doctor and Darina, who was in Rome, and I was taken to the hospital. I heard them formulate different diagnoses: thrombosis, embolism, arterial spasm. I was in the hospital for only three weeks, during which I recovered the use of my arm and my leg, and since then I am in convalescence. I get some injections and follow a diet. I hope that I won't have relapses and am resigned to a more moderate lifestyle. Yes, the last book, *The Story of a Humble Christian,* was well received. I will send you the French version that will come out next week (it will only be published in German in the spring of 1969).

Give Elsa our most affectionate regards.

Very amicably yours,

Silone

FLEISCHMANN

157

8032 Zurich
24 October 1968

My dear friend Silone,

I have chatted so often with you in my mind during the course of this year. I want to know whether Darina's and your health has improved. Your last letter worried us very much. I kept putting off writing to you, even though I knew that it only increased my fear of finding out unpleasant news. I really hope that I am wrong and that you, dear friend, are doing well. How are you?

We have many worries here. The frequency of El's "Dämmerkuren" has increased since the beginning of the year and the intervals of good periods in between have also gotten increasingly shorter. The electroshock treatments last year have had no effect. The two-week scheduled therapy at the sanatorium in Kreuzlingen has not helped at all and yesterday we cut it short.[181] El is now back at the Hirslanden Clinic in Zurich for another "Dämmer cure." She will most likely remain there for another ten days. What comes after that is still unclear.

Psychological pain is worse than any kind of physical illness, even for the sufferers. The only choice that remains is the one between hope and despair and the decision to bear one's allotted fate with dignity.

One bright spot that remains in our family is Jürg with his wife and children. He is coming this year in the winter as usual and will be combining business and pleasure during his visit.

Dr. [Lore] Hartmann forwarded Nettie Sutro's obituary to Dr. Ragaz – to whom, by the way, I also personally spoke about your contribution on the telephone.

I have been hearing such exceptional things about your newest book[182] and I am eagerly awaiting the German translation. Max Hunziker is among your admirers. I just recently read *Notausgang* for the second time, and sent it to the Birsingers who often ask about you.[183]

If you have the time and the inclination, would you mind sending El a few words? A sign that you are thinking of her would certainly cheer her up and do her a world of good right now. I would make sure that she would receive any correspondence from you at the right time – at the moment she is terribly despondent.

Maybe I should have put off writing you all this, but in your last letter in March you wrote that it is better to know what is going on, even when the news is not terribly pleasant.

Friedel Kinstetter is looking after me quite a bit. Your fortitude and composure are a blessing to me.[184]

Yours in fond friendship,

Marcel Fleischmann

FLEISCHMANN
158

HOTELalportoASCONA HOTELmuraltoLOCARNO[185]
10 November 1968

My dear friend Silone,

The news of your illness affected us very much. The ten years we spent together under the same roof cause us to be very interested in your fate. We wish we could be with you now to make sure that you are doing better. Luckily you understand what Jürg and the thrombosis in his eye [186]

SILONE
159

Ignazio Silone
36 Via di Villa Ricotti
Rome 00161
Verona, 29 May [1969][187]

My dear friend,

I have to go to Zurich, next June 10th to check the editing of the document filmed by the Westdeutsche Rundfunk. I would have preferred to go at the end of June, because of what I have to do here; but the person in charge of the documentary, in Cologne, cannot [meet me then] because he will be on vacation. So, I will be there on the 10th and will stay at the Hotel Urban. When I was leaving for Verona I received your letter informing me that on the 8th you will already be leaving Zurich to go to Davos. That's a real pity. On the other hand, even if I had not been pressed to return to Italy, Davos's altitude is forever forbidden to me. Be at least kind enough to leave me your telephone number in Davos with the doorman of the Urban. I will call you on the 11th.

Very friendly regards to you and Elsa.

Your

I. Silone

FLEISCHMANN

160

1 October 1969

My dear friend Silone,

We haven't heard anything from you in a long time and we know you weren't well for quite a while (but you did manage to make it to Israel we heard – that is, as we could tell from your postcard). Have you forgotten us completely?

Jürg turned 50 on September 23rd! He was very touched to receive tokens of affection from us and from our friends. In his heart he is still quite sad about how quickly his childhood went by, even if it was during a difficult time, and the beauty of his childhood stands in stark contrast to the hectic pace of his life in the US that is filled "only with business."

He was very attached to you, and often asks about you. It is quite sad that you weren't there at his celebration like our other friends were – but that is because we didn't let you know about it. Your silence is probably partly because we forgot to. Perhaps you would still like to send him your regards, and so we are including his address here: Mr. Werner J. Fleischmann, c/o Reeves International Inc., 14 Industrial Road, Pequannock, NJ, 07440, USA. In writing this to you, we know that you will not take it as our meddling in your personal affairs.

We have given dozens of copies of your last book to friends, but the response we received from our general practitioner pleased us the most: she immediately passed it on to her boss, Prof. Kartagener, because she wanted to make sure he didn't miss out on what she called one of the "smartest books" around. Maybe he has already gotten in touch with you?

We've both been doing very well since the beginning of July and we hope that we have made it through the hard times for a while. We've been here for three weeks now and haven't made any plans yet for our return.

Dora Mitzky spent a few wonderful days here with us, and we relived that whole intellectual world again (insofar as we took part in it back then) – Nettie – Erich – Toller – Frisch – Tscharner.* The thought that each and every one of them is gone is very hard to bear.

Please accept a warm handshake from both of us.

El and Marcel

*Your ears must have been burning as well.

SILONE

161

Ignazio Silone
36 Via di Villa Ricotti
Rome
14 October 1969

My dear friend,

Coming home from Zurich, where I stayed at the Hotel Urban from October 3 to 11, I found your letter of the first of this month. On that same day I wrote to you at Plattenstr., to inform you about the reasons for my imminent arrival. I was hoping very much to meet you, but my daily phone calls to your home were never answered. Did my letter of the 1st even arrive? The week I spent in Zurich was used by the Westdeutscher Rundfunk de Cologne to shoot one part of the telefilm about my life and my books. If Swiss TV, as is probable, picks up this film, which will be presented next spring, you will be able to see among the other places of my stay in Switzerland before the war (the Oprecht bookstore, the central library, la Langstrasse, the Schaffouse printing press, etc.) also your "little pension," and more precisely the Rigiplatz funicular – Germaniastr., the gate and the frontage of your former home. (It was closed and all the shutters were lowered.) We regretted your absence and I tried to recall your friendship and your Maecenatism towards numerous other people from Max Raphael to Manès Sperber, and towards less well-known but no less needy people. After October 20th, the same crew will go to Abruzzo to shoot the rest. Altogether the telecast cannot last more than 45 minutes, which is a lot. But the most delicate work, the decoupage and montage, will be done at the Cologne Studios and only God knows what will come out of it even though it is a friend who runs the whole thing.

I wanted first of all to bring you up to date on this, but I have copied Jürg's address from your letter, and I am writing to him immediately, apologizing for the delay. Very happy that you and Elsa are well, I hope it will last for the longest time possible.

Your

I. Silone

Darina is in Greece and will come back October 19.

FLEISCHMANN

162

26 October 1969

Dear friend Silone,

Thank you for your dear and detailed letter. Every line interested and pleased us greatly. By the end we felt connected to what has been going on with you and are very much looking forward to your movie. As you always said: Better late than never! And now your latest book is the crowning achievement to your long line of worldwide successes. (Hopefully Goldschmied is well.)

Thanks for writing to Jürg. He even mentioned your letter on the phone and sounded very happy about it.

Could you let us know when your movie will be released here? We could then watch it with our neighbour on our floor. Will it also be shown in the USA?

Too bad that you were in Zurich at the exact same time that we were in Ticino. We would have been so happy to see you. Perhaps your movie will make it possible for you to visit Zurich again, and so we could all see each other. We wouldn't monopolize too much of your time.

There's quite the uproar here about the theatre. I assume that you have been kept up to date about it. The directors and producers have actually managed to threaten its very existence! The regular theatre-goers are refusing to attend and the hippies can't make up for their absence.

A "Max Raphael Society" based in the USA issued an appeal to his friends and acquaintances to contact them if they have letters or other papers of his. I forwarded the appeal to Dora Mitzky,[188] who has corresponded with him. If you also have any material, please let me know.

Thank you again for your lovely letter – El especially thanks you – just recently she proudly unearthed her handwritten copy of *Il seme sotto la neve.*[189]

I don't feel deprived though, since I often take pleasure in rereading the nice letter you wrote to me for my birthday on January 13, 1941. I have no other letter as beautiful as that one.

El and I greet you and Darina warmly –

Marcel Fleischmann

SILONE

163

Ignazio Silone
36 Via di Villa Ricotti
Rome, Italy
1 November 1969

My dear Friend,

The TV can broadcast films the same day they are shot, especially the so-called current events; but may develop images and texts for months, until the right proportions are found. So it will be for the documentary about me. It will probably be broadcast in the months of February or March, in Germany, and in the month of May in Italy. Given the part devoted to Zurich (with the appearance of Max Bill, Bringolf, Hans Oprecht, Emmie Oprecht and of the … Germaniastrasse, including the Rigiplatz funicular) it is very probable that Swiss TV will pick up the documentary. I will keep you informed.

Many friendly regards to you and Elsa.

Silone

ELSA SCHIESS AND FLEISCHMANN

164

Marcel Fleischmann
8032 Zurich
Plattenstrasse 78
Tel. (051) 35.15.64
25 May 1970

My dear friend Silone,

We heard from Max Hunziker that you are planning to come to Zurich in June.

In that regard, I just wanted to let you know we will be going to Davos in June for 2 to 3 weeks where we will be spending time with the "Grillinos" – that is, as long as nothing unexpected comes up.

Since we missed you the last time you were here, it would be a shame if we don't get to see you during this visit. Unfortunately we can't push the date back (because part of our apartment is being painted at that time, etc.). We assume you are probably also tied to a certain date. But, we wanted to let you know our plans. Perhaps …

Very fondly,

Elsa and Marcel [190]

SILONE

165

Ignazio Silone
36 Via di Villa Ricotti
Rome
23 June1970

My dear Friend,

I confirm that Swiss TV will broadcast the documentary about me (and us) June 28th in the evening. Any listing, published in the newspapers, will tell you the precise time. I saw this documentary in Zurich. In spite of everything it is not too bad, except that I am like I am: old and ugly. Patience. But you will definitely be pleased with the part about you. So I venture to advise you to have "your" episode taped on the electromagnetic tape recorder. I suppose that you know how to use this very popular gadget. You can rent one in a store that sells similar items (phonographs, TV, etc.) But it has to be operated by someone who knows the technique. 53 Germaniastrasse is in the first part of the film, but not quite at the beginning. Unfortunately, you will not be able to record the images; only the text. Also, they can erase all that doesn't interest or concern you. I think that Jürg will be pleased to hear what they say about you.

I don't know if you remember Dr. Maria Walter who lives in Davos Platz Haus Gutemberg? [sic]. I think that she might enjoy watching the documentary and it would be kind of you to let her know.

Affectionately yours,

Silone[191]

ELSA SCHIESS AND FLEISCHMANN

166

Marcel Fleischmann
8032 Zurich
Plattenstrasse 78
Tel. (051) 34.15.64
30 June 1970

My dear friend Silone,

When one isn't a wordsmith, it is hard to know what to write to a famous author on the occasion of his 70th birthday.

The feelings that one has towards a dear friend with whom one spent a decade filled with very significant events, as well as harmony and mutual respect – well, they are best expressed in a very warm handshake from Elsa and me, along with all the best wishes for your good health.

Yours,

Elsa and Marcel

Love also to Darina[192]

FLEISCHMANN

167

Marcel Fleischmann
Zurich 32
Plattenstrasse 78
Tel. (051) 34.15.64
7 July 1970

My dear friend,

We saw your show on television while in Davos, and yesterday we heard a recording that El's nephew Jürg had made. – You can just imagine how intensely we relived and reconnected to those times.[193]

We were very happy both evenings and we thank you very much for the kind words you dedicated to your second home at the Germaniastrasse.

We agree with the review in the NZZ that this essential "film" deserved to have been shown during prime time rather in a late Sunday evening time slot, God knows.

Fräulein Dr. Walter was very happy that by mentioning us, you called attention to her – Jürg will surely also be very glad about this when he comes to visit Zurich soon.

You are so genuine in your movie: Silone, "just like in his book" (that expression is familiar, isn't it!) – such a clear representation of your intellectual attitude that your outer appearance seemed formed around it. El and I fondly shake your and Darina's hands.

Yours, Marcel Fleischmann[194]

FLEISCHMANN

168

Marcel Fleischmann 8032 ZURICH
Plattenstrasse 78
Tel. (051) 34.15.64
5 February 1971

My dear friend Silone,

I was very touched that you recently inquired about my – and our well-being. I was so pleasantly surprised to hear your voice that I could only get out a few stuttered words of French (which we so seldom have the chance to use). So please accept my belated written thanks for your kind phone call.

Afterwards I was sorry that I did not receive your acquaintances at our home. But, for over a year now, I have been suffering from bouts of depression, which makes it very difficult for me to make – or keep up – contact with others. I am especially sorry that I have brought this relative isolation on Elsa as well. Until two years ago she also suffered from this same affliction for long periods of time and now it almost seems as if I had taken it over from her. Because she is so familiar with this illness herself, she is of unbelievable help to me, even though she is also suffering from very painful, almost chronic sciatica. The therapy for us both: patience!

During the Christmas and New Year's holidays Jürg was in Arosa with his family as usual. His family has already gone home, but Jürg is still here. He has a lot of business to do in Europe, and then is planning to have Dr. Wyler operate on his hernia in the middle of this month at the Red Cross Hospital here. He prefers Swiss doctors and Swiss hospitals to American ones. His family is well. In terms of his business, he has had a difficult year behind him, just like everyone in America.

We celebrated my 80th birthday quietly at my brother's in Küsnacht. That day I also brought out again the letter that you sent me for my 50th birthday. It is so beautiful and unique in every way that I am including a photocopy of it here, since you probably don't remember its details. Don't you think it could be useful as a literary piece?

We are happy that we may have a chance to see Darina in March, even if the reason for her trip to Switzerland doesn't sound like a pleasant one. But hopefully you are doing well.

We hardly ever see the Hunzikers or other friends – due to the aforesaid isolation caused by my depression. At my age one tends to be rather sceptical about the future.

This letter has gotten longer than planned. So I will end with love from Elsa and your old

Marcel Fleischmann[195]

ELSA SCHIESS AND FLEISCHMANN

169

Marcel Fleischmann
8032 Zurich
Plattenstrasse 78
Tel. (051) 34.15.74
1 May 1971

My dear friend Silone,

It's your birthday today and we tried calling you all morning, to hear your voice and to wish you a happy birthday on the phone. But in vain!

Strangely, we have two different telephone numbers for you: 83.08.50 and 42.56.86. Both were either busy or there was no answer. I ended up calling information for international telephone numbers, but they claimed there was no Ignazio Silone in the Rome directory! Nor was there a Secondo Tranquilli. They also said that the telephone lines in Italy are so overloaded that it could take hours to even get a line, if it was even possible to get through at all. (Do let us know what your correct number is when you get a chance.)

Thus we have no other option than to send you our birthday greetings in writing and to talk to you on the phone some other time when we have your correct number and the lines aren't so busy. Hopefully you and Darina are both healthy, and you are enjoying the success of your excellent movie "Lucca" [sic].[196] As you know, I already sent you a postcard expressing our immediate joy and surprise about it. If it is shown again, we will watch it again.

We've had good news from Jürg, and would love to know if your movie will be shown in translation in America. If so, we want to make sure Jürg and his family know about it. Jürg has had two very trying years. He was being forced into a merger by his main English supplier, which luckily didn't happen in the end. We are very happy about that outcome, because the people involved were unpleasant, and now Jürg has his good old business back and it's running well, and he has regained his inner balance. It is not easy to compete against these unholy conglomerates these days. But he will manage until his children are out of school and they can resettle in Switzerland.

Did Darina end up not going to Geneva, or is she avoiding us? – Take care, dear friend – we are prouder than ever of you, if that is even possible.

Yours,

Elsa and Marcel[197]

SILONE

170

Ignazio Silone
36 Via di Villa Ricotti
Rome
12 January 1972

My dear Friend,

The publication you saw at the Hunzikers[198] was the initiative of the publisher Stefano De Luca, as he explains in his brief introduction. The limited printing was mainly reserved for those who, to some extent, contributed to the publication: writers, journalists, painters, lithographers. (Hunziker[199] received his copy because they utilized the facsimile of the message he wrote to me after reading *The Story of a Humble Christian.*) Those who received the lion's share are the three painters who deemed it to be in compensation for the etchings they gave "for free"; and also the publisher kept some for his personal friends.

I only received five complimentary copies and since it is a publication in Italian (not available in the bookstores, that is, not for sale) I had to face dozens of requests by people who felt entitled to it. But I readily admit that yours is a special case. As soon as I received your letter, I got on the phone in search of a copy for you and I was lucky enough to find it. (I will send it to you today by registered mail.)

I hope that your health is good and also Elsa's; and I wish for you that it remains good in the New Year. Darina also sends her very cordial greetings.

Your

Silone[200]

On the subject of books: My archive, that I will bequeath to the Pescina public library, lacks the first German edition of *Fontamara.* I searched for it through an antiquarian bookseller from Ascona: he found me many things, but not what I just mentioned. Don't you think that an antiquarian bookseller in Zurich might succeed? You could request it on the telephone giving my address; I would pay their bill at once. Thank you.

FLEISCHMANN

171

19 January 1972

My dear friend Silone,

Thank you for your words and your quick response to my last letter. We are really enjoying the book and have already read your personal contribution.[201] Your whole harrowing examination of life played itself out right before our eyes. We are glad that our Italian is better than we thought, and Elsa's nephew, Mundi Bolleter, has promised to go through the whole book with us to make sure we don't miss the finer points of the language. We sincerely congratulate you!

Fontamara. When the book was published, you sent Elsa and me a copy each with our own dedications inside. You dedicated Elsa's to her by name, but in mine you didn't write my name. Although it is not easy for me to be separated from my copy, I do think it is important that the body of work you are bequeathing to your hometown should be complete.[202] I am happy to let you have my copy, and it will be dispatched to you today. But if the dedication bothers you, just send it back, and I will look for another at a rare bookseller.

Yesterday our dear Carry Streuli passed away from old age, peacefully and without suffering. You can imagine how we are feeling right now.

Did you know that Professor Kartagener has been seriously ill for some time now? He is in Kantonsspital. His recovery is doubtful.

Warm regards from us both.

Yours,

Marcel Fleischmann[203]

SILONE

172

Albergo "Villa del Parco"
Fiuggi
13 April 1972

My dear friend,

I received here, in Fiuggi, your note concerning the German journalist Mytze. Fiuggi is mainly a city [known for its] water for kidney treatment. I, myself, do not need this treatment (kidneys are possibly my only organs in good shape), but the place is near Rome, about one hour away by car, at an altitude that is good for me, 800 metres; and surrounded by woods that give it an agreeable freshness. I have been here from the 16th of July and will stay for about ten more days. At the moment Darina is in Greece, after spending a week in Jerusalem. So then, this Mr. Mytze mainly deals with me from the political viewpoint. He visited me in Rome, and asked a lot of questions related to newspaper articles, brochures, etc., that I have not kept. I suppose that he visited Madame Oprecht and Emil Oprecht. I think that he is a respectable man. But, like all journalists, he tries to enrich his writing with the greatest number of names. He probably heard about my stay with you and will naturally want to say a bit more than what has already been written. He is now in Switzerland because the last time he wrote to me he gave me his address as Zurich, poste restante. May I give you some advice? If you want to avoid all risk of inaccuracy, imprecision and unintended misunderstandings on his part, tell him that you prefer to answer in writing to written questions (you can say that you are tired, for instance). I suppose that he would like to have the names of the political refugees who passed through the "petite pension" of Germaniastrasse from Max Raphael to Manès Sperber. Because they have published and will continue to publish approximate information on these matters, it is worth saying specific things.

I hope that you and Elsa are in good health and that the unavoidable inconveniences of aging are bearable. Above all I wish you, with all my heart, peace and serenity.

Your

I. Silone

FLEISCHMANN

173

Marcel Fleischmann
8032 Zurich
Plattenstrasse 78
Tel. (051) 34.15.64
1 May 1972

My dear Ignazio Silone,

Today is your birthday and you are in our thoughts with the memories of all of the friendly little parties we celebrated with you in the past, on May 1st at the Germaniastrasse.

Elsa and I wish you a very happy birthday, and good health until you are 80. After that, the aches and pains of old age set in and life gets more difficult. We could tell you a thing or two about that! So, until then, one should be grateful for every healthy day that fate bestows.

Gloria sent us the article from the *New York Times* about you and your work. We enjoyed reading it and were happy to see such a good photo of you. We sent the newspaper to the Hunzikers.

We are continuing to read *Dal villaggio all'Europa* and while we do we have the feeling of being with you. We are grateful to you for the book.

All in all we have had good news from Jürg and Gloria – except for the many problems associated with running a business today, and raising children.

I would love to have a nice long chat with you, but besides the previously mentioned physical complaints about getting older, I have been suffering from chronic depression, which robs one of the pleasures of so many things. Because of this, Elsa and I are not able to live as harmoniously as we would like.

Please tell Darina we say hello, dear friend, and as the Americans say: "all the best" from your old friends

Elsa and Marcel[204]

SILONE

174

Ignazio Silone
36 Via di Villa Ricotti
Rome 00161
25 June 1972

My dear friend,

Thank you for your news, even if it isn't joyful. Here, last week, we lost Nicola Chiaromonte.[205] Maybe you remember him: in 1935 he was one of the friends who visited me in Zurich; his wife, Annie Pohl, Austrian, had her mother living in Ascona for many years (Käte Pohl at the Bellaria Guesthouse), died in Toulouse in 1941. Chiaromonte was only 61 years old.[206] I did not know that Kartagener was as ill as you say. (In the archive of his practice, my file bears the N.2.) Thank you for your *Fontamara*, it is perfect and I don't need to search for it any longer. After some nice days, here it started to rain again.

To you and Elsa, my best friendly regards, and also Darina's.

Silone

FLEISCHMANN

175

Marcel Fleischmann
8032 Zurich
Plattenstrasse 78
Tel. (051) 34.15.64
7 August 1972

Dear friend Silone,

A short notice has appeared in various Swiss newspapers, stating that a Mr. Andreas W. Mytze from Berlin is looking for letters and documents addressed by you to various people during your time in Zurich from 1930 to 1944. A number of acquaintances have sent the ad to me.

It may be that Mr. Mytze will contact me directly, so I wanted to ask you how you would like me to respond regarding this matter.

We hope that you and Darina are doing well – we can say that we are, at least now and then.

Jürg and his family are doing well, and he is our ray of sunshine.

We live a rather secluded life, and thus have nothing new to report.

Warm regards,

Marcel Fleischmann[207]

FLEISCHMANN

176

Zurich
Plattenstrasse 78
To our friends and acquaintances
I have the sad duty
to inform you that my sweet
Elsa Schiess
Passed away on the 13th of January
After a serious and severe illness

Marcel Fleischmann[208]
gennaio [sic] 1973

My dear friend Silone,

"Mais la vie repare ceux qui s'aiment, tout doucement, sans faire de bruit." ["But life makes amends for those who love each other, very softly, without making noise."] With these simple words, our beloved El left us.

I thank you above all for your kind words, for, if anyone knew El's true nature, it was you, and that is of solace to me.

El suffered a great deal during her life, and I know I caused her much sorrow, and I have been castigating myself for not being more loving to her, for not trying harder. And now it is too late!

Our lives are now that much the poorer for Elsa's absence.

For Christmas I gave her a thin, lightweight bracelet engraved with these words: "El, je voudrais mourir pour voir si les anges te ressemblent." ["El, I would like to die to see if the angels resemble you."] She was startled by the word "mourir" but she loved it. Could it carry some blame?

Amid my tears, I now know why she left this world on my birthday.

Lately we had often been listening to "Resurrexit"[209] and now I will be waiting for the "Resurrexit" until the end of my days, because life without El has no meaning for me. I don't know what to do about it.

I am including the pastor's eulogy for you. I hope it will be meaningful to you.

It was good to talk with you about your memories of El.

Fond regards to you and Darina.

Yours,

Marcel

Friedel, who is now caring for me devotedly, sends her regards.

SILONE

177

Ignazio Silone
36 Via di Villa Ricotti
Rome 00161
6 March 1973

My dear friend Fleischmann,

I thought a lot about you on this sad occasion, – sad and expected and unavoidable.[210] If I had been in good health, I would have taken the plane or the train for Zurich; but for some time now, I have had to give up travelling. In the month of October I made the great effort of going to Lugano with the hopeful thought of continuing the journey to Zurich. It was an impossible project, alas; I barely had the strength to get on a wagon-lit to return to Rome. You know that the 13th of January is a sad day for me also; it is a day that reminds me of all the loved ones that I have lost. Now I have one more. If I think about all of those who have left us of late, I must admit that it is already the majority of our friends. It could be because of this that death has lost its lugubrious character and we wait for our call with less fear than before. At present I am much alone. This January 13 Darina was again in a clinic in Geneva (she learned about the news on the telephone from me); then she left for Dublin, to visit her sisters, whom she hadn't seen for a dozen years.

Regarding you, allow me to say that I am very reassured since I learned that Miss Friedel is back in the home. I have the greatest esteem for her; you couldn't be in better hands. My dear friend, let me embrace you in the remembrance of all the grief that we suffered together.

Your

Sil

FLEISCHMANN

178

Zurich
12 March 1973

My dear friend Silone,

Because of my failing eyesight, I have to write in pencil.

Your words moved me very much, and I need to tell you that I feel very close to you. I wish we lived closer to one another and could see each other now and then. We wouldn't even have to speak – the memories of the old days would fill the space between us.

You are also lonely these days, and wish you were in better health. I know just how you feel – although I have 10 years on you, and my complaints are more serious, and the rift that fate has caused in my life is unbridgeable. I feel closer to my grave than any necessary connection to daily life.

Thank you for your quiet embrace. I return it just as heartily.

Yours,

Marcel Fleischmann

Yes, Friedel is the best thing to come out of this unhappy time.

FLEISCHMANN

179

Zurich
23 March 1973

My dear lonely friend Silone,

Please find enclosed a photocopy of a letter from the department of the city of Zurich. The content speaks for itself and I would be grateful for a quick reply from you, and in connection with that request, I have another favour to ask, or rather a question.

Soon after El's death, while going through things with an acquaintance who was helping me with all of the formalities, I discovered a copy of your manuscript "Samen unter dem Schnee" [sic] in our library. In a fit of my habitual and often inappropriate spontaneity, I offered it to her as a token of El's memory. I didn't even consider that this precious document belonged to the Fleischmann family and should not be in someone else's possession. When Jürg was here, he was happy to come across this lovely memento of you. After all, he did grow up under your care and as you know, he has a very special and grateful relationship with you. But now, to the matter at hand:

I can give the acquaintance in question other lovely things as keepsakes, and therefore, under no circumstances give her your manuscript. But the question is: how do I tell her this? And so I wanted to ask you if you could help me out by slipping in a sentence in your reply to me that states something along the lines of how happy you are to know that this manuscript will always remain in our family, since you spent so many important years of your life with us.

I am embarrassed to include such specific details in my request, but they serve only to explain myself to you, and if this is at all awkward for you, please disregard it. Dr. Landau also asked me for the booklet *Dal villaggio all'Europa* as well as for a photo of you. I have an excellent one that you gave me in June 1961. You are sitting at your desk leaning on your arms with your library behind you. It is the best picture of you that I know and I would like to give it to him. And so I would like to ask you if it would be all right to leave out the picture (that I and some of your other friends don't find very flattering) that is in *Dal villaggio all'Europa.*

I have the last sentence of your most recent letter stuck in my head: "Dans le souvenir de toutes les paines que nous avons soufferts ensemble." ["In memory of all the sorrows that we endured together."] How true and beautiful at once, as happiness and suffering are, after all, the two ends of the spectrum of human life. I do believe though that you and we have experienced more happiness than sorrow.

You, reticent friend, you – your last lengthy letter made me very happy, and I would like to especially thank you for it. Don't take the aches and pains of old age too seriously, for it is enough that I do, with my 83 years, and it is particularly hard now that El is gone. When you write to Darina, please say hello to her from me. I am also supposed to send you much love from Friedel Kinstetter, who is taking very good care of me.

Your old Fleischmann[211]

FLEISCHMANN

180

8032 Zurich
1 May 1973

My dear friend Silone,

Today is your birthday and I simply want to say that I am with you in spirit and that now, without El, I think back more than ever to the wonderful years we spent together and am so grateful for them.

From your last letter it sounded that you are not doing very well health-wise, and I wish that that were not the case. I would be happy to hear that, in the meantime, things have improved.

I have turned into a melancholic person who has lost the will to carry on. Dear Friedel keeps me going, and won't allow me to do "anything stupid," as she calls it.

Please excuse my writing in pencil – but it matches my mood. I embrace you warmly and that expresses everything I feel for you.

Marcel Fleischmann[212]

FLEISCHMANN

181

8032 Zurich
5 July 1973

Dear friend Silone,

Please excuse the pencil – it is easier on my eyes.

When you last wrote to me, you weren't feeling well at all and said that you were only able to board the train to Rome in Lugano with difficulty.

Since then I have been worried about you; please write, even if only two words, to let me know how you are doing.

Perhaps it is also your connection with El that increases my natural interest in you. When most friends have already had to go – we hold on to the few that remain that remind us of the unforgettable good old times.

I myself have too many age-related complaints, and would be happy if fate would soon reunite me with El. I live a very lonely life and reject every visit that could distract me from it. The animals, when they are old and sick, leave the herd and withdraw into solitude.

I assume that you received a catalogue of the exhibit in the Helmhaus about the literature of exile during World War II. Your manuscript "Samen unter dem Schnee" [sic] revealed to me both your admirers and those who are jealous of you.

My family in the USA is doing well, even though the dollar crisis is not favourable to importers. But at least their health is good.

My brother Kurt underwent surgery a few weeks ago for oesophageal cancer and his convalescence sounds very difficult and his prognosis is also not good.

Dear friend, I hope that I haven't taken advantage of you by going on and on here, and I greet you and Darina fondly.

Your very old
Fleischmann

FLEISCHMANN

182

13 January 1975

My dear friend Silone,

I wrote to you on August 16 and on September 24 – by registered mail – So the letters must have arrived by now, despite the postal service debacle. – I can somewhat understand that you didn't want to respond to my questions and problems, but the fact that you haven't even sent a friendly or comforting word, well, that *hurts*.

I am writing on the anniversary of El's death, which is both my birthday and generally a day of sorrow, as dear Friedel, whom you always held in high regard, is in the hospital. She underwent an operation in August for breast cancer, which has metastasized and recently made another operation necessary.

What have I done to make you deem me unworthy of communicating with? I wish I knew. Did I forget to ask how you are doing? Are you sick? But then Darina would have probably let me know if that were the case.

Please let me know if I truly have become an expendable former friend that you have simply put on a shelf, and ended our shared connection – so late in my life, now at age 85. Can this really be so? – Do also let me know *how you are doing.*

I will wait to send this letter to you until Friedel is back from the hospital – since I am basically bedridden – which is also why I am writing in pencil – I will let you be the judge of my letters. I shake your and Darina's hands and add Friedel's kind regards to mine.

Yours,

Marcel Fleischmann[213]

SILONE

183

Ignazio Silone
36 Via di Villa Ricotti
Rome 00161
4 February 1975

My dear Fleischmann,

I regularly answered all of your letters, and I am answering also your last one with the sad news of Miss Friedel's illness. I hope that by now she is doing better. I naturally keep track of everything concerning you through other friends who have some connections with Zurich, such as, for instance, Mrs. Gabriella Maier. I know that you are at an age when one must always be careful, and am delighted that your physical strength is always good. Darina is in the Orient, first in New Delhi, then in Hong-Kong, and now in Tokyo. Of course she thinks about her friends and also about you. You should never have doubts about our loyalty. We think about you often. With the same feelings, we shake your hand. Very friendly regards.

Your

Silone

Best regards to Miss Friedel.

SILONE
184

(Postcard)
7 May 1975 [Postmarked]
Saint Mauro Reading a Book, by Pietro Perugino
To: Marcel Fleischmann, Plattenstr. 78, Zurich 32, Switzerland
From: Rome

Message, in Italian: "I reciprocate best wishes for long life, serenity and peace, Silone."

FLEISCHMANN
185

My dear friends Silone,

What a lovely surprise to hear your dear voices once again! Thank you very much for calling. – Unfortunately it was a bit hard to understand you and so my replies may have been a bit off. But next time it will surely go better.

I tend to think that our friends' devotion to us (and ours to them) is the best gift one can receive in old age. That's why I was so happy about your call, and was even somewhat confused by the unexpected gift.

If I understood correctly both of you are in relatively good health, and one should not expect more than that at our age. Our 10-year age difference, dear friend Silone, is quite apparent when it comes to the numerous ailments I am suffering from and can only just barely deal with; my mental and physical difficulties seem to be trying to outdo one another.

Luckily, despite my eye problems, I can still read, although usually I am laid up in bed while doing it. I've recently been reading autobiographies by Casals[214] and Rubinstein.[215] Such opposites! Casals is modest, sensitive, creative and noble, while Rubinstein is self-centred, brash, and embarrassing. If you haven't read Casals' book, you really should.

Friedel and I have both been battling a nasty flu, but she is finally feeling a bit better.

I didn't put a date on this letter because I have been writing it in stages. (Today is April 1st.) I wish you, my dear Tranqus, a very happy 76th birthday on May 1st – and Friedel wishes you the same. As you so often said when you lived at the Germaniastrasse: "better late than never" – I now say: "better too early than too late."

Jürg and his family are doing well, as is his business, which is no small feat given the long economic depression.

Even though I'm tired now, it was refreshing to chat with you both a bit.

With affectionate greetings, from my dear Friedel as well.

Your very old,

Marcel

I think of you whenever I read about political events in Italy in the NZZ.
Aprile [sic] 1976[216]

Additional Letters Not Included in This Volume

Three additional letters, dated 31 December 1972, July 1974, and 15 August 1974 are only found in the archives of the Fondazione Filippo Turati, in Florence. Its president, Dr. Maurizio degl'Innocenti, kindly shared them with me but could not grant me the right to publish them. Therefore, we agreed that I would merely write about them.

In the first one, (31 December 1972), Fleischmann thanks Silone for a telegram he received for the holidays and informs him that both he and Elsa are not in good health and are suffering from chronic depression. Elsa is being treated for it at the hospital in Männderdorf.

The second one (July 1974) is a very long letter. Marcel vents his disappointment for a tort he feels he has suffered from his son. He is obviously upset and, contemplating the end of his life, would like to safeguard what he deems to be his treasured possessions by donating them to those who are capable of appreciating them.

In the third one (15 August 1974) he apologizes to Silone for having "ambushed" him with the previous letter. He says that Silone can vent about injustice in his books, whereas he had to burden a dear friend. He adds that his son is apparently regretting his mistake and his daughter-in-law, Gloria Fleischmann, wrote him an affectionate letter.

Afterword

I began this work with the belief that epistolary writings are essential to our understanding of the letters' authors and history. Acting as a counterweight to the negative portrayals of Silone by some in recent years, and the previous limited knowledge of Fleischmann simply as Silone's Swiss "Maecenas" and a grain merchant turned art dealer, their correspondence provides the opportunity for more objective and much greater understanding. The personality of the two men clearly emerges from their words and their shared concept of freedom, friendship, and goodness.

Readers of the letters will have noticed how the correspondence of the first decade, beginning with Silone's letter recalling the providential coincidence of Marcel's birthday with the Abruzzo earthquake, revealed his *forma mentis.* The words he writes to his friend draw a limpid image of the man he so deeply admires. Birthdays, he says, "enable meditative souls to reassess their own spiritual lives" and, in the current "sad times," when "the spiritual balances of individuals so often end in disastrous 'deficits' and failures," Marcel's life stands out as "the example of a life that humanizes and harmonizes itself ever more each day."[1] Marcel is the man he hopes to become himself, perhaps by the end of his life. This letter mentions the approaching first anniversary of Silone's living at the Kleine Pension. Ten years later, writing from Davos where he is confined, he laments having to be away from "home" and tells Marcel that if he were to describe what his generosity meant to him, he would have to write "a resurrection narrative."[2]

It is important to recall these letters because they reveal the bond of friendship that united the two men and also their nature. The rest of the correspondence documents the precarious conditions that prevailed before, during, and after World War II and their impact. For instance, in one of his letters Silone writes that under the present conditions, "It is not enough to respect the law; it is also necessary to keep the good will of the police" because, by simply giving hospitality to someone like him one could easily "attract some of their chicanery."[3]

This comment brings to mind Bertolt Brecht's *Exile Dialogues*, where Ziffel and Kalle pointedly remark that the perception of Switzerland as "a country famous for the freedom everyone enjoys" is an illusion. In fact, the clauses that the country added in 1933 to its more liberal laws of the past deeply changed its stance regarding the admittance and treatment of refugees.

As Palmier notes, "Communist and political activists in general, were considered damaging to a good understanding with Hitler's Reich [...] Placed under police surveillance, these refugees were forbidden to practice any kind of activity, while they did not receive permanent residence permits and were always under the threat of expulsion. All political refugees were questioned about their activities [...] and their means of existence."[4] Freedom of expression was obviously curtailed. This silence, imposed on supposedly free men in a free country, was quite different from the *silence* that Silone, Marcel, and Turoldo yearned for, as indicated earlier in this work.

During the decade 1934–44, although Silone resided at 53 Germaniastrasse, he was often away for health or political reasons. His letters record his movements and the hardships he faced. The correspondence of the post-war years offers insight into the activities that he engaged in, his election to the Assemblea Costituente, his disappointment with the Italian political situation, his dedication to cultural initiatives such as the founding of *Tempo Presente* with Nicola Chiaromonte, and especially his literary production, comprising novels, essays, and a new play. Of particular interest, especially to scholars, are the letters where Silone speaks about his books and his decision to donate his archives to his hometown of Pescina.

As he travels, he records his impressions of the places he visits to share them with his friend and, in so doing, he also allows the reader to enjoy his descriptions and to learn about his perception of the places he visits. For instance, writing in 1966 he expresses his enthusiasm about America, the country whose offer of asylum he rejected during the war for patriotic reasons.

Silone never fails to write to Fleischmann about his work and sends him copies of his books as soon as they come out. His friend receives them with great interest, immerses himself in them, and shares his impressions with Silone and their friends. His literary sensitivity, as a reader and also as a writer, does not go unmentioned by Silone. In his comment on one of Marcel's letters describing a visit to the Nuremberg cemetery, he compliments his friend and encourages him to write more of such letters, suggesting that he should follow the example of Madame de Sévigné. In the same sentimental vein, when visiting the places they had known together, Silone shares his feelings with Marcel. In Vienna, for instance, his fond memories of the past are overwhelmed by the impression of its present decadence.

The many postcards that he and Darina sent to their friends are similarly valuable. As they were evidently chosen with great care, their artistic and cultural importance should not be overlooked. For instance, the one of "Roma sparita"[5] opens the readers to the artistic rendition of nineteenth-century Rome by Ettore Roesler Franz, and the ones of Abruzzo introduce them to the wonders of Silone's region and to a cultural patrimony that is still insufficiently known.

Fleischmann's letters, besides revealing the affection and admiration he has for Silone as a man and a writer, show his attachment to his family and the generous hospitality he offered to so many. A mere look at the names he mentions – the *crème de la crème* of the artistic community – offers insight into the atmosphere that prevailed at the Kleine Pension both during the first decade, when it welcomed artists and intellectuals who needed a place where they could find safety and understanding, and after the war, when it became a place where friends could reconnect and enjoy their host's gift of enduring friendship.

Marcel's letters also reveal his profound concern for Elsa's depression, his distress at having to leave the family firm, his sorrow at his friends' aging and suffering, and at having to see them die. The words he writes about the physical deterioration of Nettie Sutro and her death are exemplary in this regard. From Silone he derives the feeling of being completely understood and appreciated, and he cherishes the attention he receives. The famous letter Silone wrote to him in 1941, the dedication to him of his only novel set in Switzerland, the articles that feature the years Silone spent at the Kleine Pension, and the televised segments that revisit that same period – all these are a source of great pride to him and a consolation in his final years.

While these writings are compelling, the images of the men appear in greater focus when the content is more personal. Of particular importance in this regard are the letters Silone writes recalling his first meeting with Marcel; his arrival at the Kleine Pension; the hospitality that helped him recover both physically and spiritually while also benefiting Gabriella; his enduring admiration and affection for Marcel and his family; his participation in the happy and sad events in his friend's life; his repeated desire to share more time together – in silence; his writing from the Swiss prison to send Christmas gifts to those he loves; his describing his confinement as an occasion to realize how much others care about him; his love for Jürg; his concern for Elsa's health; his steady words to assuage Marcel's existential angst – and, above all, his willingness to let his feelings show despite his notoriously reserved nature.

Silone's affection is also shared by Darina. Upon her return to Rome and her marriage, she writes long letters describing her efforts to create a new, welcoming home so that Silone can have the serenity he needs and Fleischmann and Elsa can soon come to visit. She also shares her impressions of post-war Italy and contrasts the air of freedom that reigns with the oppressive climate she had experienced in 1941. During the following decades she joins Silone in expressing an ongoing desire to keep in touch and find ways to spend some time together. Elsa and Marcel reciprocate with similar affection.

There are only a few letters from Darina and Elsa, and as such it is hard to discern some of the less evident aspects of their personalities. At times Darina does mention her frustration at having to earn a living doing work that she does not find intellectually rewarding and also comments on Silone's difficult temperament. And when Elsa feels overwhelmed by the many emotional demands that her family's problems are making on her, she too shares her anguish with her friends. These scant details, while not terribly significant, are sufficient to discourage any perception of the two women as being "too good to be true."

Marcel's positive attitude towards all the people he mentions is certainly noteworthy. In all the letters there are only three exceptions: when Schmid advises him not to send money to Polgar, he calls him a "parasite"; when he tells Silone that Ivan Matteo Lombardo should not trust Dr Rosenstein; and when he regrets having hosted Hardekopf, who refuses to leave the Kleine Pension as it is being evacuated.

Silone, on the other hand, only expresses some contempt for Dr Carlo following the break-up between the brothers, mentions that his friend has often been deceived, and makes a disparaging comment about the Snia Viscosa project. His words and his tone are otherwise always measured.

Both friends reveal a certain sense of humour. Silone is amusing when he writes his "bruillon," attributing it to the Papal Nuncio and, with a mixture of hyperbole and irony, re-dimensions the importance of Dr Carlo. His card depicting General Guissan must also have caused his ailing friend to smile. Marcel, on the other hand, only tries to be funny with his comment about the nuns and the monastery, and in his two letters about the ownership of the razor.

Even as readers learn a lot about the events and the lives of the two men, they are left to speculate about what is not mentioned. For instance, although Fleischmann constantly boasts about his son's successes in America he does not write about the business crisis that caused the loss of the Kleine Pension. Also, while he celebrates Jürg's marriage to Jane Cook for weeks and writes words of praise about the bride, there is no mention of the end of the marriage. It is possible that he wrote other letters that we do not have (since it was Jürg who kept what we do have), but it is also in keeping with his character that he would follow Silone's suggestion that they should discuss painful events "a viva voce." This is in fact what he says he would rather do when mentioning Tscharner's agonizing death.

Most surprising about Silone is that while he writes about the loss he suffered in the 1915 earthquake on several occasions, he never mentions the loss of his brother Romolo, who died on 27 October 1932, the year after Silone and Marcel met, and the year before Silone moved to the Kleine Pension. Given this proximity, one would have expected that he would share his sorrow, as he did in recalling the other tragic event, but perhaps the wound was too fresh to put it into words.

In the *Colloqui*, and also in her recollection of the last hours of her husband's life, Darina explains that Silone blamed himself for his brother's death and was never able to speak about it.[6] In fact, he did write about Romolo's arrest and torture in *Emergency Exit*, but did not say much about the last years of his life. He was then writing *Fontamara* and was excited about his work, had his tumultuous affair with Aline Valangin, broke his relationship with Bellone, was expelled from the Communist Party, and suffered all sorts of hardship: emotional, financial, and physical. His inability to secure Romolo's release or at least provide for his basic material needs evidently caused him both suffering and remorse. But his reticence does leave this chapter of his life to be interpreted by others. As with his involvement with Bellone, it raises questions about his character that require a suspension of judgment and acceptance of Darina's suggestion that, given the times and circumstances in which the man lived, one needs to give "un senso più ampio alle cose." That is, one can only understand him by placing everything in a broader, deeper context.

Apparently Silone did not burden his friend with the specific recollection of this critical period of his life; he also did not mention all the work he did during the war to assist those who wrote to him from internment camps, nor did he mention his interaction with Allen Dulles for the sake of the Italian people. Upon his return to Italy, even when he could have boasted about the recognition he eventually enjoyed, the prestigious posts he was offered, and the prizes he was awarded, he did not. In fact he did not even mention his collaboration with Luce d'Eramo and the importance of her critical volume. Writing to Marcel, he continued to profess his unwavering affection, his nostalgia for the Swiss years, and his desire to meet again.

As we ponder this correspondence and the value that its positive messages represent for posterity, we must be mindful that both Silone and Fleischmann recognized their own shortcomings and repeatedly wrote about them.

Even though we do not have all the letters that the Silones and their friends exchanged, what Jürg and Gloria Fleischmann safeguarded allows us to see each of these remarkable individuals in a clearer, more objective light. Now that the writers are gone, the letter Darina sent to Jürg in 1981 upon returning from a visit to Marcel stands as an epilogue and as evidence that, as she believed, life can indeed be an "ethical adventure."

When she visited Marcel at the Belvoir rest home to remind him of Silone's and her enduring gratitude, he had just celebrated his ninetieth birthday and she was seventy-four and in poor health. Even so, she was still planning to write a biography of Silone. Her plan was not realized, but as readers think about Silone and Marcel in the future, it is hoped that they will find this correspondence to be both informative and insightful.

Notes

Preface

1 Previous works include: *Ignazio Silone: Beyond the Tragic Vision* (Toronto and London: University of Toronto Press, 2000) (Fontamara Prize), hereafter, ISBTV; "Ignazio Silone" and "Fontamara" in the *Encyclopedia of Italian Literary Studies*, ed. Gaetana Marrone (New York and London: Routledge, 2006); and *Simbolismo e ironia nella narrativa di Silo*ne (L'Aquila: Premio Internazionale Letterario "Ignazio Silone," 1991).

2 Darina Silone transferred the original archival material and other belongings to the Fondazione di Studi Storici Filippo Turati, Florence, 23 September 1985. See www.pertini.it/turati/a_Silone.html. Then, in 2000, to mark the centenary of Silone's birth, she donated copies of the archival material, some artwork, and other possessions to the Centro Studi Ignazio Silone. See www.Silone.it/node/93.

3 Esposito and Biondi are the authors of several books and essays on Silone and his work.

4 Rare exceptions are noted.

5 Credits for the German translation are at the end of the Editorial Note.

6 Letter dated 5 April 1981. Gratefully received from Anthony Fleischmann, with his permission to quote.

7 Wilmarth Sheldon Lewis, "Editing Private Correspondence," *Proceedings of the American Philosophical Society*, 107, 4 (August 1963): 289.

8 *Epistolario di Giacomo Leopardi*, ed. by Prospero Viani (Naples: Giuseppe Marghieri, 1860).

9 *Antonio Gramsci Epistolario*, ed. by David Bidussa et al. (Rome: Treccani, 2011).

10 *Lettere dei condannati a morte della Resistenza italiana (8 settembre 1943- 25 aprile 1945)*, ed. by Piero Malvezzi and Giovanni Pirelli (Turin: Einaudi, 1952).
11 The handwriting is the same as the one found in Elsa Schiess's application for a permit to travel to the United States.
12 The first, undated postcard brings regards from Silone's companion, Gabriella Meyer. Most of the others are written by Darina and signed by her and Silone.

Introduction

1 I refer to the long controversy, discussed later in this work, regarding Silone's letter to Guido Bellone and his alleged role as a fascist informer.
2 The novelist and literary critic. Born Lucette Mangione (1925–2001). Author of *L'opera di Ignazio Silone: Saggio critico e guida bibliogafica* (Milan: Mondadori, 1971). Hereafter LdE.
3 Quoted by Pugliese, ALIS, 144. See ALIS, 144–6, for Pugliese's excellent synthesis of Silone's manifesto.
4 A fund was established at Dwight Macdonald's initiative. See Clement Greenberg's letter to Silone, 19 August 1940, at the archives of the Centro Studi Ignazio Silone.
5 Maria Nicolai Paynter, ISBTV, 183–213, and "Dal personaggio all'autore: Tendenze degli studi siloniani dell'ultimo decennio." Trans. into Portuguese by Kátia D'Errico as "Do personagem au autor: Tendências dos estudos silonianos da última década." *Ignazio Silone: Ieri e oggi / Ignazio Silone: Ontem e hoje*, ed. by Patricia Peterle (Niteroi, Rio de Janeiro: Editora Comunità, 2010), 87–97.
6 The symposium was jointly hosted by Hunter College and the Italian Cultural Institute, 21–3 October 1998. The honorary chair was Darina Silone. The keynote speaker was Giuseppe Mazzotta. Other speakers were: Allen Mandelbaum (honoured guest); Mario Aste, Liliana Biondi, Gigliola De Donato, Maria Grazia Di Paolo, Gabriele Erasmi, Paolo Fasoli, Ernesto Livorni, Eileen Anne Millar, Maria Nicolai Paynter, Alfonso Procaccini, Gaetana Marrone Puglia, Judy Rawson, Luciano Russi, Vanna Gazzola Stacchini, William Weaver, and Giuseppe Di Scipio, who delivered the summation.
7 Interview by Liliana Biondi, *Il Tempo*, Speciale Cultura, 1 December 2001.
8 Ignazio Silone, *And He Hid Himself*, trans. by Darina Tranquilli (New York and London: Harper & Brothers, 1945), vi. Also see *Ed egli si nascose*, ed. by Benedetta Pierfederici (Rome: Città Nuova, 2000), 120, and Silone's note to the reader.

9 Carlo Levi, *Cristo si è fermato a Eboli* (Turin: Einaudi, 1945), trans. by Frances Frenaye as *Christ Stopped at Eboli: The Story of a Year* (New York: Farrar, Straus and Giroux, 1947); Ennio Flaiano, *Tempo di uccidere* (Milan: Longanesi, 1947), trans. by Stuart Hood as *The Short Cut* (Marlboro,VT: The Marlboro Press, 1992).

10 Ignazio Silone, *Fontamara*, trans. by Gwenda David and Eric Mosbacher (Harmondsworth, Middlesex: Penguin Books, 1938), 235.

11 Understood in lay terms as an echo of the medieval imitation of Christ.

12 Pope Celestine V, born Pietro Angelerio dal Morrone (1215–96). He was elected on 5 July 1294, and abdicated on 13 December of the same year. He was canonized on 5 May 1313. He was unable to reconcile his administrative duties and the power struggles he had to face with his desire for an ascetic Christian life.

13 In *Ignazio Silone. Romanzi e Saggi*, ed. by Bruno Falcetto (Milan: Mondadori, 1999), vol. II: 1607–39. Hereafter, ISRS.

14 Added in place of an illegible word.

15 The Roman emperor Flavius Claudius Julianus (Julian the Apostate, c. 331–63) supposedly cried out "Viciste Galilee" as he was dying, recognizing his error in rejecting the tenets of Christianity. The piece was written in French and bears the date "December 1942." Published by permission of the Centro Studi Ignazio Silone.

16 Turoldo gives this title to one of his collections: *Lo scandalo della speranza* (Milan: G.E.I. Grandi Edizioni Italiane, 1984).

17 LdEIS, 579.

18 See S 25.

19 See Giovanni Casoli, *L'incontro di due uomini liberi: Don Orione e Silone* (Milan: Jaka Books, 2000). Hereafter, DOeS.

20 *Luce d'Eramo* IGNAZIO SILONE, ed. by Yukari Saito (Rome: Castelvecchi, 2014). Hereafter, LdEIS.

21 *Un dialogo difficile: Sono liberi gli scrittori russi?*, ed. by Ignazio Silone and Ivan Anissimov (Rome: Opere Nuove, 1958). Also, "A Troubled Dialogue," trans. by Darina Silone, *Encounter* (June 1957): 60–7.

22 David Bidussa, "Dialogato per un rinnovamento socialista. Un carteggio degli anni Trenta tra Ignazio Silone e Angelo Tasca," *Annali del Centro di ricerca Guido Dorso* (Avellino: Edizioni del Centro D'Orso, 1986). Hereafter ISAT.

23 Margherita Pieracci Harwell, *Un cristiano senza chiesa e altri saggi* (Rome: Studium, 1991).

24 Ernest L. Bergman and Richard T. Hall, "Switzerland in World War II: Its Defense – Its Survival – Its Refugees and Internees," *Tell*, 38, 9 (March 2012): 15.

25 The art historian Max Raphael (1889–1952). In 1940 he was interned in the Gurs concentration camp, and in 1941 was transferred to Camp Des Miles. That same year he reached the United States, where he lived until his death by suicide.

26 First published in Maria Nicolai Paynter, PVSL, 24. Literal rendition.

27 F 15 and F 18; S 16.

28 Typewritten, 17 December 1974, signed "Grandpa Marcel." Quoted at greater length in the section "Marcel Fleischmann and Elsa Schiess." From "Marcel Fleischmann," by kind permission of Anthony Fleischmann.

29 David Maria Turoldo, "A Silone," PVSL, 10. In English, ISBTV, 10. The late Allen Mandelbaum kindly helped me translate these verses.

30 S 1 and S 11. For Marcel's birthday in 1937 Silone expresses a similar affection and admiration.

31 DOeS, 2–3, 106–7, 109, 117–19. Letters dated 29 October 1916; 11 February and 15 May 1917; and 29 July 1918.

32 Michele Dorigatti and Maffino Maghenzani, *Darina Laracy Silone: Colloqui* (Zevio, Verona: Perosini Editore, 2005), 68 and 81. Hereafter, *Colloqui.*

The loan afforded the Silones the possibility of living at the Hotel Plaza for two years. At the beginning of 1949 they finally went to live in an apartment at Via di Villa Ricotti 36 where they resided for the rest of their lives.

33 See the letter from the Hotel Plaza, S 48, and also S 88 from Via di Villa Ricotti.

34 The Italian conductor Arturo Toscanini (1867–1957).

35 The Austrian/Swiss musicologist Willi Reich (1898–1980).

36 See F 147, F 162, and F 168.

37 S 115.

38 Nettie Sutro (born Nanette Gerstle: 1889–1967) was Silone's friend and German translator. See the Jewish Women's Archive where her work on behalf of "nearly ten thousand refugee children in Switzerland" is remembered, together with other remarkable accomplishments: http://jwa.org/encyclopedia/article/Sutro-Katzenstein-nettie.

39 S 155.

40 Even as Darina acknowledged that Silone had a complex and at times difficult character, she also noted, both in her letters and her comments in general, how he would send her "silent" love messages by various means, and she recorded the tenderness he showed her even as he was dying in "Le ultime ore di Ignazio Silone." See *Severina* (Milan: Mondadori, 1981), 167–82.

41 S 19.

42 S 24.
43 See the "Bruillon" following S 26.
44 S 30.

Four Remarkable People

1 Giulio Raimondo Mazzarino (1602–61) succeeded Cardinal Richelieu as the chief minister of France under Louis XIII and XIV. His prominence left an imprint on the life of Pescina. A museum and the main square are named after him.
2 Quintus Poppedius Silo was a Marsican leader whom Silone admired. In the Social War of 90 BC, he fought against the Romans, ending the resistance only when the Romans passed the *Lex Julia*, granting citizenship to the conquered subjects. Ignazio, for St Ignatius of Loyola, was chosen "to add a Christian name to a pagan surname."
3 Ignazio Silone, "Visit to a Prisoner," *Emergency Exit*, trans. by Harvey Ferguson, II (New York: Harper and Row, 1968). Also, ISBTV, 24–47.
4 *Fontamara*, Meridian Classics edition, 23. Also see ISBTV, 73–167, on Silone's narrative style.
5 See also DOeS, 102–7, and Giulia Paola Di Nicola and Attilio Danese, *Silone, percorsi di una coscienza inquieta* (L'Aquila: Fondazione Ignazio Silone, 2006), 85–97. Hereafter SPCI.
6 DOeS, 114–15.
7 Ibid., 119.
8 See ISRS, I: lxxvi–vii, and ALIS, 80–1.
9 Posted in the Centro Studi museum. Also see *Quaderni Siloniani* (Jan. 1998). The entire issue is dedicated to Romolo Tranquilli.
10 A note written to Mussolini by Chief of Police Bocchini informs the Duce that Silone, "one of the communist leaders," is trying to meet with Bellone: "In via assolutamente riservata informo poi la E.V. che l'ispettore generale di P. S. Comm. Guido Bellone ha ricevuto da Basilea da Tranquilli Secondino – uno dei capi dei comunisti – un telegramma che gli preannuncia la sua venuta in Italia" [I inform Your Excellency, in strict confidence, that the Inspector General of Police, the Commissioner Guido Bellone received a telegram from Basel from one of the communist leaders announcing his coming to Italy].
11 See www.amici-silone.net/cronologia. Hereafter, *Amici*.
12 The French novelist, essayist, art historian, and Nobel laureate Romain Rolland (1866–1944), and the French novelist, communist, and pacifist Henri Barbusse (editor of *Le Monde*) (1873–1935).

13 See ALIS, 84–91, regarding Romolo's arrest. Silone's comments about his brother's death are quoted in SPCI, 229.
14 See p. 28, where the letter is quoted at length.
15 See ALIS, 95.
16 The chief of the fascist police, Guido Bellone (1871–1948). Following the 1915 earthquake he was in Pescina assisting the survivors. He might have met Silone at that time. See Documento 1, Archivio Centralle dello Stato, Interno, Direzione Centrale Amministrazione Civile Terremoti (1908–17) Busta 201, found by Diocleziano Giardini and quoted by him in *Quaderni Siloniani,* 1–2 (2000): 10.
17 The letter, without an addressee, is handwritten and signed "Silvestri." See Dario Biocca and Mauro Canali, *L'informatore: Silone, i comunisti e la polizia* (Milan: Luni Editrice, 2000), 26–7. Hereafter, SCP. For my English translation see ISBTV, 14–15.
18 The strongest arguments are found in SCP; in Giuseppe Tamburrano, *Il "caso" Silone* (Turin: UTET, 2006); and Giuseppe Tamburrano, Gianna Granati, and Alfonso Isinelli, *Processo a Silone. La disavventura di un povero cristiano* (Rome: Piero Lacaita, 2001). Also see: Maria Moscardelli, *La coperta abruzzese* (Rome: Aracne, 2004), and her well-argued rebuttal of the accusations in www.amici-silone.net; and Ottorino Gurgo and Francesco de Core, *Silone. L'avventura di un uomo libero* (Venice: Marsilio, 1998). For contributions in English, see Stanislao G. Pugliese, ALIS, 295–330, and Michael P. McDonald, "Il caso Silone," *National Interest* (Fall 2001): 77–89.
19 Mimmo Franzinelli, "Sull'utilizzo (critico) delle fonti di polizia," *Percorsi Storici,* 0 (2011).
20 Matteo Collura, "Luce d'Eramo, l'ultima difesa della spia," *Corriere della Sera* (8 March 2001): 37.
21 Christopher Hitchens, "Ignoble Ig-Nazi-O?" *The Nation,* 270, 23 (12 June 2000): 9; and his retraction, 271, 12 (23 October 2000): 9.
22 Ignazio Silone, *Ed egli si nascose,* ed. by Benedetta Pierfederici (Rome: Città Nuova Editrice, 2000), 3–8.
23 Darina Silone, Pescina, 1 May 2000. From a copy of the speech I received from her.
24 Alberto Moravia, *La ciociara* (Milan: Bompiani, 1957). Trans. by Angus Davidson as *Two Women* (South Royalton, VT: Steerforth Italia, [reissued] 2001).
25 Alexander Stille, "The Spy Who Failed," *The New Yorker,* 15 May 2000: 44. And my comment, published in the June 19 and 26 issue: 16.
26 Prior to 1947 he signs only two letters with the new name. See Silone to MF, S 10 and S 23. Fleischmann only began to address him as Silone after 1945.

27 Camilla Ravera, "Quegli anni con Silone nel PCI," *Misura*, 1978. Kindly shared by Maria Moscardelli.
28 Quoted in SPCI, 253.
29 Cited by Dario Biocca in *La doppia vita di un italiano* (Milan: Rizzoli, 2005), 161–2. Hereafter, LDV. The nicknames "Buba" and "Cucchila" have no English equivalents.
30 Ignazio Silone, *Memoriale dal carcere svizzero*, trans. by Stanislao G. Pugliese as *Memoir from a Swiss Prison* (Merrick, NY: Cross Cultural Communications, 1005), 25–6. Hereafter MSP.
31 ALIS, 95–6.
32 See S 14 about his residence permit. Also, Maria Moscardelli shared a "Legitimation-Karte," released to Silone in 1940, reminding me that residence permits had to be renewed and could be revoked. Thus, Silone was in a precarious situation for the duration of his stay.
33 See Vittoriano Esposito, *Ignazio Silone e la rivolta del "terzo fronte"* (Avezzano: Centro Studi Ugo Maria Palanza, 2007). Also see Liliana Biondi's thesis on the Mazzinian source of Silone's nationalistic stance, "Valori mazziniani rivisitati e condivisi da Ignazio Silone," in *Unità d'Italia e Massoneria* (Bologna: Acadèmia Editrice, 2011), 99–107.
34 MSP, 25. Also, Patricia Peterle, "Da politica à literatura: O percurso de Ignazio Silone," *Alea: Estudos Neolatinos* 2, 1 (January–June 2009): 99–110.
35 ISRS, vol. I (1998): 1375–8.
36 S 97.
37 Aline Valangin (born Ducommun) (1889–1985). The "Fondo Aline Valangin" at the Lugano Cantonal Library contains a remarkable collection of her writings, including novels, short stories, poetry, travel notes, diaries, articles, and correspondence. Her memoirs are in *Mutter* (Zurich: Limmat Verlag, 2001). Also see Peter Kamber, *Story of Two Lives – Wladimir Rosenbaum and Aline Valangin* (Zurich: Limmat Verlag, 1990).
38 http://amicisilone.altervista.org//ilfilodellavita/aline.htm.
39 The letter, dated Monday 3 and Tuesday 4 April 1933, was written in French. See Vincenzo Todisco's Italian translation in "Una lettera inedita di Ignazio Silone ad Aline Valangin," *Quaderni grigionitaliani*, 28 July 2012: 339–42.
40 ISBTV, 11.
41 Valangin's letters to Silone are at the Centro Studi archives.
42 Edy Meyer (1877–1967) was a typographer. His file is in the Schweizerisches Sozialarchiv. He was also known as Eduard Mayer, Meier, or Maier. Gabriella married him in June 1933 and they divorced in October 1934. For this period in Gabriella's life, see Franca Schiavetti Magnani, *Una famiglia italiana* (Milan: Feltrinelli, 2002), 104.

43 Gabriella Seidenfeld, "Le tre sorelle" (manuscript), 27. Read by kind permission of the Centro Studi Ignazio Silone.
44 Ibid., 54.
45 Antony Fleischmann confirmed that this is what Marcel affectionately called his home and that his numerous guests were simply that. As further evidence that it was never a place of business, no correspondence is ever addressed to the "Kleine Pension."
46 MF to Andreas Mytze, 3 October 1972. Centro Studi archives.
47 I learned from Eithne Laracy Kavanagh that this is how the name appears in the baptismal records.
48 William Weaver (1923–2013) superbly translated many of Silone's works. He met the Silones in Rome in 1946 and draws brief but poignant sketches of them in *Open City: Seven Writers in Postwar Rome* (South Royalton, VT: Steerforth Press, 1999), 11–14.
49 Courtesy of Maria Moscardelli.
50 S 29.
51 "Infante" is the name of the man whom Pietro Spina rescues from a subhuman existence in *The Seed beneath the Snow.* The choice of this nickname might allude to the role that Gabriella played in Silone's life.
52 *Colloqui,* 61. While skiing in Arosa, Darina broke her leg and spent five weeks in Bern during her recovery before rejoining Silone in Baden.
53 SPCI, 139–40.
54 S 34.
55 Elinor Lipper (1912–2008) was the author of *Eleven Years in Soviet Prison Camps.* Her letters to Silone, found at the Centro Studi archives, attest to the attention she received from the writer. In one (1 December 1948), she thanks Silone for all his help with the manuscript. In another (1 May 1949) she thanks him for his long letter and all of his suggestions. On 20 June 1949 she asks him to review the manuscript, and on 23 June she writes that Oprecht (Silone's publisher) has offered her a contract. Her words, such as "it would be a gift to see you again" or "are your eyes always so sad?" and her wish to meet him – in Switzerland or northern Italy – are evidence of an ongoing relationship.
56 See LdEIS, where the friendship between the two intellectuals and their mutual admiration is documented in their correspondence.
57 *Colloqui,* 137.
58 Lamentably, Malik's letters to Darina Silone went missing prior to her final hospitalization, and a public appeal I made for their return to Eithne Laracy has thus far gone unheeded. See "Lettere sottratte alla moglie di Silone. Appello per la restituzione": www.abruzzo24ore.TV/news/Pescina-sottratte-lettere-a-darina-moglie-di-ignazio-silone-l-appello-per-la-retituzione/96124.htm.

59 Keshav Malik (1924–2014) was one of India's foremost poets and art critics. A fellow of the Lalit Kala Akademi (Indian Academy of Art), he received the Padma Shri award for literature.

60 The comments and the two poems, written in English, were e-mailed to me by the poet on 10 February 2013 with his permission to publish them.

61 S 155.

62 I am thankful to Maria Moscardelli for sharing Silone's unpublished letters with me.

63 Diocleziano Giardini also published *Ignazio Silone: Cronologia della vita e delle opere* (Cerchio, Aquila: Adelmo Polla, 1999), and made other important contributions to Silonian scholarship including "Alcune novità sul 'caso Silone,'" *Quaderni Siloniani*, 1–2 (2000): 10–12.

64 Darina Silone, "Ignazio Silone, Allen Dulles and the CIA," *Times Literary Supplement*, London, 1 December 2000.

65 The American diplomat Allen Welsh Dulles (1893–1969) worked in Switzerland for the American OSS (Office of Strategic Services), the precursor of the CIA.

66 Both quotations are from Darina Silone's handwritten letter, in my possession, dated Rome, 15 June 2000. For Silone's interaction with Dulles see "OSS Documents on Ignazio Silone". Available at: http://peterkamber.de/index.php?option=com_content&view=category&layout=blog&id=41Itemid=59. Also see ALIS, 156–61.

67 The essayist and art critic Clement Greenberg (1909–94); the editor of *Partisan Review*, writer, art critic, and philosopher Dwight Macdonald (1906–82), and his wife, Nancy Gardiner Rodman (1910–96); the Croatian politician Ante Ciliga (1898–1992).

68 The Spanish communist journalist Juan Andrade (1898–1981).

69 The Italian Communist Party leader, Senator Umberto Elia Terracini (1895–1983).

70 S 20 and S 21.

71 The Italian painter Emilio Vedova (1919–2006). On 12 December 1952 he writes that Silone's appeal in defence of the Sevillian prisoners inspired him to paint a work that has been acquired by the Museum of Modern Art, Sao Paulo, Brazil.

72 F 35.

73 See Ignazio Silone Web for a detailed chronology, ISBTV, 20–3, for the years 1944–78, and ISRS, vol. II: 1013, for Silone's warning.

74 ISRS, vol. I: 1385–91.

75 See *Nicola Chiaromonte, Ignazio Silone: L'eredità di "Tempo presente,"* ed. by Goffredo Fofi, Vittorio Giacopini, and Monica Nonno (Rome: Fahrenheit 451, 2000). See also ALIS, 239–50.

76 ISBTV, 13.

77 Ignazio Silone, "et in hora mortis nostrae," *Severina*, 63–4.
78 StAM, 384.
79 See *Colloqui*, 125, for her complete comment translated in the epigraph of this work.
80 On her passing, Italian and English media paid her tribute, recalling her many gifts and talents. For warm testimonials by Maffino Redi Maghenzani, Maria Nicolai Paynter, Vittoriano Esposito, Liliana Biondi, Don Flavio Peloso, and Giulia Paola Di Nicola see "Ricordando Darina Silone" in *Prospettiva Persona*, 45-46 (2003): 57–70.
81 Giorgio Bassani, *Il Giardino dei Finzi-Contini* (Turin: Einaudi, 1962). Trans. by William Weaver as *The Garden of the Finzi-Continis* (New York: Harcourt, 1977).
82 See the illustrations for a picture of the tomb.
83 Names and dates are in the chronology.
84 Michael Fleischmann was first a director of a Zurich grain-trading company owned by Jacob Koch, Albert Einstein's uncle. In 1893 he established his own company. See the "Municipal Police Detective's Report," dated 4 July 1900, in John Stachel, David C. Cassidy, and Robert Schulmann, eds, *The Collected Papers of Albert Einstein*, vol. 1, 246 n2. The report also mentions Einstein's weekly visits to the Fleischmann firm at 65 Banhoffstrasse, Zurich. In a letter dated 14 July 1919, Einstein informs his wife that, "Mrs. [Helene] Fleischmann has died – of cancer": Diana Kornos Buchwald, Robert Schulmann, and Jószef Illy, eds, *The Collected Papers of Albert Einstein* , vol. 9, 125.
85 See "Some Eighty Years Ago (1). First Romanian Visit of State to Switzerland," *Quarterly Bulletin* 2 (2004), the Embassy of Romania to Switzerland, 8, n6. Carlo's credentials might have been enhanced by his publication of *Die auslandischen Konsulate in der Sweiz: Insbesondere die deutschen* (Leipzig: Dathe, 1920).
86 See the "Monthly Interview April: Kaspar M. Fleischmann": www.xecutives.net/interviews/alle/241. Kaspar is the son of Marcel's brother Kurt and Nelly Schmid.
87 S 25.
88 S 161.
89 A documentary by Andreas Myntz on Silone's Swiss years includes a segment on the Kleine Pension and, as such, is one notable exception.
90 *Colloqui*, 68.
91 F 93 and F 94.
92 According to Iris Schmeisser, MoMA provenance specialist, Braque's *Man with a Guitar* and Picasso's *Ma Jolie* have been on extended loan to the MoMA since 1939, and "were acquired through Fleischmann's agent Paul Drey, New York, in 1945." These are still held by the museum.

93 *Colloqui*, 45.

94 See Philippe Dagen, "L'enigme du 'Joeur de guitar' de Georges Braque," *Le Monde*, 27 January 1998. Retracing the provenance, the author states: "Restent les annés obscures, de 1940 à 1948, d'Alphonse Kann à André Lefèvre" [There remain the dark years from 1940 to 1948, from Alphonse Kann to André Lefèvre]. These include the dates concerning Fleischmann's ownership and the related data.

Iris Schmeisser, provenance specialist at the MoMa, kindly informed me that Braque's *The Guitar Player*, created in 1914, and reclaimed by the heirs of Alphonse Kann, from whom it was confiscated by the ERR in 1940, was in Fleischmann's possession "after it was exchanged with Rochlitz and sold to Pétridès." This would suggest that Fleischmann bought the painting from Pétridès and sold it to Lefèvre shortly before 1943 when the Allies declared all transactions that had occurred during the war to be null and void. (This is the only trade that appears to have been made before the end of World War II.)

95 Alex Danchew, *On Art and War and Terror* (Edinburgh: Edinburgh University Press, 65).

96 *Art Looting Intelligence Unit (ALIU) Reports*, 1945–6, and ALIU Red Flag Names List and Index. Marcel Fleischmann is not on the list. See www.lootedart.com/MVI3RM469661.

97 See Swiss Reports, p. 118: https://www.fold3.com/image/.

98 See the *Jacques Seligmann & Co. Records, 1904–1978* regarding Germain Seligmann and the above-mentioned correspondence: www.aaa.si.edu/collections/container/viewer/Fleischann-Marcel-288234.

The art dealer Paul Drey (1885–1953), who was acting as Marcel's agent, is listed in the *Archives Directory for the History of Collecting* as "a senior partner at the Paul Drey Gallery, in New York, founded in 1920. [...] He was responsible for selling artwork to Museums in the United States, including the Metropolitan Museum, the National Gallery, the Chicago Art Institute and the Boston Museum of Art": www.libumma.org/portal/archives-directory-for-the-history-of-collecting in america.

99 The German Jewish criminal defence lawyer and scholar Max Hirschberg (1883–1964). As shown by the *Seligmann Records*, he interacted with Seligmann on behalf of his client Marcel Fleischmann.

100 Hirschberg is referring to the *Inter-Allied Declaration against Acts of Dispossession Committed in Territories under Enemy Occupation and Control* (London: H.M.S.O., 1943). The report was released in London on 5 January 1943 and is commonly known as "The Declaration of London." Although Switzerland is not a signatory of the declaration, the stipulations

also extend "in particular to persons in neutral countries." See *Declaration*, second paragraph.

101 F 58.

102 Héctor Feliciano, *The Lost Museum: The Nazi Conspiracy to Steal the World's Greatest Art* (New York: Basic Books; Harper Collins, 1997).

103 Jonathan Petropoulos, *The Faustian Bargain: The Art World in Nazi Germany* (Oxford: Oxford University Press, 2000).

104 Ibid., 70, and 297 nn35, 36.

105 S 7.

106 F 87.

107 F 150.

108 For Elsa's birth date, see www.Ancestry.com, *Ueberseeische Auswanderung*, 1947, Elsa's handwritten application for travel from London to New York. Also, the "Information Sheet," dated 22 February 1947, for birthplace, residence, profession, and destination.

109 S 14.

110 F 55, F 57, F 62.

111 F 93.

112 Darina Silone 92. The italics are mine.

113 F 147.

114 F 176.

115 The letter is in English, and the passages are as they appear in the original.

116 The letter bears Marcel's handwritten signature.

117 Used by kind permission of Anthony Fleischmann. As Marcel states in the postscript, he dictated this letter to his nephew's secretary, hence the lack of accuracy, including in the spelling of Silone's and Elsa's names.

118 See F 150 and Silone's and Darina's comments in card 151.

119 Darina Silone's letter to Jürg, dated 5 April 1981. Used by kind permission of Anthony Fleischmann.

The Correspondence

1 The German/Swiss writer Hans Mühlestein (1887–1969).

2 The spelling of this surname is not consistent. It also appears as Meyer, Meier, and Maier.

3 The Russian Marxist politician Leon Trotsky (1879–1940). Nettie Sutro Katzestein, born Nanette Gerstle in Germany (1989–1967). Writer, translator, and founder of the Schweizer Hilfswerk fur Emigrantenkinder (SHEK).

4 The German writer and novelist Jacob Wassermann (1873–1934).

5 *The Swiss painter Nicklaus Stöcklin (1896–1982) and family member(s).
6 The letter ends without salutations.
7 No year is given. 11 October 1934 was a Thursday. See Fleischmann 3. Hereafter, F and letter number.
8 Anita is Mühlestein's wife.
9 Tony Degen was a friend of Marcel Fleischmann. F 6.
10 Silone, 5. Hereafter, S and letter number.
11 The Austrian-Swiss painter Johann Wilhelm Von Tscharner (1886–1946).
12 No year. Under the date "3 Juin" there is, in pencil, "1935 ?" In 1935 Silone was in Ascona on several occasions and, having benefited from his publication of *Fontamara*, had begun to write his second novel, *Bread and Wine*. The concerns he expresses about the harm he could do by remaining at his friend's house are not without cause. Writing to Emmie Oprecht, his publisher's wife (July 1935), he says: "In Ascona I have had some Fascist difficulties, and from today I am in the Massagno Alps above Lugano ..." ISBTV, 18.
13 Silone uses Italian to say: "So, then, goodbye and good wishes."
14 The modernist art historian and philosopher Max Raphael (1889–1952).
15 Addressee shown at the bottom of the page.
16 "For me." Added by hand after the salutation and the note: *"Diverse Zettel."*
17 Nettie Sutro and her husband, Erich Katzestein.
18 Serena (Gabriella Seidenfeld) and Silone never married, but some of his relatives refer to her as his wife. Their relationship changed when Silone met Aline Valangin, but they now appear to be together again.
19 "Herrr Kapitalist!!!" added by hand.
20 Typed. Handwritten salutation and signature.
21 The trial of the "Anti-Soviet Trotskyist Centre" held in Moscow 23–30 January 1937. Thirteen of the seventeen defendants were found guilty and executed.
22 The French writer André Paul Guillaume Gide (1869–1951). Initially an admirer of Russia and a communist, when he travelled to Moscow in 1936, Gide was horrified by the Stalin trials. He wrote *Retour de l'U.R.S.S.* (Paris: Gallimard, 1936), as well as articles denouncing the situation. Like Silone, he later contributed to *The God That Failed: Six Studies in Communism*, edited by Richard Crossman (New York: Harper and Brothers, 1949).
23 "Fraulein" is used here for Gabriella. Cf F 12 where she is "Frau" Serena.
24 Cf F 18.
25 Dr Carlo Fleischmann, Marcel's brother, was an honorary consul. See S 27.
26 Silone's second novel, published first in German as *Brot und Wein* (Zurich: Oprecht, 1936); in English as *Bread and Wine* (London: Methuen, 1936; New York: Harper and Brothers, 1937).

27 Latin for "destruction, ruin, extinction, death." Handwritten at the bottom of the first page.
28 The Austrian journalist and writer Alfred Polgar (1873–1955).
29 Possible year. Silone writes from Le Cannet, 17 February 1938.
30 Marie de Rabutin-Chantal, marquise de Sévigné (1626–96).
31 The Austrian musicologist and critic Willi Reich (1898–1980). Swiss citizen, 1961.
32 The Italian musician and conductor Arturo Toscanini (1867–1957).
33 The Austrian writer Stefan Zweig (1881–1942).
34 The Swiss physician Manes Kartagener (1897–1975).
35 *La scuola dei dittatori* was first published in German as *Die Schule der Diktatoren* (Zurich: Europa Verlag, 1938). The Italian original version was published by Mondadori in 1962.
36 Fleischmann might have lent Silone this amount, or could have forwarded copyright proceeds received on Silone's behalf from his publishers. Miss Hegnauer apparently handled administrative matters.
37 Handwritten at the end of the letter.
38 The German psychologist and philosopher Erich Seligmann Fromm (1900–80).
39 The Czechoslovakian-American social and political scientist Karl Wolfgang Deutsch (1912–92).
40 No year given. Silone was probably reacting to the 1940 battles of Taranto (11–12 Nov.) and Cape Teulada (Battle of Spartivento, 27 Nov.) during which the Italian Navy suffered tremendous losses.
41 This institution was eventually cited for abuse and liquidated.
42 Silone adds a typewritten page, in French, with the following heading: "Première épître de Paul, apôtre, aux Corinthiens. Chapitre XIII: Caractère et excellence de l'amitié, *" followed by verses1–13 and this remark: "*Au lieu d'amitié, certains auteurs traduisent le mot charité, d'autres le mot amour; mais, puisque charité a un peu change di [sic] signification dans les temps modernes et puisque Paul ne pensait pas seulement aux rapport entre homes et femmes, peut-être le mot amitié convient le mieux" [In place of friendship, some authors translate the word charity, others love; but charity has changed somewhat in meaning in modern times and since Paul was not only thinking of the relationship between man and woman, maybe the word friendship is best suited].
43 Date suggested by the content of Silone's humorous "Brouillon" handwritten on the back of this letter and occasioned by Dr Carlo's approaching fiftieth birthday, 28 April 1942. See S 26.

44 This is likely written to comment humorously on Dr Carlo's role as "Ancien Consul" and the importance that Marcel's father attributed to his and Marcel's younger brother's diplomatic appointments.
45 Saint Nicholas of Flue (1417–87) is the patron saint of Switzerland. He was beatified in 1669 and was canonized in 1947 by Pope Pius XII.
46 Silone refers to the 1924 Romanian royal state visit to Switzerland, which Michael and Carlo attended as "Consul General" and "Ancien Consul," respectively.
47 The error is intentional, as is the hyperbolic treatment of Carlo's and Michael's attributes.
48 Silone's handwritten letter, in German, follows this handwritten message in the same language by Friedel Kinstetter.
49 Silone writes from the Swiss prison.
50 Emmie Oprecht, née Fehlmann (1899–1990), was the wife of Silone's publisher, Emil Oprecht (1895–1952). See *The University of Zurich Romanisches Seminar*, at the Zurich Central Library: Correspondence, 4:48 Oprecht, The Verlagsarchiv Oprecht/Europa-Verlag, 1942–3 correspondence, 14.24 Silone, Ignazio (26 documents in the Steinbeck dossier).
51 On his release from the Swiss jail, Silone was confined to Davos. The Pension Strela was in Davos.
52 The note about the weather in Zurich is handwritten in the margin. Such comments were at times used to signal other precarious conditions.
53 "or Dr. Huber" added by hand.
54 The letter bears this date added in pencil: "9-IV-43." 9 April 1943 was indeed a Friday.
55 No year given. Upon release from prison Silone was confined to Davos and then to Baden.
56 This comment probably refers to aging in a general sense, since Marcel's first grandchild, Jessica Fleischmann, was born in 1952 to Werner Jürg and his second wife, Gloria Goldberg Fleischmann.
57 The Swiss physician, writer, and libertarian socialist Fritz Brupbacher (1874–1945). Silone met him soon after his arrival in Zurich. In 1931 Brupbacher sponsored him for membership at the Museumsgesellschaft. See ISiE, 41. For Silone's epistolary exchanges with Brupbacher and his wife, Paulette, see the Brupbacher file at the Schweizerisches Sozialarchiv, Zurich.
58 The Swiss lawyer Max Huber (1874–1960) and his wife.
59 Year suggested by the content.
60 Film director Klaus Witting was a trustee of the Bavaria Filmkunst from 1 April to 1 November 1946, when he was replaced by Fritz Thiery. He lived for many

years at the Kleine Pension, becoming part of Fleischmann's Germaniastrasse "family."

61 Marcel's letters may have been typed by an assistant or Elsa Schiess, hence the note.

62 Silone returned to Italy on 14 October 1944.

63 Date suggested by the content of F 41. Letter by Elsa Schiess typed on the back of F 38.

64 Probably Klaus Witting. He was not a brother, but was treated as a member of the family. See note 60.

65 The Austrian tenor Richard Tauber (1891–1948).

66 The Swiss lawyer Hans Ebrard (1894–1978).

67 Klaus Witting.

68 Handwritten signature: Marcel Fleischmann.

69 The publisher, film producer, and philanthropist Cino del Duca (1899–1967), whose real first name was Gino. See *Colloqui,* 141.

70 On the back, the text of a "4.3.46" (4 March 1946) telegram, in French, informs Silone that "the suitcase has arrived" and asks him to "please respond to the 12 February letter regarding Gino."

71 Umberto II of Savoy (1904–83) became King of Italy on 9 May 1946 and left the country on 12 June 1946.

72 The Swiss painter Max Hunziker (1901–76) and his wife, the psychoanalyst Gertrud Hunziker-Fromm (1915–2012), a cousin of Erich Fromm.

73 The Swiss painter Johann (Wilhelm Jan) von Tscharner (1886–1946).

74 The Swiss architect Carl Theodor Hubacher (1897–1990).

75 The German playwright, novelist, and poet Ernst Toller (1893–1939). He was arrested and tortured by the Nazis. A most welcomed guest at the Kleine Pension. Unable to overcome the depression caused by the events, he committed suicide.

76 The Italian socialist leader Giacomo Matteotti (1885–1924). A member of the Italian Parliament, he spoke against Mussolini and was assassinated on 10 June 1924.

77 No year given. *Fontamara*'s first Italian edition was published by Faro in October 1947.

78 The Italian film director Luigi Comencini (1916–2007) or his wife, the noblewoman Giulia Grifeo. Silone was also well acquainted with Marie Magdaleine Hefti, the director's mother. Her personal card, with this handwritten note – "Bücher fur Silone abgeholt 6.1.47" [books collected for Silone] – is in the Centro Studi archives.

79 Illegible handwritten note follows.

80 The German art historian, collector, and art dealer Wilhelm Uhde (1874–1947). Listed in the *MoMA Provenance Research Project* as the seller of Braque's *Man with a Guitar* to Marcel Fleischmann in 1924.
81 The German theatre director Jürgen Fehling (1885–1968).
82 "Success" is written in English. The word "alter" [old] in the salutation is handwritten.
83 Cf U.S. Department of Justice Information Sheet regarding passengers arriving on aircraft.
84 Possibly alludes to the need to sell the Kleine Pension, since the street name never changed.
85 This identifies the two women from Zofingen mentioned in F 55.
86 Dr. Hans-Jorg Brunner, the director of the Brunner Sanatorium.
87 Tony Degen.
88 Handwritten comment regarding Lia Ritter.
89 Printed stationery, hereafter all in capital letters. Salutation in the second page, left margin. In the front, in pencil "R nicht beant coolen" [R cold, no answer].
90 A probable allusion to the money that Fleischmann lent Silone to help him resettle in Italy. See *Colloqui*, 68.
91 Darina writes in German.
92 S 58 and S 59.
93 The Swiss lawyer and investor Jacques Rosenstein (1900–79). Based on establishment of IKAP (International Kapital Anlagen Gesellschaft) of which Rosenstein was a partner, by Bank La Roche.
94 Followed by illegible handwritten line.
95 The Italian socialist politician Ivan Matteo Lombardo (1902–80). In 1943 he spearheaded the reconstitution of the PSI. In 1946 he was elected to the Assemblea Costituente. He served as Italian "Undersecretary of Industry" 1945–6 and "Minister of Foreign Trade" 1950–1. As Silone states, Lombardo was then chief of the Italian delegation to the treaty negotiations with the United States; hence, he could possibly have helped Jürg by writing on his behalf.
96 Typed. Handwritten signature. Stamp-dated "12. SEP. 1947."
97 Followed by two illegible handwritten words.
98 Silone does not include the year, but the letter is stamped: "3.Okt.1947."
99 See F 67.
100 No year is given.
101 The French pacifist, poet, and writer Jean-Paul Samson (1894–1964). He was Silone's French translator.

102 No year. Front page, in pencil: "R 20.11.47." There was a general strike in Rome on 15 November 1947.
103 The German playwright Bertolt Brecht (1898–1956).
104 Handwritten note.
105 There is no trace of the Marchesa. I contacted the Santasilia family, and they too could not identify her.
106 Handwritten note added at the bottom of the page. A "Casa Grillino" still operates today as a small hotel and art gallery in Brione sopra Minusio.
107 The Baroness Irene von Guttry ([?] –1950) was the German translator of several novels by Anatole France and Claude Ferrère.
108 Handwritten note.
109 The Romanian actress Joana Maria Gorvin (1922–93) was Fehling's companion.
110 A psychiatric clinic in Zurich.
111 The German writer, poet, journalist, and translator Ferdinand Hardekopf (1876–1954) and family member(s).
112 Not dated. "2 IX 48." added in pencil.
113 Egidio Reale (1888–1958) was a founder, with C. Rosselli and G. Salvemini, of the antifascist movement Giustizia e Libertà. At the time of this writing he was the Italian ambassador in Bern.
114 StAM, 13–17.
115 Undated. Top front page, in pencil, "1.1.48."
116 Handwritten note.
117 The noted Swiss doctor Luzius Rüedi (1900–93). He was head of the ear, nose, and throat (ENT) department of the Zurich University Hospital. He also conducted research in the field of tuberculosis and in 1941 opened a clinic in Davos. Silone may have consulted him there.
118 F 78.
119 Miss Frisch was possibly related to Fega Frisch (1878–1964) and her husband, Efraim Frisch (1874–1942), whom Silone knew well. See the *Efraim Frisch Collection,* Personal Correspondence, 17 October 1939, Silone to E. Frisch, proposing the translation of *The Seed beneath the Snow,* and Silone's card to Fega for her eightieth birthday.
120 The well-known artists' model Tylia Perlmutter (1904–72). Together with Suzanne Lombard, she translated the *Diaries of Anne Frank* from Dutch to French under the pseudonym Tylia Caren. Her identity was kindly confirmed by Eithne Laracy, who was in Paris in 1949 and became well acquainted with Tylia Perlmutter.
121 DS 89.

122 Regarding the loss of 53 Germaniastrasse to repay Carlo. Marcel writes from his new address at 78 Plattenstrasse on 9 February 1950.
123 "In best terms" written in English.
124 The Baroness Irene von Guttry.
125 Typed. Handwritten signature.
126 Fleischmann's former business address.
127 "Closed door": i.e., remains closed.
128 Illegible handwritten note follows.
129 The Italian writer and literary critic Giovanni Papini (1881–1956). Silone refers to the fictitious interviews published in Papini's *Il libro nero. Nuovo diario di Gog* (1951).
130 The novel *Eine Handvoll Brombeeren* (*A Handful of Blackberries*).
131 Silone's novel *A Handful of Blackberries,* first published in Italian in 1952 as *Una manciata di more*, translated by Hann Elise Hinderberger as *Eine Handvoll Brombeeren* (Zurich: Europa Verlag, 1952).
132 Carry Streuly was co-author with Pierre Benoit of the novel *Alzira* (1948).
133 The island of Ischia is a renowned thermal springs location. "I fanghi" are spas for mud therapy.
134 Second page, top left, in pencil: "Hotel Eden Rom b. Pincio." Left margin: "empfohlen durch Morgenthal oder Rom" [Recommended by Morgenthal or Rome].
135 Klaus Witting.
136 S 107, S 111.
137 Typed. Handwritten signature.
138 The year 1955 is derived from the content of the previous letter.
139 No date or place. Year derived from note in S 107.
140 The Swiss dermatologist Werner Jadassohn (1897–1973), who practised in Geneva.
141 The note, apparently photocopied, is written on Silone's personal letterhead.
142 The Swiss Dr Paulette Brupbacher, born Paula Raygrodski in Belarus (1880–1967). With her second husband, Dr Fritz Brupbacher, she worked in the field of sex education and marriage law. The Brupbacherplatz, in Zurich, is named after the couple.
143 Added on the front page, left margin.
144 F 118.
145 The Baron Raul Kuffner von Diószek (1886–1961) and his wife, the Polish painter Tamara De Lempicka (1898–1980). Tentative identification is based on the baron's Austrian origins, the couple's association with the art circles also frequented by Marcel Fleischmann, and common

acquaintances such as the Paul Drey Gallery named as dealers for both Kuffner and Fleischmann in the *MoMa Provenance Research Project.*

146 Tony Degen Kesse.

147 The British director Thorold Barron Dickinson (1903–84) and his wife, the architect (Irene) Joanna MacFadden ([?] –1979).

148 The German conductor Martin Rich (1905–2000). Cf S 134.

149 Followed by illegible handwritten note.

150 *The Fox and the Camellias* was first published in Italian as *La volpe e le camelie* (Milan: Mondadori, 1960), with the following dedication: "Al mio amico Marcel Fleischmann" [To my friend Marcel Fleischmann]. Fleischmann received his copy for approval before the official publication.

151 *Viaggio a Parigi,* translated by Nettie Sutro, was first published in German as *Die Reise Nach Paris* (Zurich: Verlag Oprech und Helbling, 1934). "Der Fuchses" [The Fox] is one of the short stories in the collection.

152 "The Journey to Paris" a short story in the volume of the same title.

153 *Il Mondo,* a weekly political, cultural, and economic journal published from1949 to 1966. See the issues of 17 March and 7 April 1959.

154 F 122.

155 S 20.

156 A private hospital in Zurich.

157 F 121 and S 127.

158 *Tempo Presente* letterhead; heading crossed out.

159 Professor Albert Bolleter was a nephew of Elsa Schiess.

160 Handwritten in Italian. Gratefully received from Anthony Fleischmann with permission to publish.

161 Silone does not write a transitional sentence, but is apparently speaking about Darina.

162 The envelope, photocopied on the back of the letter, is stamped "May 26, 1963."

163 Silone was Kartagener's patient for the treatment of bronchiectasis, one of the conditions associated with the Kartagener Syndrome.

164 Personal stationery. At the end, a handwritten signature.

165 See S 25.

166 See F 49.

167 The Swiss neurologist Herbert Binswanger (1900–75).

168 Handwritten.

169 The date is suggested by the message. The card bears a fictitious address followed by the inverted order of the real one. Silone may have sent the card as a humorous note to his convalescent friend. In F 147, Fleischmann speaks about his prostate surgery.

170 "Emergency Exit" is an essay in the volume by the same name. First published in Italian as *Uscita di sicurezza* (Florence: Vallecchi, 1965); and in German as *Notausgang* (Cologne: Kiepenheur & Witsch, 1966). The English version, *Emergency Exit*, was published in New York by Harper and Row, 1968.
171 The Reverend Paul Vogt (1900–84), head of the Zurich Fluchtlingshilfe [Refugee Aid]. In 1947 he received a doctorate *honoris causa* from the University of Zurich for his work on behalf of refugees during World War II.
172 The Swiss Jewish scholar Dr Lore Hartman von Monakow, president of the Kinderhof [Children's Village] and author of several books, including *The Jerusalem Biblical Zoo* and *Pathways in the Dispersal.*
173 The Swiss textile industrialist, art expert, and collector Georges Bloch (1901–84).
174 Handwritten.
175 Message typed on a blank card. Handwritten initals: "M.F."
176 See F 152, F 153, and S 156. Nettie Sutro's life was to be celebrated. See "Nettie Sutro-Katzenstein" (1889–1967) in the *Jewish Women's Archive*, where her work on behalf of "nearly ten thousand Jewish refugee children in Switzerland" is remembered together with her other remarkable accomplishments: http://jwa.org/encyclopedia/article/sutro-katzenstein-nettie.
177 The Swiss theologian Leonhard Ragaz (1868–1945). Co-founder of religious socialism with Hermann Kutter. His thought greatly influenced Silone.
178 The pastor Max Gerber (1887–1949).
179 Typed. Handwritten signature.
180 F 157.
181 Elsa was a patient of Dr. Herbert Binswanger (1900–75), a member of the Binswanger medical dynasty, owners of the noted Kreuzlingen Sanatorium.
182 *L'avventura di un povero cristiano* (Milan: Mondadori, 1968). Translated by William Weaver as *The Story of a Humble Christian* (London: Gollancz; New York: Harper and Row, 1971).
183 The Swiss painter Hans Birsinger (1903–91) and family member(s).
184 The last two comments and the salutation are handwritten in the left margin.
185 Written on hotel stationery with both hotels' names.
186 Handwritten on hotel stationery. The rest of the letter is missing.
187 No year. The documentary was occasioned by Silone's upcoming seventieth birthday.
188 The translator and writer Dora Mitzky.
189 See F 181.
190 Handwritten, on personal stationery.

191 Typed. Handwritten signature.
192 Handwritten, on personal stationery.
193 S 159.
194 Handwritten, on personal stationery.
195 Handwritten, on personal stationery.
196 The TV film *Il segreto di Luca,* from the novel of that title, directed by Ottavio Spadaro.
197 Typed, on personal stationery. Handwritten signature.
198 *Dal villaggio all'Europa (Omaggio a Silone)* (Rome: De Luca Editore, 1971). The work included texts by Giovanni Cristini, Ernesto Buonaiuti, Nicola Chiaromonte, Geno Pampaloni, Luce D'Eramo, Bruno Corbi, and Ignazio Silone; etchings by Gian Battista Salatino, Riccardo Tommasi Ferroni, and Giovanni Gromo. It was initiated by Stefano De Luca, Antonietta Leggeri, and Franco Simongini, to honour Silone on his seventieth birthday. The volume was printed in a limited edition. Maria Moscardelli, who received a copy from Silone, kindly shared the information with me.
199 The surrealist artist Max Hunziker (1901–76) and his wife, the psychoanalyst Gertrud Hunziker-Fromm (1915–2012) ,were good friends of Silone and Marcel. Hunziker illustrated one of the covers of *The Seed beneath the Snow.*
200 Typed. Handwritten signature.
201 The book is *Dal villaggio all'Europa,* cf note 198.
202 S 170.
203 Handwritten.
204 Handwritten, on personal stationery.
205 The Italian antifascist and anti-Stalinist writer and art critic Nicola Chiaromonte (1905–72).
206 Silone misstates Chiaromonte's age.
207 Typed on personal stationery. The signature is handwritten.
208 Folding card: Left side announcement and Fleischmann's handwritten signature. On the right the letter to Silone.
209 *Et Resurrexit* by Johann Sebastian Bach.
210 Regarding Elsa's death.
211 Typewritten, with a handwritten signature and correction from April to March.
212 Handwritten.
213 Handwritten.
214 The Catalan cellist and conductor Pablo Casals (1876–1973).
215 The Polish-American classical pianist Arthur Rubinstein (1887–1982).
216 Handwritten on lined paper.

Afterword

1 S 1.
2 S 30.
3 Silone to MF, S 16. Also, ISiE. 25–58.
4 Jean-Michel Palmier, *Weimar in Exile. The Antifascist Emigration in Europe and America* (London: Verso, 2006), 154–6.
5 See https://www.google.com.search?q=ettore+rosen+franch+roma+sparita.
6 Silone speaks about him to Darina in his final hours. See her *Severina*, 170–4. Also, Moscardelli's recollection in the Ignazio Silone Web.

Selected Bibliography

Selected Works by Ignazio Silone[1]

Autobiographical Writings and Essays

Il fascismo. Origini e sviluppo. Translated into German by Gritta Baerlocher as *Der Faschismus: Seine Entstehung und seine Entwicklung.* Zurich: Europa Verlag, 1934. Latest Italian edition, translated by Marina Buttarelli and edited by Mimmo Franzinelli: Milan: Mondadori, 2002.

Uscita di sicurezza. Florence: Vallecchi, 1965. Trans. into English by Harvey Ferguson, II, as *Emergency Exit* (except for the last essay, for which no indication is given). New York: Harper and Row, 1968.

Uscita di sicurezza. Milan: Longanesi, 1979.

THE SHORT STORIES: *The Journey to Paris/Mr. Aristotle*

Trans. into German by Nettie Sutro. *Die Reise nach Paris.* Zurich: Verlag Oprecht und Helbling, 1934.

Trans. into English by Samuel Putnam. *Mr. Aristotle.* New York: Robert McBride, 1935.

Trans. into Danish by Maria Garland. *Den tragiske Idyl.* Copenhagen: Fremad's Forlag, 1935.

Trans. into English by John Lehman. *The Journey to Paris.* London: Penguin, 1936.

Trans. into Italian by Silvia Carusi and Karin Wiedemeyer Francesconi. *Viaggio a Parigi.* From German ed., 1934. Ed. and with introduction by Vittoriano Esposito. Pescina: Centro Studi Siloniani, 1993.

1 For a complete bibliograpy see ISRS, II: 1607–64.

THE SATIRE: *The School for Dictators*

Trans. into German by Jacob Huber (pseudonym for Rudolf Jacob Humm). *Die Schule der Diktatoren.* 1st printing. Zurich: Europa Verlag, 1938.

Trans. into English by Gwenda David and Eric Mosbacher. *The School for Dictators.* New York: Harper and Brothers, 1938; London: Jonathan Cape, 1939.

La scuola dei dittatori. Rev. ed. Milan: Mondadori (Narratori Italiani), 1962. Reprint: Milan: Mondadori (*Scrittori Italiani e Stranieri*), 1978.

THE NOVELS OF EXILE (in chronological order of writing)

Fontamara

Trans. into German by Nettie Sutro. 1st printing. Zurich: Verlag Oprecht und Helbling, 1933.

Zurich and Paris: Nuove Edizioni Italiane (original Italian version), 1933.

Trans. into English by Michael Warf. New York: Harrison Smith and Robert Haas. 1st American edition. 1934.

Trans. into English by Gwenda David and Eric Mosbacher. London: Methuen, 1934. Reprint: Harmondsworth, Middlesex: Penguin, 1938. 3rd and final rev. Italian version. Milan: Mondadori, 1953.

Trans. into English by Eric Mosbacher, with an introduction by Irving Howe. Trans. of Mondadori, 1953. New York and Toronto: A Meridian Classic, New American Library, 1984.

Bread and Wine

Brot und Wein. 1st printing. Zurich: Oprecht, 1936.

Trans. into English by Gwenda David and Eric Mosbacher. *Bread and Wine.* London: Methuen, 1936; New York: Harper and Brothers, 1937.

Pane e Vino. Original Italian version. Lugano: Nuove Edizioni di Capolago, 1937.

Vino e pane. Rev. Italian version. Milan: Mondadori, 1955. Reprint, 1976 (11th printing). Milan: Mondadori (Oscar), 1981.

Trans. into English by Eric Mosbacher. *Bread and Wine.* New York: Atheneum, 1962; Signet Classic, 1986.

The Seed beneath the Snow

Trans. into German by W.J. Guggenheim. *Der Samen unterm Schnee.* 1st printing. Zurich: Oprecht und Helbling, 1941.

Il seme sotto la neve. Typescript, Zurich Central Library, [1942 ?].

Il seme sotto la neve. Lugano: Edizioni di Capolago; Zurich: Verlag Oprecht, 1942.

Trans. into English by Francis Frenaye. *The Seed beneath the Snow.* New York and London: Harper and Row, 1942.

Il seme sotto la neve. Rome: Faro, 1945; Milan: Mondadori (Medusa), 1950.
Trans. into English by Harvey Ferguson, II. *The Seed beneath the Snow.* Trans. of Mondadori, 1950. New York: Atheneum, 1965.
Milan: Mondadori (Narratori Italiani), 1961. Reprint, Mondadori (Oscar), 1979.

THE POST-EXILE NOVELS

A Handful of Blackberries

Una manciata di more. Milan: Mondadori, 1953. Reprint (4th printing). Milan: Mondadori (Oscar), 1980.
Trans. into English by Darina Silone. *A Handful of Blackberries.* London: Jonathan Cape; New York: Harper and Brothers, 1953.

The Secret of Luca

Il segreto di Luca. Milan: Mondadori (Narratori Italiani), 1956. Reprint (16th printing). Milan: Mondadori (Oscar), 1985.
Trans. into English by Darina Silone. *The Secret of Luca.* London: Jonathan Cape; New York: Harper and Brothers, 1958.

The Fox and the Camellias

La volpe e le camelie. Milan: Mondadori, 1960. Reprint (3rd printing). Milan: Mondadori (Oscar), 1979.
Trans. into English by Eric Mosbacher. *The Fox and the Camellias.* London: Jonathan Cape; New York: Harper and Brothers, 1961.
Severina. [Posthumous.] Edited and completed by Darina Silone. Milan: Mondadori, 1981.

THE PLAYS

And He Hid Himself

Trans. into German by Lotte Thiessing. 1st printing. *Und er verbarg sich.* Zurich: Verlag Oprecht, 1944.
Ed egli si nascose. Italian original. Zurich and Lugano: Ghilda del Libro, 1944.
Trans. into English by Darina Tranquilli. *And He Hid Himself.* New York: Harper and Brothers, 1945.
Trans. into English by Darina Laracy. *And He Did Hide Himself.* London: Jonathan Cape, 1945.
Ed egli si nascose. Rev. ed. 1966. Reprint, Milan: Cino del Duca, 1966.
Ed egli si nascose. Ed. by Benedetta Pierfederici. Rome: Città Nuova Editrice, 2000

The Story of a Humble Christian

Trans. into English by William Weaver. *The Story of a Humble Christian*. London: Gollancz; New York: Harper and Row, 1971.

L'avventura di un povero cristiano. Milan: Mondadori, 1968. Reprint, 1975.

Selected Other Writings

The Living Thoughts of Mazzini. New York and London: Longmans, Green, 1939.

"Visit to a Prisoner." *Emergency Exit*. New York: Harper and Row, 1968.

Memoriale del carcere svizzero. Ed. Lamberto Mercuri. Milan: Lerici, 1979.

Memoir from a Swiss Prison. Translated into English by Stanislao G. Pugliese. Merrick, New York: Cross Cultural Communications, 2006.

Habeas animam! Speech delivered at the Congress for Cultural Freedom. Brussels, 3 November 1950. In Vittoriano Esposito, *Attualità di Silone*. Rome: Edizioni dell'Urbe, 1989.

Secondary Sources

Bidussa, David. "Dialogato per un rinnovamento socialista. Un carteggio degli anni Trenta tra Ignazio Silone e Angelo Tasca." *Annali del Centro di ricerca Guido Dorso*. Avellino: Edizioni del Centro Dorso, 1986.

Biocca, Dario. *Silone. La doppia vita di un italiano*. Milan: Rizzoli, 2005.

Biocca, Dario, and Mauro Canali. *L'informatore: Silone, i comunisti e la polizia*. Milan and Trento: Luni, 2000.

Biondi, Liliana. "Darina: Custode fedele della memoria di Ignazio Silone." *Prospettiva Persona*, XII (2003): n.45, 65–8.

— "1929–1944: Il quindicennio svizzero di Ignazio Silone tra narrativa e cultura europea." In aa.vv. *Per Ignazio Silone*, 49–63. Fondazione Spadolini Nuova Antologia. Florence: Edizioni Polistampa,2002.

— "Le radici e la terra d'origine nella scrittura di Ignazio Silone." In aa.vv. *Ignazio Silone: La letteratura come fonte di nuova vita*. Lugano: Banca Popolare di Sondrio, 2010.

— "Silone Ignazio (scrittore): Lettere a Don Orione." *Messaggi di Don Orione*, 33 (2001) N.106: 79–87.

— "Silone lettore dei segni della storia." *Regione Abruzzo* XXVI (Nov.-Dec. 1998): 28–30.

— "Valori mazziniani rivisitati e condivisi da Ignazio Silone." *Unita d'Italia e Massoneria*, 99–107. Bologna: Acadèmia editrice, 2011.

Bolognese, Giuseppe. "Silone's Modern Quest and Primordial Discovery." *Perspective on Contemporary Literature* (1982): 106–14.

Bondy, François. "L'engrenage de l'existencé entretien avec Ignazio Silone." *Preuves*, 186–7 (1966): 39–44.

Bria, Camillo. *Ignazio Silone.* Bresso, Milan: Edizioni Cetim, 1977.

Brown, Robert McAfee. "Ignazio Silone and the Pseudonyms of God." In Harry J. Mooney, Jr, and Thomas F. Staley, eds, *The Shapeless God,* 19–40. Pittsburgh: University of Pittsburgh Press, 1968.

Buchwald, Diana Kornos, Robert Schulmann, József Illy, Daniel J. Kennefic, and Timan Sauer, eds. *The Collected Papers of Albert Einstein. Volume 9. The Berlin Years: Correspondence, January 1919–April 1920.* Princeton: Princeton University Press, 2004.

Canali, Mauro. *Il caso Silone. Le prove del doppio gioco.* Rome: Liberal, 2000.

— *Le spie del regime.* Bologna: Il Mulino, 2004.

Casoli, Giovanni. *L'incontro di due uomini liberi: Don Orione e Silone.* Milan: Jaca Book, 2000.

Cassata, Maria Letizia. *Ignazio Silone: Paese dell'anima.* Milan: Mursia, 1968.

— *Gli uomini di Silone.* Gubbio: Oderici, 1967.

Castagnola Rossini, Raffaella. *Incontri di spiriti liberi. Amicizie, relazioni professionali e iniziative editoriali di Silone in Svizzera.* Rome: Piero Lacaita, 2004.

Chiaromonte, Nicola. *Il tarlo della coscienza.* Bologna: Il Mulino, 1992.

Coleman, Peter. *The Liberal Conspiracy: The Congress for Cultural Freedom and the Struggle for the Mind of Postwar Europe.* New York: Free Press, 1989.

Collura, Matteo. "Luce d'Eramo, l'ultima difesa della spia." *Corriere della Sera* (8 March 2001): 37.

Crossman, Richard, ed. *The God That Failed: Six Studies in Communism.* New York: Harper and Brothers, 1949.

Cucchiarelli, Paolo. "Ignazio Silone e il silenzio sul periodo svizzero." *Ignazio Silone clandestino nel Novecento. Materiali su un personaggio scomodo anche dopo la caduta del muro,* 73–83. Rimini: Editori Riminesi Riuniti, 1996.

Dagen, Philippe. "L'enigme du 'Joeur de guitar' de Georges Braque." *Le Monde,* 27 January 1998.

Danchew, Alex. *On Art and War and Terror.* Edinburgh: Edinburgh University Press, 2009.

Danese, Attilio, ed. *Laicità e religiosità in Ignazio Silone.* Teramo: Edigrafital, S. Atto, 2001.

d'Eramo, Luce. *Ignazio Silone.* Rimini: Editori Riminesi, 1994.

— *Ignazio Silone.* New edition, ed. by Yukari Saito. Rome: Castelvecchi, 2014.

— *L'opera di Ignazio Silone.* Milan: Mondadori, 1976.

d'Eramo, Luce, intro. *Ignazio Silone: Clandestino del Novecento,* aa.vv. Rimini: Editori Riminesi, 1996.

Di Nicola, Giulia Paola, and Attilio Danese. *Silone, percorsi di una coscienza inquieta.* L'Aquila: Fondazione Ignazio Silone, 2006.

Di Paolo, Maria Grazia. "Silone's Celestino V and the Fabula of the Evolution of a Soul." *Forum Italicum* (Spring 2005): 73–82.

Dorigatti, Michele, and Maffino Maghenzani. *Darina Laracy Silone: Colloqui.* Zevio (Verona): Perosini Editore, 2005.

Embassy of Romania to Switzerland. "Some Eighty Years Ago (1). First Romanian Visit of State to Switzerland." *Quarterly Bulletin* 2, 6 (2004): 8.

Esposito, Vittoriano. *Attualità di Silone.* Rome: Edizioni dell'Urbe, 1989.

— *Ignazio Silone ovvero un "caso" infinito.* Pescina: Centro studi Siloniani, 2000.

— *Ignazio Silone. La vita, le opere, il pensiero.* Rome: Edizioni dell'Urbe, 1985.

— *Silone vent'anni dopo.* L'Aquila: Amministrazione Provinciale, 1998.

Falcetto, Bruno. "Un'esigenza di intervento sociale." In Aldo Forbice, ed., *Silone, la libertà. Un intellettuale scomodo contro tutti i totalitarismi,* 33–41. Milan: Guerini, 2007.

— "Lo scrittore Silone, i delatori e la denuncia." *L'indice dei libri del mese,* 6 (June 2000): 10–11.

Falcetto, Bruno, ed. *Ignazio Silone. Romanzi e saggi.* 2 vols. Milan: Mondadori, 1999.

Feliciano, Héctor. *The Lost Museum: The Nazi Conspiracy to Steal the World's Greatest Art.* New York: Basic Books/Harper Collins, 1997.

Fleischmann, Carlo. *Die auslandischen Konsulate in der Sweiz: Insbesondere die deutschen.* Leipzig: Dathe, 1920.

Fleischmann, Edgar, and Carlo Fleischmann. *Theoretischer Unterricht an Soldaten.* In *Scheizeriche Militärbücherei.* Vol. 1. Leipzig: Grethlein, 1925.

Fofi, Goffredo, Vittorio Giacopini, and Monica Nonno, eds. *Nicola Chiaromonte, Ignazio Silone: L'eredità di "Tempo presente"* Rome: Fahrenheit 451, 2000.

Forbice, Aldo, ed. *Silone, la libertà. Un intellettuale scomodo contro tutti i totalitarismi.* Milan: Guerini, 2007.

Franzinelli, Mimmo. "Sull'utilizzo (critico) delle fonti di polizia." *Percorsi Storici,* 0 (2011).

— *I tentacoli dell'OVRA.* Turin: Bollati Boringhieri, 1999.

Galli, Sara. *Le tre sorelle Seidenfeld: Donne nell'emigrazione politica antifascista.* Florence: Giunti, 2005.

Garosci, Aldo. *Storia dei fuorusciti.* Bari: Laterza, 1953.

Gasbarrini, Antonio, and Annibale Gentile, eds. *Ignazio Silone. Comunista, 1921–1931.* L'Aquila: Angelus Novus Edizioni, 1989.

— *Silone tra l'Abruzzo e il mondo.* L'Aquila: Regione Abruzzo, 1979.

Giardini, Diocleziano. "Alcune novità sul 'caso Silone.'" *Quaderni Siloniani*, 1, 2 (2000): 10–12.

— *Ignazio Silone: Cronologia della vita e delle opere*. Cerchio, Aquila: Adelmo Polla, 1999.

— *Scorre la vita*. Trieste: Trieste Grafica, 2005.

Giardini, Diocleziano, ed. *Viaggio letterario: La storia di Pescina e i suoi personaggi*. Avezzano: DVG Studio, 2015.

Granati, Gianna, and Alfonso Isinelli. *Processo a Silone. La disavventura di un povero cristiano*. Rome: Piero Lacaita, 2001.

Gravagnuolo, Bruno. "Ignazio Silone e il ricatto del Fascismo." *Unione Sarda*, 30 April 1996: 2.

Gurgo, Ottorino, and Francesco de Core. *Silone. L'avventura di un uomo libero*. Venice: Marsilio, 1998.

Herling, Gustavo. "Quell'impero della menzogna che Silone combatteva." In Aldo Forbice, ed., *Silone, la libertà. Un intellettuale scomodo contro tutti i totalitarismi*, 255–64. Milan: Guerini, 2007.

Hitchens, Christopher. "Ignoble Ig-Nazi-O?" *The Nation*, 12 June 2000.

Holmes, Deborah. *Ignazio Silone in Exile: Writing and Antifascism in Switzerland, 1929–1944*. Burlington, VT: Ashgate, 2005.

Howe, Irving. "Socialism and Sensibility." *New Republic*, 26 October 1987.

Inter-Allied Declaration against Acts of Dispossession Committed in Territories under Enemy Occupation and Control. London: H.M.S.O., 1943.

Kadosh, Sara. "Nettie Sutro-Katzenstein." In Paula E. Hyman and Dalia Ofer, eds, *Jewish Women: A Comprehensive Historical Encyclopedia*. Brookline, MA: Jewish Women's Archive, 2009. Accessible via the JWA website. Also see the Nettie Sutro Collection at the Archiv fur Zeitgenschichte, Zurich.

Kazin, Alfred. "A Dialogue on Dictatorships." *New York Herald Tribune*, 12 December 1938.

— "From an Italian Journal." *The Inmost Leaf*. New York: Harcourt, 1956.

— "Ignazio Silone's Compassionate Parable." *New York Herald Tribune Books*, 11 April 1937.

Krieger, Murray. "Ignazio Silone. The Failure of the Secular Christ." *The Tragic Vision: Variations on a Theme in Literary Interpretation*. Chicago: University of Chicago Press, 1966.

— "Northrop Frye in Modern Criticism: Ariel and the Spirit of Gravity." In Murray Krieger, ed., *Northrop Frye in Modern Criticism: Selected Papers from the English Institute*. New York and London: Columbia University Press, 1966.

Leake, Elizabeth. *The Reinvention of Ignazio Silone*. Toronto: University of Toronto Press, 2003.

Leone, Giuseppe. *Ignazio Silone scrittore dell'intelligenza*. Florence: Atheneum, 1996.

Lewis, R.W.B. *Ignazio Silone: Introduzione all'opera*. Rome: Ragionamenti, 1978.
— "Ignazio Silone: The Politics of Charity." *The Picaresque Saint*. Philadelphia: Lippincott, 1956.
Lewis, Wilmarth Sheldon. "Editing Private Correspondence." *Proceedings of the American Philosophical Society*, 107, 4 (August 1963): 289–93. http://www/jstor.org/stable/985671.
Magnani, Franca Schiavetti. *Una famiglia italiana*. Milan: Feltrinelli, 1991.
Martelli, Sebastiano, and Salvatore Di Pasqua. *Guida alla letteratura di Ignazio Silone*. Milan: Mondadori, 1988.
McDonald, Michael P. "Il caso Silone." *National Interest* 65 (Fall 2001): 77–89.
Millar, Eileen Anne, ed. *The Legacy of Fascism*. Glasgow: University of Glasgow Press, 1989.
Modigliani, Vera. *Esilio*. Rome: Garzanti, 1946.
Moscardelli, Maria. *La coperta abruzzese*. Rome: Aracne, 2004.
Mytze, Andreas. *Ignazio Silone zum 75. Geburstag*. Berlin: Europäische Ideen, 1975.
Nicoli, Giovanni, and Thomas Stein, eds. *Zurigo per Silone: Atti delle Giornate Siloniane in Svizzera*. Zurich: L'avvenire dei lavoratori, Tragelaphos, 2004.
Origo, Iris. "Ignazio Silone: A Study in Integrity." *Atlantic Monthly* (March 1966): 86–93.
— *A Need to Testify*. San Diego, CA: Harcourt, 1984.
Orth-Veillon, Jennifer Aileen. *Ignazio Silone, Albert Camus and Manès Sperber: Writing between Stalinism and Fascism*. PhD diss., Emory University, 2011.
Padovani, Gisella. *Letteratura e socialismo: Saggi su Ignazio Silone*. Catania: Aldo Marino, 1982.
Palmier, Jean-Michel. *Weimar in Exile. The Antifascist Emigration in Europe and America*. London: Verso, 2006.
Pampaloni, Geno. "L'opera narrativa di Ignazio Silone." *Il Ponte* (January 1949).
Paynter, Maria Nicolai. "Ignazio Silone." In Luca Somigli and Rocco Capozzi, eds, *Dictionary of Literary Biography: Italian Prose Writers 1900–1945*, Vol. 264, 302–13. Detroit: Gale, 2002.
— "Ignazio Silone" and "Fontamara." In Gaetana Marrone, ed., *Encyclopedia of Italian Literary Studies*. New York and London: Routledge, 2006.
— *Ignazio Silone: Beyond the Tragic Vision*. Toronto: University of Toronto Press, 2000.
— *Perché verità sia libera. Memorie, confessioni, riflessioni e itinerario poetico di David Maria Turoldo*. Milan: Rizzoli, 1994.
— "Do personagem ao autor: Tendências dos estudos silonianos da última década." Trans. by Kátia D'Errico. In Patricia Peterle, ed., *Ignazio Silone: Ontem e hoje*. Niteroi, Rio de Janeiro: Editora Comunità, 2010.

— *Simbolismo e ironia nella narrativa di Silone*. L'Aquila: Premio Internazionale Letterario "Ignazio Silone," 1992. Originally, "Symbolism and Irony in Silone's Narrative Works." PhD diss., University of Toronto, 1989.

Peterle, Patricia, ed., *Ignazio Silone: Ontem e hoje*. Niteroi, Rio De Janeiro: Editora Comunità, 2010.

— "Da politica à literatura: O percurso de Ignazio Silone." *ALEA*, 2, 1 (January–June 2009): 99–110.

Petersen, Neil. *From Hitler's Doorstep: The Wartime Intelligence Reports of Allen Dulles*. University Park: Pennsylvania State University Press, 1996.

Petropoulos, Jonathan. *The Faustian Bargain: The Art World in Nazi Germany*. Oxford: Oxford University Press, 2000.

Pieracci Harwell, Margherita. *Un cristiano senza chiesa e altri saggi*. Rome: Studium, 1991.

— "Silone e Simone Weil." *Annali – 1999/2000*, 285–314. Naples: Istituto Universitario Suor Orsola Benincasa, 2004.

Rahv, Philip. "The Revolutionary Conscience." *Nation*, 10 April 1937.

Ravera, Camilla. "Quegli anni con Silone nel PCI." *Misura*, 4 (1978).

Rigobello, Giuliana. *Ignazio Silone*. Florence: Le Monnier, 1981.

Rousseaux, André. "Les vérités terriennes d'Ignazio Silone." *Le Figaro Lettéraire*, 17 May 1953.

Ruberti, Antonio. "L'umanesimo Siloniano." Proceedings of the convention on *Ignazio Silone scrittore politico e politico*, Pescina, 15–16 November 1991. *Oggi e Domani* (special supplement, March 1992): iii.

Ruggeri, Antonio. *Don Orione, Ignazio Silone e Romoletto*. Tortona: Edizione Don Orione, 1981.

Saito, Yukari. "La presunta doppiezza della vita vissuta." In Aldo Forbice, ed., *Silone, la libertà. Un intellettuale scomodo contro tutti i totalitarismi*, 115–46. Milan: Guerini, 2007.

Scott, Nathan A. "Ignazio Silone: Novelist of the Revolutionary Sensibility." *Rehearsals of Discomposure*. New York: King's Crown Press, 1952.

Scurani, Alessandro. *Ignazio Silone: Un amore religioso per la giustizia*. Milan: Edizioni Letture, 1991.

— "La religiosità di Silone." *Letture* (July 1966): 485–504.

Signori, Elisa. *La Svizzera e i fuorusciti italiani*. Milan: Angeli, 1983.

Silone, Darina. "Ignazio Silone, Allen Dulles and the CIA." Letter to *Times Literary Supplement*, 1 December 2000.

— "Letter to Tamburrano." In Aldo Forbice, ed. *Silone, la libertà. Un intellettuale scomodo contro tutti i totalitarismi*, 283. Milan: Guerini, 2007.

— "Il mio primo incontro con Ignazio Silone." In Antonio Gasbarrini and Annibale Gentile, eds, *Silone tra l'Abruzzo e il mondo*, 19–22. L'Aquila: Regione Abruzzo, 1979.

— "Un nuvola nera ha offuscato il centenario." *Quaderni Siloniani,* 1, 2 (2000): 2–3.

— "Le ultime ore di Ignazio Silone." *Severina,* 165–82. Milan: Mondadori, 1981.

Slochower, Harry. "Absolute Doubt: André Gide, Ignazio Silone, Johns Dos Passos." In *Literature and Philosophy between Two World Wars.* New York: Citadel Press, 1964.

Soave, Sergio. *Senza tradirsi, senza tradire. Silone e Tasca dal comunismo al socialismo cristiano (1900–1940).* Turin: Nino Aragno, 2005.

Spadolini, Giovanni, ed. *Ignazio Silone in Svizzera.* Lugano: Associazione Carlo Cattaneo, 1994.

Spriano, Paolo. *Storia del partito comunista italiano.* 7 vols. Turin: Einaudi, 1967–98.

Stachel, John, David C. Cassidy, and Robert Schulmann, eds. *The Collected Papers of Albert Einstein. Volume 1, The Early Years, 1879–1902.* Princeton: Princeton University Press, 1987.

Stille, Alexander. "The Spy Who Failed." *The New Yorker,* 15 May 2000: 44. And comment from Maria Paynter, *The New Yorker,* 19 and 26 June 2000, 16.

Tamburrano, Giuseppe. *Il "caso" Silone.* Turin: UTET, 2006.

Tamburrano, Giuseppe, Gianna Granati, and Alfonso Isinelli. *Processo a Silone: La disavventura di un povero cristiano.* Rome: Piero Lacaita, 2001.

Todisco, Vincenzo. "Una lettera inedita di Ignazio Silone ad Aline Valangin." *Quaderni grigionitaliani,* 28 July 2012: 339–42.

Togliatti, Palmiro. "Contributo alla psicologia di un rinnegato. Come Ignazio Silone venne espulso dal Partito comunista." *L'Unità,* 6 January 1950.

Tranquilli, Romolo. "Perché Silone tacque." Interview by Mariangela Di Cagno. In Antonio Gasbarrini and Annibale Gentile, eds, *Silone tra l'Abruzzo e il mondo,* 344. L'Aquila: Regione Abruzzo, 1979.

Turoldo, David Maria. *Lo scandalo della speranza,* Milan: G.E.I. Grandi Edizioni Italiane, 1984.

— "A Silone." *Regione Abruzzo,* 12 December 1989: 15.

Valiani, Leo. *Sessant'anni di avventure e battaglie.* Milan: Rizzoli, 1983.

Vigorelli, Giancarlo, ed. "Per i settant'anni di Silone." *Il Dramma,* 5 (May 1970): 71–87.

Virdia, Ferdinando. *Ignazio Silone.* Florence: La Nuova Italia, 1985.

Voigt, Klaus. "Ignazio Silone e la stampa tedesca dell'esilio." In Gaetano Arfè, ed., *L'emigrazione socialista nella lotta contro il fascismo (1926–1939),* 105–36. Florence: Sansoni, 1982.

Wacks, Penelope Jaffe. "Conflict and Commitment in Ignazio Silone's *Ed egli si nascose.*" *A.T.I. Journal,* 31 (July 1980): 26–34.

Warner, Michael. "Origins of the Congress of Cultural Freedom, 1949–50." *Studies in Intelligence,* 38, 5 (unclassified 1955 ed.). https://www.cia.gov/.../v.38i5a10.pdf.

Weaver, William. *Open City: Seven Writers in Postwar Rome.* South Royalton, VT: Steerforth Press, 1999.

Zirardini, Alessandro. "Le role de l'intellectuel – Silone s'explique." *L'Express,* 9 February 1961.

Websites

www.aaa.si.edu/collections/jacques-seligmann–co-records-9936. Records of Seligmann-Fleischmann interaction.

www.aaa.si.edu/collections/container/viewer/fleischmann-marcel-288234. 24 documents regarding Seligmann-Fleischmann art dealing.

www.abruzzo24ore.TV/news/Pescina-sottratte-lettere-a-darina-moglie-di-ignazio-silone-l-appelllo-per-la-restituzione/96124.htm. Media report to denounce the disappearance of personal letters.

www.amici-silone.net. Italian/English website created and managed by Maria Moscardelli, Silone's grandniece.

www.fold3.com/image/#291836599. Declassified documents on the "visit of Investigators into looted works of art and their whereabouts in Switzerland."

www.lootedart.com/MVI3RM496661. ALIU (Art Looting Intelligence Unit) reports including red flag list and index.

www.nybooks.com/articles/2002/06/27. William Weaver discusses the "caso Silone" with Biocca and Canali.

www.pertini.it/turati/a_silone.html. Website of the Fondazione di Studi Storici Filippo Turati, Florence. Silone's archives were donated to this socialist institution by Darina Silone.

www.peterkamber.de/silone. Documents regarding Ignazio Silone and the OSS (Office of Strategic Services).

www.silone.it. Website of the Centro Studi Ignazio Silone.

www.xecutives.net/interviews/alle/241. Website of the Swiss Management Network with an interview with Kaspar Fleischmann.

Acknowledgments

My greatest debt is to Darina Silone for generously granting me assistance and advice. She helped me understand Silone and her life with him, offered comments on others' scholarship, and shared her thoughts on the controversies that developed about Silone. Her greatest gift to me was her listing me among her friends. After Darina's death, her sister Eithne Laracy Kavanagh was similarly generous. I am deeply indebted to her for her encouragement and generous assistance.

Gloria Fleischmann's altruistic concern for safeguarding the correspondence made this project possible. I am indebted to her for stipulating that I could publish it, and I am grateful to Dr Maurizio Di Nicola, president of the Centro Studi Ignazio Silone, for honouring her request. Anthony Fleischmann's generosity in sharing memories, letters, photographs, and information with me was of essential help, as I was writing about his grandfather. He has my deepest gratitude. I also thank his associate Samantha Pearce for her kind assistance. Kaspar Fleischmann has my sincere appreciation for providing me with additional information.

As a relative of Ignazio Silone and the person who dedicated important scholarship to him, Maria Moscardelli was instrumental in my research. She granted me total cooperation. She spoke to me about her personal relationship with Silone and his wife, and about the Tranquilli family, and shared unpublished letters and documents that she has in her possession. No expression of gratitude can satisfy the debt that I incurred, so I will simply say: *grazie infinite*!

I am profoundly grateful to the Indian poet the late Keshav Malik for his remembrance of Darina Silone, the affectionate comments that he e-mailed to me, and the poems that he allowed me to publish.

I will never forget the late Ron Schoeffel, editor-in-chief of the University of Toronto Press, and my chairpersons and friends the late Xoán González-Millán and Giuseppe Di Scipio. Their knowledge, kindness, and professionalism enriched many lives, including mine.

Dr Richard Ratzlaff, who succeeded Ron Schoeffel, has my deep appreciation for helping make the publishing process as seamless as possible. He was also responsible for selecting external readers who earned my gratitude for their diligent work and constructive criticism. My special thanks to Anne Laughlin, managing editor at the Press, for her caring professionalism and for assigning the copy-editing task to Margaret Allen, who has my admiration and gratitude.

I am deeply indebted to state archivists Drs Martorano Di Cesare and Sebastiana Ferrari for their professional expertise and for granting me access – together with Dr Franca Mazzali – to the Centro Studi archives. I thank Professor Walter Capezzali and Drs Aurora Boticchio and Stefano Iulianella for facilitating the initial presentation of my findings, and the Centro Studi's volunteers, Paola Di Mascio and Lorenzina Simboli, for their generous assistance. I also thank Professor Maurizio degl'Innocenti and Professor Giuseppe Muzzi for their kindness in our interaction and for granting me access to material held at the Fondazione Filippo Turati.

Iris Schmeisser, the provenance specialist at the MoMA archives, has my gratitude for her invaluable help during my research regarding Marcel Fleischmann as an art dealer. I also thank Professor Alex Danchev, the author of *On Art and War and Terror,* for his response to my inquiry about Marcel Fleischmann.

A very special thanks goes to Diocleziano Giardini, whose work to protect Silone's archival material began many years ago when, at the inception of the Centro Studi, Darina Silone entrusted him with the task of helping scholars with their research. He shared information, sent me pictures, and answered my questions with his usual generosity. I am also grateful to Silone's relative Romolo Tranquilli for the information he gave me when I first began my research in Pescina.

Many colleagues and scholars have facilitated my work with their writings, comments, advice, or assistance. Professor Maddalena Kuitunen was my first mentor. Professors Giuseppe Mazzotta and Stanislao Pugliese offered me advice and were of significant help with their scholarship. They both have my deepest appreciation. I have also benefited from the work of Professors Bruno Falcetto, Paolo Fasoli, Deborah Holmes, Liliana Biondi, Maria Passaro, Patricia Peterle, Carmela Scala, Attilio Danese, and Giulia Paola Di Nicola, and also of Mimmo Franzinelli, Marfino

Maghenzani, Michele Dorigatti, Giovanni Casoli, Michael McDonald, Yukari Saito, and Paolo Cucchiarelli. Florinda Iannace offered me encouragement at the beginning of my career. My colleagues Marlene Barsoum and Julia Przybos gave me friendship and advice; Elke Nicolai and Eckhard Kuhn-Oslus helped me find German translators. Prabha Lakshmanan kindly provided information about Keshav Malik.

Professor Maria Cornelio has my deep gratitude for reading my rendition of Silone's letters and offering her comments as an expert translator. I am also indebted to Emma Paynter for her professional input when rereading the manuscript.

I thank Laura Visco, Jesse Tandler, Lucrecia Aviles, Jeanette Abreu, and Fatema Begum for their assistance.

The unsung heroes in any enterprise are usually those whose care enriches our lives in subtle ways. They are our family members, relatives, and friends. Their kindness and their words of encouragement and appreciation are as important as volumes of scholarship. The list is long, but it is well justified. Thank you for caring: Filippo and Nicoletta Carnevale; Gabriella and Victoria Galante; Sandro and Linda Carnevale; Nicola, Mario, John, and Colleen Di Lello; Patricia Di Lello and Greg Robinson; Graziana Di Lello and Daniel Weidner; Benito Santone and Grazietta D'Amore; Esterina D'Amore; Giuseppe Galliani and Cecilia Santone; Fabio Santone and Angela Flacco; Corrado Martini and Emanuela Vivarini; Maria Grazia and Carla Galliani; Fabrizio Vivarini; Mario, Rino, and Derna Santone; Paola and Rachele Spilla; Maria Fulvia and Camilla Mammarella; Chiara Di Biase; Alfredo and Bridget D'Amore; Adriana Nicolucci D'Amore and the entire, exceptional McGowan family.

A million thanks to my very special friends Eugenia and David Askren, Jelica and Velimir Ristic, Gianni Ferrara, Anna Aguzzi, Nanda Botticelli, Melva Eidelberg, Violet and Tony Oliveira, Mercedes and Herman Steiner, the Salernos, Giacinta Di Battista, and Chiara Di Biase.

Donald, my husband and best friend, was my mentor and sounding board; as well as my travel guide, research partner, and official photographer. He sustained me, as always, in every possible way, with his intelligence and infinite patience. Emma, Joseph, Alessia, and Sofia were my essential motivators. All five of them have my eternal love and gratitude. I also thank the Nicolai cousins, the West Coast Paynters, and the entire, exceptional, McGowan family.

The realization of this work was made possible in part by a grant from the Professional Staff Congress-City University of New York (PSC-CUNY) Research Foundation.

Index